THE LIFE OF
SIR GEORGE WILLIAMS

"*The course of this man's life had been very simple and yet crowded with events and with manifold activity. The element of his energy was an indestructible faith in God, and in an assistance flowing immediately from him.*"

GOETHE.

"*For whom thanks be to our Lord Jesus Christ.*"

SIR GEORGE WILLIAMS

THE LIFE

OF

SIR GEORGE WILLIAMS

FOUNDER OF THE YOUNG MEN'S
CHRISTIAN ASSOCIATION

BY

J. E. HODDER WILLIAMS

*"A whole Christ for my salvation
A whole Bible for my staff
A whole church for my fellowship
A whole world for my parish"*

**Fredonia Books
Amsterdam, The Netherlands**

The Life of Sir George Williams:
Founder of the Young Men's Christian Association

by
J. E. Hodder Williams

ISBN: 1-4101-0228-9

Copyright © 2003 by Fredonia Books

Reprinted from the 1906 edition

Fredonia Books
Amsterdam, The Netherlands
http://www.fredoniabooks.com

All rights reserved, including the right to reproduce this book, or portions thereof, in any form.

In order to make original editions of historical works available to scholars at an economical price, this facsimile of the original edition of 1906 is reproduced from the best available copy and has been digitally enhanced to improve legibility, but the text remains unaltered to retain historical authenticity.

𝕿𝖍𝖎𝖘 𝕭𝖔𝖔𝖐 𝖎𝖘 𝕯𝖊𝖉𝖎𝖈𝖆𝖙𝖊𝖉

TO

THE MEMBERS OF THE YOUNG MEN'S CHRISTIAN ASSOCIATION
ON THE CONTINENT OF AMERICA, AND TO
TWO OF THEM IN PARTICULAR

TO THE HON. JOHN WANAMAKER

AND

TO JAMES STOKES

TWO LIFE-LONG FRIENDS OF SIR GEORGE WILLIAMS

PREFATORY NOTE

THIS biography has been written at the request of the family of Sir George Williams, and I have to express my thanks to his sons, and particularly to Mr. Howard Williams, for placing at my disposal all available papers as well as affording me assistance in the preparation of the book.

Owing to the fact that Sir George Williams destroyed all his corespondence, and only kept a diary for a short period after he came to London, I have been compelled to rely chiefly upon the reminiscences and co-operation of those who knew and loved him. It would be impossible to acknowledge in anything like detail the help I have received from all quarters, but I take this opportunity of recording my indebtedness to Mr. Edwin Catford, of Dulverton, to Mr. George B. Sully, of Burnham, and to the Rev. Harry Butler, of Bridgwater, for their kindness in assisting me to picture Sir George Williams's early years; to Mr. William Creese, one of the twelve first members of the Association, who has taken the greatest interest in the work, giving me the benefit of his recollections of the early meetings, and ensuring the

PREFATORY NOTE

correctness of what is, I believe, the first authentic account of the beginning of the Young Men's Christian Association, in the upper room in St. Paul's Churchyard; to my grandfather, Mr. M. H. Hodder, a life-long friend of Sir George Williams and among the earliest members of the Association; to my father, who was for nearly forty years so closely connected with him in business and in private life; to Mr. Walter Hitchcock and to Mr. Amos Williams.

I am indebted to many unknown correspondents who have written to me of the state of affairs in London warehouses at the time Sir George Williams came to London, and especially to Mr. H. W. Wrench, Mr. W. C. Collins, Mr. P. Joyce, Mr. Chas. A. Mace, and Mr. J. H. Norris.

Mr. W. H. Mills, Mr. Basil Hewer, and Mr. Frank Howe of the Young Men's Christian Association, Mr. L. L. Catt, Sir George Williams's private secretary, Mr. Edgar Rowan, Mr. J. G. Oddy, Mrs. Hindley, the Rev. G. J. Hill, the Rev. Nevile Sherbrooke, the Rev. E. J. Jones, the Rev. H. Epworth Thompson, Mr. A. F. Borton, Mr. J. Marshall Badger, Mr. P. J. Whittaker, Mr. A. Greenwood, Mr. R. Poynton, and Mr. J. A. Stacey have, in ways too numerous to mention, helped by placing at my disposal the materials for the composition of this book.

In writing of the history of the Young Men's Christian Association I have constantly made use

PREFATORY NOTE

of the excellent Historical Record by the Rev. J. G. Stevenson, M.A.

To Mr. W. Hind Smith, who has in the most generous manner given into my hands his unique collection of reminiscences, reports, and original documents; to Mr. R. C. Morse, of New York, who has spent much time and thought over the chapter dealing with the Young Men's Christian Association in America; to Mr. J. H. Putterill, of Exeter Hall, who has accorded me his advice and help throughout the work; and to Monsieur E. M. Soutter, of Paris, and Monsieur Sarasin-Warnery, President of the World's Alliance, I wish to express my gratitude.

My brother, Mr. Percy Hodder Williams, has been at great pains in revising the proofs and has assisted me in many ways. To him I tender my warmest thanks.

Of what I owe to one other, without whose constant aid and encouragement this work, written "after business hours," would never have been accomplished, I cannot write. She knows.

J. E. HODDER WILLIAMS.

Bromley Common,
    Kent.

CONTENTS

CHAPTER I
THE SOIL AND THE CITY 3

CHAPTER II
THE SPIRITUAL HOMELAND AND THE FATHERS IN CHRIST 21

CHAPTER III
A YOUNG MAN FROM THE COUNTRY 45

CHAPTER IV
THE WORLD AND A YOUNG MAN 67

CHAPTER V
THE UPPER ROOM IN ST. PAUL'S CHURCHYARD . . 95

CHAPTER VI
THE EARLY DAYS OF THE YOUNG MEN'S CHRISTIAN ASSOCIATION 125

CHAPTER VII
THE WORLD-WIDE GROWTH OF THE YOUNG MEN'S CHRISTIAN ASSOCIATION 149

CHAPTER VIII

The Critical Years of the Young Men's Christian
Association 175

CHAPTER IX

The Years of Progress 203

CHAPTER X

The Religion of a Successful Merchant 239

CHAPTER XI

The Years of Triumph 271

CHAPTER XII

From Jubilee to Jubilee 295

CHAPTER XIII

Rest 313

CHAPTER XIV

The Master Builder 333

INDEX 351

ILLUSTRATIONS

SIR GEORGE WILLIAMS . . . . *Frontispiece*	
	FACING PAGE
ASHWAY FARM, NEAR DULVERTON, THE BIRTHPLACE OF SIR GEORGE WILLIAMS	8
SIR GEORGE WILLIAMS'S HOMELAND	16
A view from the window of the farm on the hill	
THE VILLAGE STREET AT DULVERTON	32
Showing the Church where Sir George Williams was baptised, and the house where he first went to school.	
THE MOTHER OF SIR GEORGE WILLIAMS	40
From a coloured miniature in the possession of Amos Williams, Esq.	
HIGH STREET, BRIDGWATER, IN WHICH MR. HOLMES'S SHOP WAS SITUATED	56
From an old drawing in the possession of George B. Sully, Esq.	
THE FRIENDS' MEETING-HOUSE, BRIDGWATER	72
Where, at the age of eighteen, Sir George Williams signed the "Teetotal Pledge."	
THE BRIDGE ACROSS THE RIVER AT BRIDGWATER	80
At the end of the bridge now stands the George Williams Memorial Building of the Young Men's Christian Association. From an old drawing in the possession of George B. Sully, Esq.	
SIR GEORGE WILLIAMS AS A YOUNG MAN	96
The earliest known photograph, taken soon after he entered Messrs. Hitchcock & Rogers's.	
WILLIAM CREESE AND JOHN C. SYMONDS	112
The first Secretaries of the Young Men's Christian Association.	
EDWARD VALENTINE	112
"My friend Val"—First Treasurer of the Association.	

ILLUSTRATIONS

	FACING PAGE
EDWARD BEAUMONT	112

    To whom the idea of the Association was first mentioned by George Williams.

A FACSIMILE OF THE LETTER ANNOUNCING THE FORMATION OF THE YOUNG MEN'S CHRISTIAN ASSOCIATION 128

C. W. SMITH 144

    Who gave the name to the Association.

EDWARD ROGERS 144

    One of the twelve original members of the Association.

THE ORIGINAL CARD OF MEMBERSHIP OF THE YOUNG MEN'S CHRISTIAN ASSOCIATION 144

J. H. TARLTON 160

    First Paid Secretary of the Young Men's Christian Association.

W. EDWYN SHIPTON 160

    Mr. Tarlton's successor and one of the great organisers of Association Work.

HELEN HITCHCOCK (LADY WILLIAMS) AND SIR GEORGE WILLIAMS (AT THE AGE OF THIRTY-TWO) 176

    From photographs taken at the time of their marriage.

SIR GEORGE WILLIAMS 192

    From a photograph taken about 1870.

SIR GEORGE WILLIAMS IN 1876 196

    From a photograph taken during his visit to America.

SIR GEORGE WILLIAMS IN 1898 208

SIR GEORGE WILLIAMS AT THE AGE OF SIXTY 208

EXETER HALL 224

    Opened as the headquarters of the Young Men's Christian Association on March 29, 1881.

SIR GEORGE WILLIAMS 240

    From a photograph taken soon after the opening of Exeter Hall as the headquarters of the Young Men's Christian Association.

SIR GEORGE WILLIAMS IN COURT DRESS 272

    Photographed on the day he received the honour of knighthood from Queen Victoria.

ILLUSTRATIONS

FACING PAGE

THE CASKET ENCLOSING THE SCROLL CONFERRING THE FREE-
DOM OF THE CITY OF LONDON ON SIR GEORGE WILLIAMS
PRESENTED AT THE GUILD-HALL, JUNE 4, 1894 . . . 280

THE FUNERAL OF SIR GEORGE WILLIAMS AT ST. PAUL'S
CATHEDRAL, NOVEMBER 14, 1905 320

THE LAST RESTING PLACE OF SIR GEORGE WILLIAMS IN ST.
PAUL'S CATHEDRAL 328

THE LAST PHOTOGRAPH OF SIR GEORGE WILLIAMS 336

THE SOIL AND THE CITY

CHAPTER I

THE SOIL AND THE CITY

AS they turned the corner and the spire of Bridgwater Church rose into view against the evening sky, the boy's heart beat fast. They had come within sight of the end of their journey.

And at the journey's end was the beginning of the world.

It had been a long ride. Father and son had started in the moorland mist of the early morning from the home hidden among the hills some four miles above Dulverton. They had made their way slowly, for roads were bad in those days, along the narrow cart-track which leads from the farmhouse to the rough country lane, with its treacherous borders of ditch and gully. You will not fail to notice these if you happen to pass this way; they must be carefully watched if you would escape an ugly fall; and they are worth some attention, for, as you shall presently hear, they played a strange part in the career of the hero of this book. They rode down the steep hill to Dulverton Church, whose bells were supposed to chime out the quaint rhyme —

"Old John Wesley's dead and gone,
　　He left us in the tower;
　'T was his desire that we should play
　　At eight and twelve and vower"—

and where even now the curfew is tolled morning and night. They passed the house at the head of the narrow village street where the boy had first gone to school, following the road of which you may read in the pages of *Lorna Doone*, where Jan Ridd first caught sight of " a little girl, dark-haired, and very wonderful," across the old stone bridge over the River Barle, through Tennyson's " land of bubbling streams," and then into that wonderful open meadow-land, which lies on the borders of Somerset and Devon, the like of which exists nowhere else in the world. Here the fields are billow upon billow of brightest green, such green as you may only see in the West country, and between the meadows and orchards so " full of contentment," in an almost oriental contrast of colour, lie patches of red earth, earth red as brick, red as the dust of an African desert, sometimes tinged with coral or shaded in chocolate. The chalky road brought them to little townships, sheltering among a cluster of trees, and in the distance, hidden in some unexpected corner, they caught glimpses of those thatched farmsteads, the time-worn homes of the yeomen of old England, where only a few years back you might still hear the thud of the flail on the threshing-floor. Everywhere was the sound of brooks, and beyond and above rose the grey-brown Brendon and Quantock hills.

At last the fertile land was left behind. Late in the day they reached the town of Bridgwater, and came to a halt outside the drapery establishment of Mr. Holmes, which stands at the head of the High Street, near the statue of Admiral Blake, that gallant old Republican who fought with equal spirit and glory on land and sea.

George Williams was going out into the world. The phrase is so simple that its significance is often forgotten, but it pictures one of the supreme moments of life — a moment as solemn, as critical, as full of joy and sorrow, as birth or death. Sir George Williams, as we remember him, seemed to belong to London, to be a very part of the City, as if the noise and dust of its streets had been breathed into him with the breath of life; but to George Williams, the boy of fourteen, Bridgwater, the quiet country town, which the man of the cities would now speak of as belonging to some far-off land of repose — Bridgwater was the world.

For the farm where George Williams was born lies at the end of everything, lies on the confines of the country. Its isolation, even to-day, is complete. It is the last farmstead before you reach a pathless moorland, and the loneliness of that land, especially in winter, when the glory of gorse and heather and fern has faded and the hills are shrouded in mist, is almost intolerable.

True, it was little more than a twenty-five-mile ride from the home on the hills to Bridgwater, but as I stood in the room where George Williams slept as a boy and looked out on the silent land, rugged, large, and desolate, where the eye searches longingly for some sight of man, and thought of the place of his last rest at the very heart of crowded life, I wondered in what terms one might measure the vast country that lies between the farm and the town, between the country town and the Metropolis, between the farmhouse and St. Paul's Cathedral.

George Williams was the youngest of the eight sons of Amos and Elisabeth Williams, of Ashway Farm, Dulverton, in the county of Somerset, and was born on October 11, 1821. The family came of generations of yeoman farmers, and to this day, in spite of the ills that have fallen in England upon the men of the open life, the grandchildren of Amos Williams have never lost their affection for the soil; to this day you will find his descendants fighting the everlasting battle upon the land of their fathers against the elements of the Almighty and the stress of foreign competition. Amos Williams belonged to the days when British farming was an honourable and honoured profession. He lived before the time when it degenerated, as he certainly would have thought, into a mere business, when machinery and chemistry reduced it to the level of a factory. To his generation farming was almost a form of sport, not, of course, to be taken too seriously, for "no Devonshire man or Somersetshire either ever thinks of working harder than his Maker meant for him," and only in most untoward circumstances would the work on the land be allowed to interfere with the day's hunting. His home was in the heart of the country of the wild red deer and of the hunting farmer; of the famous Exmoor ponies, in build like a miniature cart-horse, in colour "bay or brown mouse," a herd of which was bred by Sir Thomas Acland on old Ashway Farm. Families then lived easily, though without luxury, on the land, while the shadow of the future was as a man's hand in the sky. Wheaten bread was unknown; the food was coarse, though abundant. In many of the farmhouses plates were seldom used. Instead of these the table was carved throughout its length into a series of mock plates, and on these, according to a recent historian, the meat was placed. Every day the table was washed with hot water, and covers were set over the imitation plates to keep off the dust. It was the custom to serve the pudding and treacle first, so as to lessen the appetite and effect a saving in the meat, which consisted for the most part of salt pork.

George Williams must have seen in his early boyhood much of the rough and rude side of life. Men were still hanged for sheep-stealing, and smuggling was carried on vigorously in the neighbourhood. The moral state of the lower classes was pitifully low, their habits so degraded and depraved that Devonshire and Somerset were classed in the unenviable category of counties presenting the agricultural labourer in his most deplorable circumstances. Certainly the surroundings of George Williams's boyhood were not calculated to foster false notions of the gross and brutal passions of his fellows. It is often suggested that such a young man as George Williams became must be ignorant of life, innocent of the temptings of the flesh, and in innocence and ignorance finding security. Such a charge could never be brought against the son of a West country farmer.

You may be sure that these men of the soil belonged heart, body, and soul to the old school of traditional Toryism. Their daily round was bound up in a thousand traditions. They were nursed on legends, cradled in the superstitions of the West country. The times, they were forced to admit, were moving. After almost a century of discussion the first Reform Act had been passed. Whispers of Chartism were in the air. But they thanked God that the land, the soil, did not move with the times, and they belonged to the land. A sturdy, courageous, fiery race was this; slow to move, but terrible when roused,

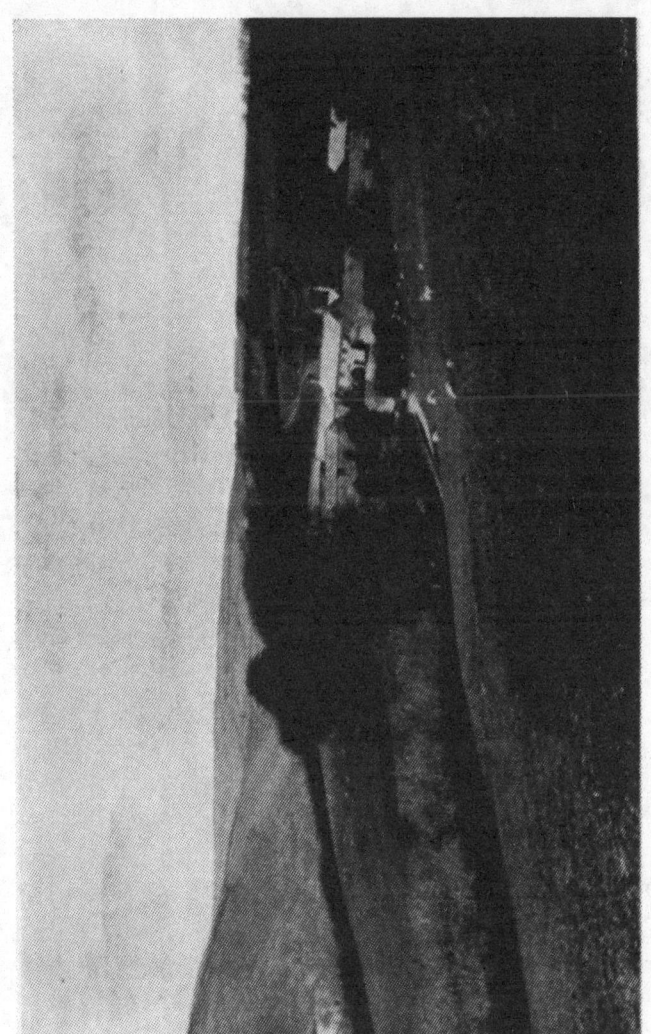

Ashway Farm, near Dulverton, the Birthplace of Sir George Williams

proud as the king, strong with the strength of mountain and moor, a race that had existed unchanged for centuries, but which has been crowded out of existence in less than fifty years by the force of steam and the whirr of machinery. On first acquaintance you might be tempted to judge an Exmoor man, as you might a Highlander, dull-witted on account of his deliberate manner of movement and of speech, but while the shrewdness of the North is proverbial, it may at least be matched in the West, and it is no fancy to suppose that as George Williams grew to boyhood, his father, as keen at a bargain as at following the hounds, realised that the glory was gradually fading from the life on the farm and was not altogether sorry when circumstances suggested another calling for his youngest son.

George Williams's mother is remembered in Dulverton as a small and dainty old lady, simple and charming, who, after her husband's death, caused by the bite of an adder at the comparatively early age of sixty-three, passed her days among her children and children's children: always bright, always sunny, always willing and anxious to help everybody in every possible way. That was the memory I found of her in her own country, and her youngest son would have coveted no nobler epitaph for himself although he moved in a different and greater world. From his mother George Williams certainly inherited his cheery character, his winning manner; from his father his indomitable will, the tremendous power of quiet determination, and unquenchable enthusiasm which belongs in special degree to that countryside which fathered the men who, under Blake, defended Taunton for nearly a year against overwhelming odds, who fought and died like heroes at Sedgmoor, and who never quailed or flinched before all the horrors of the Bloody Assizes.

It cannot be said that the experience of George Williams's boyhood on the farm played any great part in his subsequent career. It seems, indeed, almost out of place to picture him in surroundings that will always be associated with the chase of deer and fox, otter and hare. There is no story to tell of nights spent in study, of splendid dreams and thoughts of greatness among the hills, no record of fierce longings and aspirations or precocious sayings treasured up in family lore. You might sum up these early days in the one sentence: He was an ordinary, though somewhat nervous and highly strung boy, living the rather monotonous and unexciting daily life of the school and the farm. He was the liveliest member of the household, and, as is often the case in a large family, the youngest son, whose wits had been sharpened by constant contact with his elders, was allowed special license and was particularly smart of speech and quick at repartee. His brothers evidently looked to him to provide the fun of the farm, and he was ever ready with some droll story or song when they called upon him as they sat round the great open log fire in the winter evenings. His cheerfulness, indeed, in a country where moroseness has become something more than a pose, is the one thing that seems to have impressed those who can still call his boyhood dimly to mind — that, and the ruddy countenance, the high colour of health, which he only lost during the last months of his life.

The sons did most of the work of the farm, and when, a few years ago, George Williams visited his early home, he took particular delight in pointing out the path along which he drove the sheep and the cattle to the famous Torr Steps, that relic of a prehistoric causeway across the Barle which lies at the bottom of the hill on which stands Ashway Farm, and how, fearful of ghosts and goblins — for the weirdest superstitions abound in this neighbourhood — he used as a boy to call to mind the old story of the way in which the devil himself built the bridge for a wager. Tennyson records a visit to these steps — "if it were only to see them the journey is worth while" — and his son describes how delighted the poet was with the sight of the tawny cows cooling themselves in midstream, of the green meadows leading to Ashway on one side, and of the great wooded slope which faces the farm.

George Williams obtained his first education at

the hands of Mrs. Timlett, who kept an old-fashioned dame school in Dulverton High Street. It was a rough four-mile ride from Ashway, and one of his earliest recollections was of riding to school in the early morning behind one of the farm hands, tightly clasping the man's leather belt. At an early age he was sent to Gloyn's Grammar School at Tiverton, the town of the two fords — following that same road from Dulverton which Jan Ridd describes as "not very delicate, yet nothing to complain of much — no deeper indeed than the hocks of a horse except in the rotten places." This is not the actual establishment described in the first chapter of *Lorna Doone*, but Blackmore, who drew the picture from the remembrance of his own school days, must have come to Tiverton only a year or two after George Williams left, and there can be little doubt that Gloyn's and the famous "school of Blundell's" had much in common. School life was hard and harsh everywhere then, and Tiverton had a reputation for roughness — it was Archbishop Temple who told how at Blundell's he used to chastise Blackmore by striking him on the head with a brass-headed hammer — so that it is no wonder that George Williams's recollections of those days were for the most part of privation and suffering. From time to time Amos Williams would ride over to Tiverton to visit his son, and in this connection a story is told of another farmer from the neighbourhood of Dulverton who, on one occasion, took the father's place and in parting with the boy gave him a shilling. George Williams never forgot, and many years afterwards, when the farmer's son came to London and applied for a situation at the house in St. Paul's Churchyard, the head of the establishment recognised the name and went out of his way to give the young fellow an excellent position, inquired constantly after his welfare, and did everything in his power to advance his prospects.

George Williams's religious upbringing as a boy was of the type that sufficed for the country farmer, then, as now, a determined upholder of all the traditions of Church and State. He was baptised and confirmed in the Church of England, and attended Dulverton Church with his family at somewhat irregular intervals. No one can be charged with prejudice in suggesting that the Church at that time had sunk very low. It was the day of the sporting parson, who was a sportsman first of all and last of all, a man upon whom the responsibility of a cure of souls weighed with amazing lightness, a day of the driest husks of religion. A typical clergyman of the West country in the days of George Williams's boyhood has been pictured by Whyte Melville in his Exmoor story *Katerfelto*, the scene of which is laid close to George Williams's home. "Parson Gale," he says, "was one of those ecclesiastics who looked upon his preferment and his parish as a layman of the present day looks upon a sporting manor and a hunting box. There were few men between Bodmin and Barnstaple who could vie with the parson in tying a fly, tailing an otter, handling a gamecock, using the fists, cudgelling, wrestling, and on occasion emptying a gallon of cider or a jack of double ale. And to these accomplishments must be added no little skill in doctoring and some practical knowledge of natural history. It is not to be supposed that the Rev. Abner Gale found much time for those classical and theological studies, to which he had never shown the slightest inclination." The religious atmosphere, of which so much is heard to-day, was unknown to George Williams's early boyhood, and often he must have seen the prizes for the village sports displayed within the church itself, the white hat decorated with ribbons in the place of honour by the reading desk, and have joined the procession led by the parson to the village green, where the wrestling and running matches were held immediately after the Sunday morning service.

It was a time of great stirrings and strife in the Church, a time when England was in the throes of a new birth, religious, social, and political, and soon after George Williams left school the sound of these things reached Dulverton. The feeling of expectation and unrest penetrated even to the farm on the hill. The family was outgrowing the home. The great polished table, the pride of every West country housewife, was overcrowded. The overworked land yielded more grudgingly; prices ruled high when the farmer bought and low when he sold. One of the sons was thinking of starting a business for himself at Dulverton, and round the family board there was no small discussion as to George's future. After leaving school at the age of thirteen he took up the work of the farm in earnest, but the brothers were not altogether satisfied with the way he was shaping. Had he, after all, the making of a farmer in him? For some reason he did not take kindly to the land, it actually seemed as if the love of the chase had not been bred in his bones. The desire for the larger life — a feeling almost inexplicable to the true British farmer who, to this day, in spite of all his grumblings, is unable to conceive how any sensible creature can choose the town when he might live on the land, and who even now, as I myself have heard, wonders what a man can find to do with himself all day long in London — was beginning to stir his fancy and dominate his dreams. And then, as he would tell in after years, a load of hay and a rut in the road settled the question. George was leading a cart of hay home to the rick in the yard. The clouds were coming over the hills and everything was being pressed forward to escape the storm. He was not watching his horses with the necessary care — one would like to imagine that he had lost himself in visions of great work in the future, but he himself has admitted that he could find no such excuse and that the accident arose from pure thoughtlessness — and in a moment the cart was overturned and horses, hay, and the boy were in the ditch. That, said the father and elder brothers in solemn conclave, ends the matter once and for all. George will never make a farmer. He is fit only for the town, and to town he shall go. In their judgment they could not have meted out a more severe punishment. It was a sentence of banishment. The brother in Dulverton was consulted, and suggested that George might be apprenticed to a draper with whom he was acquainted in Bridgwater.

And outside this draper's shop father and son drew rein on this evening in the summer of 1836.

George Williams had entered the world.

This book, which is a tribute to a man of the city, a man who for more than half a century worked day and night in the crowded, throbbing shadow of the Cathedral, raised upon the very heart of the world, begins then with a tribute to the man of the soil, to the soil itself. We know a little of the falseness of the picture of simple life on the land so beloved of poets and a certain class of social reformer; we have learnt something of its sordid side, of the meanness of its petty interests, of its viciousness, its narrowness, and the tragedy of an endless struggle to wake a tired soil into fruitful

SIR GEORGE WILLIAMS' HOMELAND
A view from the window of the farm on the hill

activity. But we men of the smoke and grime, of the narrow, noisy street and stifling warehouse, realise, too, how intolerable a thing this feverish life of ours will be for the children of those whose blood has never been purified by the rare, keen air from a thousand hills, whose sinews have never fought their way to strength and toughness against the wind and the storm, whose whole being is builded on the lines of least resistance. The men from God's out-of-doors, these are the men who have done and will do the great things for God and man in the world of the strenuous life. Watch how the children's children are paying the price of the city born and you will realise what a mighty part physical force is playing in this fight for existence. Look out for the man who has the brain of the city in the body from the country; he is the man who wins. From the bleak wilds of the North and the open lands of the South, day by day men are still pouring in to the cities and towns, all dowered with the supreme gift of good health, still pouring in as they did seventy years ago when George Williams arrived in Bridgwater.

George Williams owed something to the soil, more perhaps than he admitted to himself, for he was a townsman bred if not born, a man with all the instincts of the city. None who knew him could fail to be impressed by his extraordinary physical energy, by his power of endurance even to the end, by the mighty reserves of force that lay in the little frame and held disease at bay and again and again defied even Death. He took no exercise, no recreation. He never attended to his bodily well-being or comfort. He laughed at any suggestion of harbouring his strength. From morning till night, throughout the years, he toiled with body and brain, taking no thought of health, ignoring, it seemed, the simplest precautions, stretching and straining every nerve to its utmost limit, allowing himself no moment for recuperation. And yet he lived to be eighty-four, and crowded into his life the work of ten.

God-given this power was, we know, but something of its secret lay in his " Exmoor toughness," in the deeps of his chest and the mighty capacity of his heart and lungs, in that splendid inheritance from the men of the moors, from his boyhood on the hills.

THE SPIRITUAL HOMELAND AND
THE FATHERS IN CHRIST

CHAPTER II

THE SPIRITUAL HOMELAND AND THE FATHERS IN CHRIST

"I ENTERED Bridgwater a careless, thoughtless, godless, swearing young fellow" — thus George Williams made confession in after years.

He left Bridgwater an earnest, enthusiastic, whole-hearted worker for Christ and His Kingdom.

The change was wrought very quietly. It was the outcome of no sudden shock of emotion, no visible upheaval of spirit. George Williams had, it is true, an unswerving faith in the efficacy of "religious excitements," as the old preachers called them. In his time he witnessed many such revivals, at which multitudes were stirred, as by the voice of a prophet, into an agony of abasement and terror, when the Spirit strove openly with men and demons were publicly cast out. He took a personal and prominent share in some of the most wonderful of these missions. He was largely instrumental in arranging for Moody and Sankey's campaigns, and one of his last public appearances was connected with the work of Messrs. Torrey and Alexander. But he himself was not called by earthquake, fire, or great and strong wind. He was the child of the still small Voice.

Of the first two years spent with Mr. Holmes, the Bridgwater draper, we know little, except that the boy was uniformly attentive to his duties in the shop, a favourite with the other apprentices, and remarkably successful behind the counter, particularly in serving lady customers. In some inexplicable manner this farmer's son was born to the business, his knowledge and taste were intuitive. One of the assistants, Miss Thomas, who afterwards married George Williams's friend and fellow-worker, Mr. Beaumont, of Oxford, recorded some years since that her memory of the young apprentice was of a remarkably active, ruddy-faced boy, very diligent and persevering, and especially clever at haberdashery. In his spare hours he would make up lists of every detail he could lay hands on as to prices and customers, and his pockets were generally filled with business papers of all kinds.

In those days the drapery trade was not often specialised in departments. The country apprentice had to begin at the beginning and enjoyed the enormous advantage of being compelled to learn every detail of the business. As the youngest and last comer George Williams swept out the shop, ran errands, and filled his time with odd jobs of various kinds. There were twenty-seven assistants in Mr. Holmes's house, for he was the principal draper in the neighbourhood, and all "lived in." It is not a little curious that the old custom which prevailed in London in the time of Dick Whittington, of forming the employees in a drapery establishment into a kind of large family, has survived all these years. The system has many crying disadvantages, is open to much abuse, and is rapidly passing out of favour, but in the case of a master who regarded his responsibilities with just seriousness it was not without compensations, for in such instances there was a wholesome element of control and discipline in the arrangement. The hours of work were excessive, and the morals and conversation of many of the assistants in the Bridgwater shop anything but inspiring. Still there was in this establishment a definite religious atmosphere, due no doubt to the influence of Mr. Holmes, who was a regular attendant at the old Zion Congregational Chapel, and whose custom it was to insist that all the members of his staff should attend his own place of worship each Sunday morning. A clause to this effect was included in the apprenticeship indentures, and this rule greatly annoyed George Williams, brought up as he had been in the Establishment. He has recorded, however, that when he was inclined to protest against such a stipulation his mother very characteristically remarked that he could go to the parish church in the afternoon "to make up for it."

In a letter which has come into my possession

George Williams writes: " There were two other apprentices whom I soon found were different to myself. I was much given to swearing, and I saw increasingly that they were going to heaven, but that I was on the downward road to hell. I now began to pray, but, even on my knees, oaths would come into my lips. I had been brought up a Churchman, but my master required all his assistants to attend his own chapel. The gentleman who introduced me to the Bridgwater draper was himself a Unitarian, and on Sundays would invite me to dine with him, and then take me to his own chapel. But gradually I began to see that the doctrine which made light of the sacrifice of Christ could not be right, and one Sunday when there had been an eclipse of the sun I told the gentleman there was a new minister at the Congregational Chapel and I intended to go there. 'Oh, nonsense!' he replied, 'our minister is going to preach on the eclipse of the sun; you must come and hear him.' 'No,' I said, 'I will not.' 'Well,' said the gentleman, 'go if you like, but I will have nothing more to do with you.' He went to my parents and said he was afraid George would be no more good, as he had turned 'Methody.' So the whole family consulted together as to what had better be done, and at last one of my brothers wisely remarked, 'I should advise you to leave George alone, as it is possible he may be right and we may be wrong!'"

Of those who so greatly influenced him at this

time I can learn but little, and yet I would write the names of his fellow-assistants, Miss Harris, Miss Gerard, Miss Thomas, and William Harman, large across this chapter, for, unknowing, they played their part in the moulding of a great man and in the making of a great movement. Surely they have their reward, the reward laid up for those who make ready the ground for the sower of the seed. George Williams had many earnest talks with his fellow-apprentice, William Harman, who afterwards was prominent in the religious life of Bridgwater, "a man," as one who knew him writes, "of earnest piety, great energy and determination, with the heart of a child," and to this young man George Williams often expressed deep gratitude. But it was the life, not the word, that first attracted him, and that, I doubt not, was one of the reasons why the founder of the Young Men's Christian Association ever dwelt on the supreme importance of living Christ, ever preached the immeasurable possibilities of a single Christian life. "I felt," he said once in speaking of these days, "that there was a difference between me and these other assistants, and I tried to discover what it was." The doctrines of Unitarianism, which at that time had a large and influential following in the West country, failed to answer his questionings, and if, in after years, he was a strenuous foe to all that savoured of minimising the importance of the deity of Christ and

His vicarious, atoning sacrifice, it was because in his boyhood, when seeking for light, he found only greater darkness in humanitarianism.

One Sunday evening — it was in the winter of 1837, when he was just sixteen years old — he sat alone in a back seat in the little Congregational Chapel now used as the barracks of the Salvation Army. The minister was the Rev. Evan James, a man " of gentle spirit and holy life, whose grasp of principle was very firm," who had established a great hold on the young people of the town. Nothing is known of the sermon preached that evening, even the text is unrecorded, and it does not appear that the preacher was possessed of any special gift of eloquence, of any outstanding power of persuasion. No one can tell what arrow from God's sheaf entered the boy's heart. You must remember that he was seeking Christ, and was placing himself in the way of finding Him. George Williams did not make the mistake, so common with young men, of requiring some special dispensation, some peculiar heavenly vision; to make use of the old phrase, he did not despise the means of grace. Many years later at the opening of the splendid building devoted to the work of the Young Men's Christian Association which now overlooks the river at Bridgwater, and which was erected mainly by his efforts as a thank-offering for his spiritual homeland, he said: " It is not easy to forget one's first love. I first learnt in Bridgwater to love my dear Lord and Saviour for what He had done for me. I learnt at Bridgwater to see the vital importance, the tremendous importance, of the spiritual life. I saw in this town two roads, the downward road and the upward road. I began to reason, and said to myself, 'What if I continue along this downward road, where shall I get to, where is the end of it, what will become of me?' Thank God, I kept in the clean path, nevertheless I was on the downward road. I saw that this road would certainly lead me to spend my eternity with the devil and his angels, and I said, 'Cannot I escape? Is there no escape?' They told me in this very town of Bridgwater how to escape — Confess your sins, accept Christ, trust in Him, yield your heart to the Saviour."

Some men may write of the psychology of conversion, but I would not attempt to probe and search the great secret which a man may share only with his Maker. This only need be said: that night was the beginning, the point of turning. On his return from Zion Chapel George Williams knelt down at the back of the shop and gave his heart to God. "God helped me," he said very simply, in speaking of his conversion, "to yield myself wholly to Him. I cannot describe to you the joy and peace which flowed into my soul when first I saw that the Lord Jesus had died for my sins, and that they were all forgiven."

George Williams was admitted a member of the Church on February 14, 1838. The record runs: " Proposed by Rev. E. James . . . dismissed (transferred) to London the Rev. T. Binney." He attended his first Church meeting on the end of March, 1838, and at once took a prominent part in the work of the Church, indeed at the first meeting he is noted as seconding the motion for the election of deacons. Immediately afterwards he joined some others in the establishment of a prayer meeting in a room adjoining the business premises, and after attending for a time the Bible Class conducted by the father of James Sully, the eminent psychologist, became an ardent worker in the Sunday School.

" It is not how little but how much we can do for others " — that was the motto of every moment from sixteen to eighty-four. His being was tuned to that keynote at the very moment he made his great decision, and through all his days you might hear the insistent refrain: " He lived not unto himself but to the glory of God and in the service of men."

A man never escapes altogether from the influence of his first heart's home, and it is true in the realm of religion that the child is father to the man. The spiritual history of the great religious teachers and workers through the ages bears witness that, in spite of turmoil within and controversy without, of change in doctrine and outward semblance of belief, in spite of the wider range of intellect which grows with the years and which might well blot out the recollection of the early home, these men never escape, nor, in their heart of hearts, wish to escape, from the vision which came to them in the birthplace of their souls. There is in the new birth more than a verbal resemblance to natural birth, the expression " Fathers in Christ " is more than a beautiful phrase. And in all our roamings of spirit there's no place like home.

George Williams's spiritual homeland was a shop. The silent, mighty power of the Christian life lived under the ordinary commonplace circumstances of business, that was the memory of his homeland which he carried with him through changing scenes and years. Although he was one of those happy men who can point to the hour and place of the changed life, of the end and the beginning, it was the life, not the word, of other Christians that first prepared the way of the Lord to his heart. Did he ever forget?

And the Fathers in Christ? First of all, the Rev. Evan James, the man of no reputation, and, as far as we know, of no peculiar talents. Let the servant of the Most High, who labours in that most barren land of country church and chapel, often, it seems, more barren of hope than the most unlovely lands of heathenism, wearily waiting and watching for sign of harvest among the decorous respectability which listens to him Sunday after Sunday, men and women of such cramped hearts and souls that in them he is sometimes tempted to think the Son of Man hath not where to lay His head — let him, in the heaviness of his spirit, take heart of grace. George Williams is the brightest gem in the unfading crown of a simple country minister of the Gospel, who, in the common round of his work, without taking special thought or making special appeal, was the means of leading him to the Master.

Did George Williams ever forget? When riches and honour came to him it was ever one of his chief delights to help and encourage the humblest minister of the Gospel wherever he might be stationed. He believed, with all the certainty that came from the memory of the little chapel in Bridgwater, that the service for Christ unceasingly rendered in pulpit and on platform, by minister and missioner, is never wasted, never lost, never in vain.

And then, following this unknown minister, there enters the homeland the famous and startling figure of the Rev. Charles G. Finney, the great American evangelist. Years afterwards, when Finney was conducting his second campaign in London, George Williams attended his meetings, but it was through Finney's books — his *Lectures to Professing Christians* and his *Lectures on Revivals of Religion* — that this man's remarkable personality first entered the spiritual homeland of George Williams. No one shall ever measure the power for good that lies and shall

ever lie in a good book. To Law's *Serious Call* we
owe George Whitefield, and to these printed lectures
by Finney is certainly due much of the zeal and passion which produced the Young Men's Christian Association. These books were first published in 1837,
and must have fallen into George Williams's hands
in the first glow of his religious faith. They fanned
it into a flame which became a devouring fire. For
such a young man no more inspiring works could
have been found. George Williams was not a student,
not a great reader; matters of criticism and details
of doctrine always failed to excite his interest. He
knew nothing and cared nothing about the results of
linguistic or historical enquiry into the authenticity
of the Scriptures. There was neither poetry nor
mysticism in his being, and only a very practical
religion would have appealed to him. He belonged
to that generation of great men who in the twink-
ling of an eye were born, it would seem, into the fulness of their faith. Once the decision made, no
questionings seemed to trouble him. He was disturbed by no doubts. What he believed, he believed
with all his might. For a man whose aim was to
make others believe, no endowment could compare with
this power of unshaken, unshakable faith. And yet
there was nothing of complacency in his nature, his
conscience was very tender. What was the secret
of these men — for George Williams was typical of
many others of his time? They worked — all their

energies, spiritual, mental, physical, were concentrated in doing things. They had no time to talk or dream. For good or for evil they had little time even to think. There was, of course, more than a touch of harshness and of hardness in this certainty of belief which is peculiarly unattractive to these latter days when men sometimes place Charity on the throne of the Almighty. In Finney's books you will find the secret, not only of George Williams's certainty of belief, but also of his absorbing passion for souls and for the work that wins souls. As you read these addresses you will note phrases, sentences, points of view which will at once be recognised as having been adopted in their entirety by George Williams, and, more than that, there are episodes recounted by Charles Finney, episodes connected particularly with the visible and tangible results of prayer, which might be matched, almost word for word, from the experiences of George Williams.

Prayer — that was the rock upon which Charles Finney built, upon which he taught George Williams to build. "I heard," he said in one of his addresses, "of a person who prayed for sinners, and finally got into such a state of mind that she could not live without prayer. She could not rest day or night unless there was some one praying by her side; she would shriek in agony if the prayer ceased, and this continued for two days until she prevailed in prayer and her soul was relieved." George Williams knew

THE VILLAGE STREET AT DULVERTON

Showing the Church where George Williams was baptised, and the house where he first went to school

THE SPIRITUAL HOMELAND

what it was to experience that deep travail of spirit when a man lays hold on God for a blessing and will not let Him go until he has received it. There came a time when he, too, agonised in spirit for the souls of men, separately, individually; and would cease suddenly from this wrestling with Jehovah, cease because he knew, with an absolute certainty which no man can explain, that a soul was his to give back to God.

Prayer with a definite object was Finney's text; he was always pleading against the random prayer which accomplished little or nothing. Unceasing prayer, too, he taught; he was an apostle of the callous knees. He would often speak of him of whom it was written that his knees were callous, like a camel's, for he had prayed so much.

And with all his fervour and burning zeal, Finney was a man of the utmost practical common sense. To him the man who did not make the business in which he was engaged a part of his religion, did not serve God; such religion was "the laughing-stock of hell." There was good, sound common sense, too, in much of his advice as to the way of speaking to men on the subject of Salvation — advice George Williams certainly laid to heart. "Take him," says Finney, "when he is in a good temper. If you find him out of humour very probably he will get angry and abuse you. Better let him alone for that time or you will be likely to quench the Spirit. It is possible that you may be able to talk in such a way as to cool his temper — but it is not likely."

And, above all, Finney was never weary of pressing upon men the awful responsibility of each single individual. In one tremendous passage he cries: "Here you are, going to the judgment, red all over with blood. Sinners are to meet you there; those who have seen how you live, many of them already dead, and others you will never see again. What an influence you have exerted! Perhaps hundreds of souls will meet you in the judgment and curse you (if they are allowed to speak) for leading them to hell by practically denying the truth of the Gospel."

To Finney the great business on earth of every Christian was to save souls. "If you are thus neglecting the main business of life," he writes, "what are you living for?"

I have quoted these few phrases from Finney's books because they are little known by the younger generations, and because, as can easily be seen, they did much to mould and make George Williams what he was. He adopted, he absorbed Finney's creed. To him, from the day of his conversion, to live was Christ and to bring to Christ all with whom he came in contact; in season, out of season, always, everywhere, to preach Christ.

There was another side to Finney's teaching of which it would not be so pleasant to write. He was

THE SPIRITUAL HOMELAND 35

at times intolerant and bitter, and even the Rev. J. Barker, who wrote the preface to the collected addresses, finds him "infested with the errors of religious fatalism." He attacks, for instance, the humble habit of drinking tea and coffee, which are "well known to be positively injurious; intolerable to weak stomachs and as much as the strongest can dispose of," and points out how fearful a thing it is to think of the Church alone spending millions on its tea tables, when a world is going to hell for want of their help. "Parties of pleasure, balls, novel-reading, and other methods of wasting time" are unreservedly condemned. "Practise the worldly customs of New Year's Day," he says, "if you dare — at the peril of your soul." "Christians ought to be singular in dress as becomes a peculiar people, and thus pour contempt on the fashions of the ungodly in which they are dancing their way to hell." "Christian lady," he writes, "have you never doubted whether it be lawful to copy the extravagant fashions of the day brought from foreign countries and from places which it would be shame even to name? And if you doubt and do it you are condemned and must repent of your sin or you will be lost for ever." I am compelled to note these examples of Finney's extreme narrowness because this aspect of his teaching undoubtedly had its influence upon George Williams. It might have had a still greater effect, a very damaging effect upon his life and work, if it

had not been that he was privileged to come under
the sweet and mellowing teaching of a second Father
in Christ. It is hard to imagine a man who adopted
everything from Charles Finney and still kept his
hold upon young men throughout two generations
of intellectual progress. If George Williams had
been fashioned only by Finney, how he would have
antagonised and alienated some of the finest characters he attracted to his side. But all that was for-
bidding and harsh in the teaching of Charles Finney
was smoothed and polished and rendered beautiful by
the influence of Thomas Binney. Here, of course,
we anticipate a little, for it was after he left Bridgwater for London and became a regular attendant
at the Weigh House, whose pulpit was at that time
" beyond all question the most attractive and most
important in its moral influence in the City of London," that he fell under the spell of one who rounded
off and completed the work that Charles Finney had
hewn in the rough. These two men, Charles Finney
and Thomas Binney, great men both in their several ways, who thus met and joined in the heart and
life of George Williams, had hardly a trait in common, except devotion to a common Master. And the
order of their coming was of God. A man upon whom
Binney had first laid his hand would no doubt have
been repelled by the unattractive side of Finney's
religion, so repelled that he would probably have been
untouched by its inspiring power, and without Charles

Finney — "I report as a man may of God's work" — there had been no George Williams.

Do not let me be misunderstood. I am not exalting one Father in Christ above another. Some element of fanaticism, of exaggeration, of bigotry, if the word must be used, is essential in the initial stages of every great movement. That element Thomas Binney could never have supplied. It is true that there was a time when he was engaged in controversy of a particularly bitter nature, but into this he was forced by an unguarded phrase, and his whole being was compact of sympathy and broadest tolerance.

No need to write of Thomas Binney for the older generation which knew and revered him, and rejoiced even in his eccentricities and extravagances. Let those to whom he is but a name refer to the description given by Mark Rutherford, who was a devoted admirer, in his *Revolution in Tanner's Lane*, where, under the guise of the Rev. Thomas Bradshaw of Pike Street Meeting House, is pictured the Thomas Binney of George Williams's day. "He was," we read, "tall and spare, and showed his height in the pulpit, for he always spoke without a note, and used a small Bible, which he always held close to his eyes. He had a commanding figure, ruled his Church like a despot, had a crowded congregation of which the larger portion was masculine, and believed in predestination and the final perseverance of the saints. Although he took no active

part in politics, he was a Republican through and
through, and never hesitated for a moment in those
degenerate days to say what he thought of any
scandal." Thomas Binney's preaching and teaching
brought the fervid enthusiasm of Finney into touch
with the realities of a young man's life in London.
Probably no man of his time developed so pre-
eminently in the pulpit the tendency of the thinking
and reading of the age. He preached the reality of
the battle that is life, and as he pictured it the fight
was glorious, the victory sure. He had the greatest
sympathy with the aspirations of young men, with
their hopes, their intellectual and moral efforts, and,
withal, he was gifted with just that touch of sarcasm
which seems to be an essential part of a young man's
religious, as of his secular, education. The story
has often been told, for instance, of the way in which
he replied to certain young men who had spoken
with undue positiveness at a Church meeting, by
the suggestion that they should make a study of
2 Sam. x. 5, "Tarry at Jericho until your beards
be grown, and then return."

There was in his preaching, too, a fine scorn of
the tendency to belittle trade, which was prevalent
in those days. He hated hypocrisy, and said so in
unmeasured phrase. Character was his favourite
text, and he had a right to preach from such a text,
for he was a man every inch of him — " a king of
men," according to Archbishop Tait. Sir George

Williams learnt something of his pride of business from Thomas Binney, through whose discourses rang a constant endeavour to maintain the nobility of the commercial character. There was nothing petty or sentimental in his theology; he taught the dignity of manhood, the splendour of the life of honest work. "How the devil must chuckle," he once said, "at his success when he gets a fellow to think himself wonderful because he can dress in scarlet or blue, and have a sword by his side and a feather in his hat; and when he says to him (and the poor fool believing it), 'Your hands are far too delicate to be soiled by the counter and the shop'; and then whispers to him, 'Keep them for blood — human blood!' Fifty to one, as Buxton says of Plaistow and the Pope, fifty to one on the great unknown; on Brown, Smith, and Jones, or any one of them, against Cæsar and Napoleon; Wood Street against Waterloo the world over."

Perhaps the favourite theme of Thomas Binney, especially during the later years of his ministry, when George Williams came under the spell of his vivid eloquence, undimmed to the last, was sympathy, charity, love to the brethren. "Oh! let us have more faith in one another, though we sometimes lean on a reed that will pierce our hand, and perhaps pierce our heart; still do not let us give up faith in man — in Christian man. Do not let us give up a hearty and honest faith in manhood, truth, sincerity, righteousness, and purity of motive and purpose. Let us live with one another as if we really believed there was such a thing as brotherhood; and do not let us go through the world always frowning with suspicion, and always acting towards others as if we were afraid of what they would turn out. I think that if we are 'simple concerning evil,' there will not only be guilelessness in ourselves, but there will be an honest, noble, hearty, candid, confiding faith in one another."

It was through the influence of Thomas Binney, too, that that other noble merchant and philanthropist, Samuel Morley, was moulded to his broad sympathies and capacity for service. It was no wonder that a preacher who more than any one else in his generation made men think for themselves, take large views of life, attempt great and generous things, was followed to his last resting-place by such men as Dean Stanley, Dr. Stoughton, the Earl of Shaftesbury, Dr. Moffatt, Samuel Morley, and George Williams.

George Williams was to the end strict, stern, positive in his religious beliefs. He belonged to the old Evangelical school of thought, and he held to its creed with intensity and intense sincerity. But his heart was so great, his charity so broad, that the austerity of his doctrine was covered by the gracious mantle of kindness and sympathy. Sympathy could never have produced the Young Men's Christian

THE MOTHER OF SIR GEORGE WILLIAMS

Association, Calvinism could never have produced the Young Men's Christian Association. But these two, peace and the sword, love of the sinner and hatred of the sin, were welded and fused in the steadfast and loving heart of George Williams, who clung with fierce tenacity to the rigorous doctrines of the guilt of man and the wrath of God, but was so full of pity that under most bitter provocation he would think no evil, and was ever seeking for the face of goodness behind the mask of sin.

His was the ardour and passion of Charles Finney, but Thomas Binney taught him to draw men to Christ with cords of love.

A YOUNG MAN FROM THE COUNTRY

CHAPTER III

A YOUNG MAN FROM THE COUNTRY

WHEN, at the age of nineteen, George Williams's apprenticeship at Bridgwater came to an end, he was for a time undecided as to his future plans. His brother Fred, who was one of the first to leave the farm, had been for a short time in the employ of Messrs. Hitchcock & Rogers, a firm of retail drapers on Ludgate Hill, London. During his brother George's apprenticeship Fred Williams returned to Somersetshire and started for himself as a draper in North Petherton, a small village a few miles distant from Bridgwater. To him George Williams repaired after leaving Mr. Holmes's establishment, and for about six months he helped in his brother's shop, and was there "blessed to my brother's wife, who was a Unitarian and whose eyes were opened so that she owned Christ as her Saviour," while in his spare time he was much occupied with Sunday School work in the neighbouring villages. When Fred Williams next visited London, in October, 1841, to buy the new season's goods, he took George with him and introduced him to Mr. Hitchcock. At first the head of the London establishment declared that he could not find an opening for him. "No," he said in his abrupt way — and the boy's face fell — "I've no place for him. He's too small." The brother pleaded that, though there might be little of him, it was very good, and after some discussion Mr. Hitchcock went so far as to promise that if they would come again next morning he would see what he could do. "So," writes George Williams, "in fear and trembling I went again, and then Mr. Hitchcock said, 'Well, you seem a healthy young fellow! I will give you a trial.' I entered the establishment and began work behind the counter, where I remained a few years, until one day a buyer was seen cutting off a piece of silk and hiding it in his drawer. Mr. Hitchcock found this out and dismissed him, and I was put in his place. I succeeded so well," he adds, "that in a few years' time I had increased the turnover more than £30,000 a year."

Messrs. Hitchcock & Rogers, when George Williams entered their employ at a salary of £40 a year, did not confine themselves entirely to the retail trade, although this was then the principal part of their business. Mr. Hitchcock was himself a Devonshire man, and had gone through much the same routine of training as George Williams. He had been apprenticed to a draper in Exeter, and, after serving for some time in various London establishments, entered into partnership with Mr. Rogers in St. Paul's Churchyard, then, as now, a leading mart for drapery goods and a favourite shopping resort for ladies. Mr. Rogers was compelled at an early age to retire from active control in the business, but under Mr. Hitchcock's guidance the firm soon acquired a reputation for energy and enterprise, and became one of the leading retail houses in the City. So quick was the growth of the business that ten years after it had been established it was found necessary to employ a staff of about 140 assistants drawn from all parts of the country. Milliners and dressmakers and country drapers, attracted by the opportunity of a large selection of varied goods and by the convenience of lengths cut to suit their requirements at a low trade price, often visited the business, and in this manner a semi-wholesale trade of considerable magnitude was done, Messrs. Hitchcock & Rogers making a specialty of silk goods and shawls. Their windows were among the most noted in London at that time, and the business was of the best class and without competition in the neighbourhood.

The hours were then from seven to nine in the summer months and from seven to eight in winter, shorter hours than in many other houses. Mr. Hitchcock informed all newcomers that they were expected to attend church, but it was said that only a single pew was provided for the 140 assistants!

Needless to add that the custom was more honoured in the breach than in the observance. Whenever a new hand was engaged he had to sign a book agreeing to take his discharge at a moment's notice if required. All young men in the establishment wore black broadcloth coats, and a white tie was essential, while a moustache, if it was not, as in most similar establishments, a sin " beyond the imagination of the wildest youngster," was at least so uncommon that the sole assistant allowed the privilege was quite noted throughout the City as " Hitchcock's Frenchman." In those days a red tie or a tweed coat would have ruined the credit of any drapery house. Although Messrs. Hitchcock & Rogers's establishment was among the most progressive in London, one who entered the house about the same time as George Williams writes that there were two or three beds even in the smallest rooms, each bed occupied by two assistants. " On the last stroke of eleven bang went the outer door, and any on the wrong side of it were reported next morning. Many were the amusing scenes caused by the young fellows scurrying across the Yard to get in before the fated stroke, though the prolonged chiming and deliberate striking of the Cathedral clock gave timely warning to those in the neighbourhood. Soon after closing time, 10.30 for the apprentices and 11 o'clock for the other assistants, the shopwalker would come round to see that lights were out, and then, of course, when his back was turned, they were soon lit again, and we began to spend the evening." Of course, there was the inevitable public-house adjoining the shop — the famous "Goose and Gridiron" — which was used as an office by Wren when rebuilding the Cathedral, and which has now been absorbed in the establishment of Hitchcock, Williams, & Co. This place was, writes my informant, "a sad thorn in the side of Hitchcock & Rogers, for the young fellows, under pretence of going to see if the windows were properly dressed, would slip in for a drink. The woollen cloth shop at the Paternoster Row end of the building had rather a bad name in this respect. One or two bedrooms having windows overlooking the 'Goose and Gridiron' were occupied by young men who had an understanding with the landlord, so that when he heard a whistle he was to be on the *qui vive*, and the coast being clear, a Wellington boot was lowered at the end of a string, and bottles of beer having been placed in it, another whistle was the signal to heave it up again."

There is no reason to believe that at the time this young man from the country arrived in London he had formed any very definite or exalted ambitions. He was not one of those who, from the start, map out a brilliant future for themselves, who fix the goal of their ultimate ambition and work steadily towards it — and sometimes reach it. Although George Williams has been likened by some to Dick

Whittington, herein at least there was nothing in common between them. As a matter of fact, a few years later, while in the employ of Messrs. Hitchcock & Rogers, he gave serious consideration to the question of returning to Bridgwater and purchasing Mr. Holmes's business, then in the market, and it was due to the very strenuously worded advice of some of his older Bridgwater friends that he abandoned the idea of settling down as a country draper. There can be little doubt that the determining factor in his decision to enter London was not so much a desire to better his position as a deep conviction that in the City he would find larger opportunity, a wider field, of work for Christ.

Within a few months of his conversion he had changed the whole aspect of the Bridgwater shop. It was said in after years that when he joined Messrs. Hitchcock & Rogers it was almost impossible for a young man in the house to be a Christian, and that, three years afterwards, it was almost impossible to be anything else. This was certainly the case in Bridgwater, for in a few months the prayer meeting and the Bible class had become almost a part of the business routine. The passion of the pioneer was consuming him. He yearned for greater and grander conquests. And the call came to him from London. He had prayed for wider opportunities, for more arduous work for his Master, and the Master opened the way to the city of cities. In the fulness of years all things — wealth, honour, and the rich pleasures of success — were added, but this young man from the country entered London seeking first the Kingdom of God.

The London that George Williams came to was a hard place for a Christian young man. London will always typify all that is fiercest and most glorious in life's battle. It will ever be the place of heroes and of hideous failure, where everything that is good and evil in man is magnified. There is little enough of heaven in the great City to-day; there is, at least, less of hell than there was sixty years ago. Sir George Williams was right when he said, speaking of his early experiences in the City warehouse, that the first twenty-four hours of a young man's life in London usually settled his eternity in heaven or hell. In those days a young man was either burning hot or ice-cold, was utterly and completely possessed of God or just as completely given over to the powers of darkness. There was no middle road between the saint and the sinner. In the strictest sense that is ever so, but we of this generation have many resting-places on our Hills of Difficulty, many arbours set up in recent years by good men at the order of the Lord of the Hill. I know well that these may be, for some, places of slothful ease, that not a few linger now on the hill and fail to reach the highest heights. But it is surely better to have climbed half-way than never to have climbed at all. This is no place for a defence of that vast host of commonplace lives which some, not knowing the heart, would judge as Laodicean. I would rather bless the means, sacred and secular, which have made it possible for a man to live a clean and honest life before God without setting himself apart from his fellows. It is well enough to say that persecution and the brutal onslaughts of unrighteousness made heroes in the days that are past. That is true. They make heroes still. But it is well to remember that in ten thousand cases they damned those who had not in them the stuff of martyrs and saints. I would not make little of the strength that comes from resisted temptation, but we are none the less Christian because we pray to be led in a smooth path rather than across the rock-strewn hills.

Such paths run the length and breadth of London to-day. Sixty years ago you would have had to search diligently to discover a single one.

It is difficult to realise that little more than half a century separates us from the London which greeted the apprentice from Bridgwater. Most of the conveniences and luxuries of present-day life, to us the obvious necessities of existence, were then either unknown or in a vague experimental state. In many respects we are further removed to-day from the early Victorian age than that age was from the time of the Norman Conquest. Roughly speaking, the early nineteenth century was only the better of the eleventh to the extent of printing and gunpowder. The throb of steam was just beginning to shake the country, the hand loom in the worker's cottage was giving way to the power loom in the factory, the flail to the threshing-machine, the sewing-machine was just emerging from the scientific toy stage to the sphere of practical use, and it was not, as Sir Walter Besant has pointed out, until the year 1837 that the eighteenth century truly came to an end.

The light of the greatest revolution the world has ever seen, the morning of our modern renaissance, was breaking. A great darkness still shrouded London, and the life of the City shop assistant was still little removed from that of a slave.

To-day nearly every young man has attained his ideal of a forty-eight-hour week, and although longer hours prevail in suburban establishments, it will be generally admitted that the early-closing movement has brought about a fairly satisfactory and equitable state of affairs. In the early forties things were indeed different. The living-in system was conducted on lines that contemptuously ignored the moral and physical welfare of young men. Many striking and terrible pictures of these days are given in the reports and other publications of the Metropolitan Early-Closing Association, established the year George Williams came to London under the title of "The Metropolitan Drapers' Association." This Association offered a prize of twenty guineas for "the best practical essay on the evils of the present protracted hours of trade generally, but more especially as they affect the moral, physical, and intellectual condition of the drapers of the Metropolis." The prize essay, published in the following year, was the work of one who wrote from his own bitter experience, and affords a vivid picture of life as George Williams found it when he reached London. The hours varied from six, seven, and eight in the morning to nine, ten, and even twelve at night. Even in Messrs. Hitchcock & Rogers's the first batch of assistants had to be at work at seven o'clock to dust the warehouse. These were known as the Literary Squad, a name taken from a comic song, "The Literary Dustman," then greatly in vogue. The shop would be closed at from eight to nine P. M. in winter and from nine to ten P. M. in summer, but on busy days, and during nearly the whole of the spring and summer seasons, the young men were seldom at liberty to leave until two or three hours after closing time, for much of the work now done by porters fell to the lot of the junior assistants, who had to put every article — from a piece of silk to a paper of pins — into its appointed place, and clean out the premises in readiness for the morrow. During the busiest part of the year it was a common thing for these young men to be penned in the unhealthy atmosphere of the shop from six or seven o'clock in the morning until ten or eleven o'clock at night. "This," says the writer, " presents the business of the day in its most favourable aspect." There were many shops in which the young men were employed for a period of seventeen hours out of twenty-four. On Saturday, as if in mockery of preparation for the Sabbath, the closing hours were in all cases later, and the assistants were often unable to retire to rest until one or two o'clock on Sunday morning.

In few houses of business was there any sitting-room other than the dining-room, which was often a basement kitchen, while the sleeping apartments were small and badly ventilated.

The harmful effect upon health and morals of such long confinement, of the foul air and lack of exercise, of hurried meals — the average time spent at three meals, breakfast, dinner, and tea, was often not more than half an hour [1] — are so obvious that we need not follow the writer in his attempt to make a case in favour of a shorter working day. One of

[1] This almost incredible statement is vouched for by the writer of the " Prize Essay on the Evils which are produced by Late Hours of Business" (London : James Nisbet & Co., 1843). He writes : " To sit down (in the shop) for any period, however short, is universally forbidden. Be it also observed that while the mechanic or day labourer has half an hour allowed him for breakfast, and an hour for dinner, out of his twelve hours of labour, the assistant draper has no fixed time for either. Five or ten minutes is the usual time spent at breakfast or tea ; and dinner is hurriedly snatched as it can be during some momentary intermission of business. We may safely assert that in nineteen shops out of twenty the average time spent at the *three meals* — breakfast, dinner, and tea — is not more than half an hour."

the evil results of this tyranny was that the men were, of necessity, withdrawn from most opportunities of reading and study, and the lack of popular newspapers deprived them of any intelligent participation in the movements of the day. Even when the tone of the establishment was not actively immoral, life was lived on a low, dull plane. Business, supper, a walk, and then to bed — that was the daily round. Of these young men it might truly have been said that no man cared for their souls. And when George Williams came to London there were at least 150,000 such assistants in the City of London. The essay contains the significant statement that in a prominent Mechanics' Institute there was only one linen-draper out of nearly seven hundred members. Worse still, this system was a direct incentive to vice. Young men engaged in shops do not differ from their fellows in their craving for some kind of recreation and amusement. Their late hours prevented them from the enjoyment of what little rational and wholesome recreation was available at that time in London, with the natural result that the desire for something which would take them, even for a few moments, out of themselves and away from the restrictions and sordid grind of their work, found gratification in the lowest form of sensual enjoyment. When at last they were free, they turned, by an irresistible impulse, to the tavern, to strong drink, to the grossest forms of immorality. Surely, says the author of this essay,

HIGH STREET, BRIDGWATER, IN WHICH MR. HOLMES' SHOP WAS SITUATED
From an old drawing in the possession of George B. Sully, Esq.

the ruin of their souls was chargeable, in no slight degree, to that system which furnished at once temptation and excuse.

This tale of long hours does not, unfortunately, exhaust the evils peculiar to the shop life of the period. The new reign had brought with it a great revival of trade. As a result new hands were constantly being taken on, and little or no care was given to the selection of the men who offered themselves, for the employer always guarded himself by the stipulation that any one might be dismissed literally at a moment's notice. Thus these houses of business generally contained a very mixed set of men. Those of pure mind and high ideals were forced to associate in closest intimacy with the vicious and depraved. In this way every possible aid was given to the corruption of good manners by evil communications. In the conduct of business the code of commercial morality was degraded in the extreme. It was a time when all scruples of truth and honesty were ignored when a sale was to be effected, when a premium was set upon misrepresentation, when intemperance and dissolute living were winked at in the case of a skilful salesman, when in one large West End house the example of a man, notorious for the unblushing lies he told and for the unmerciful way in which he fleeced customers, was held up for imitation by the junior hands. "There was," wrote one who was at that time employed in St. Paul's Churchyard and who afterwards entered the ministry, "no class more degraded and dissolute, none who were sunk deeper in ungodliness and dissipation than the shopmen of London." The subject does not bear enlarging upon. The effect upon a boy fresh from the country of being compelled to live and work, to share a bedroom, and in many cases the bed itself, with veterans in vice — men so sunk in debauchery that they took a hellish delight in contaminating and defiling all around them — these things are best left to the imagination.

Here, surely, was a condition of life which might drive the best meaning of young men, through sheer desperation, into grossness and depravity. With no time for wholesome intellectual or physical recreation, even were such facilities available, no place to spend a quiet hour other than a reeking dining-room or the barest of bedrooms, it is little wonder that they were driven out into the street, to seek there such ignoble joys and pleasures as might be found. And there, you may be sure, the pleasures were indeed ignoble enough. Nowadays, if a young man determines to go to the devil, he must first deliberately, and of free choice, reject a thousand and one opportunities of good. But in the early part of the nineteenth century he had to scheme and hunt for such opportunities, and all round him men were playing fast and loose with the little time they had not sold to their employers.

The young fellow of the period, in search of a moment's freedom from the cares and trammels of business, found his way, as a matter of course, to the tavern with its sing-song and free-and-easy. Here heavy drinking was the rule — heavy in quality and quantity. Gambling was rampant everywhere. The place reeked with tobacco smoke, the songs and conversation were coarse even beyond the bounds of obscenity. In the summer Highbury Barn and Cremorne Gardens, pleasure grounds of very doubtful reputation — " for one man that is ruined in a gin-shop there are twenty that are ruined at Cremorne " — were sometimes patronised by those fortunate individuals who could escape for a few hours. Tavern life was then near its end, and the last days of a popular institution are rarely its most attractive. The tavern, as Dr. Johnson knew it, was little changed in outward appearance, but for intellect and wit had been substituted the inane vulgarity of the so-called comic song, roared out in chorus by young and old to the accompaniment of clattering pewter and glass. The public-houses, which prospered so greatly in the neighbourhood of every large warehouse, were not unlike the supper-rooms patronised by the young bloods of the period, differing only in degree of freedom and ease. Unfortunately few of them could boast of even an occasional visit from a Colonel Newcome. It was seldom that any voice was raised in protest, seldom that the " harmony " was disturbed by such an outburst as was called forth from that gallant gentleman by a similar entertainment at the " Cave." " Does any man say ' Go on ' to such disgusting ribaldry as this? For my part I am not sorry that my son should see for once in his life to what shame and degradation and dishonour drunkenness and whisky may bring a man." It was to such places that the young men of the City had to turn to escape the counter and the dormitory.

It was in surroundings such as these, among men such as these, that the Young Men's Christian Association saw the light. And not the Young Men's Christian Association only, for while London life in the early forties was, for the most part, low in standard, while morals were coarse and appetite unrestrained, there were many who had already seen and hailed the star of the morning, many who had watched the faint streaks of light on the horizon, the radiance on the distant hills, and rejoiced in the certainty that midnight was passed. These prophets of the days of the Son of Man were as yet scattered and lonely, but as the years passed they caught sight of many " lights at other windows," and took courage and worked even more strenuously for the coming of righteousness and justice. It was, as we have said, a period of strange contrasts. A man's conversation was devout or filthy, his recreation the service of Christ or the amusement of Satan. It was at once a time of sloth and fiery energy, of ignoble ideals and loftiest ambitions. From the point of view of material success it was a time full of good hope, for to those who won through its temptations the business life of those days was a splendid training, while the chances of promotion were much greater than they are to-day. There was a mighty uplift in British trade, and young men of quickness and ability were wanted everywhere. Determination, hard work, integrity, and energy reaped an immediate and rich reward. It was the day in which the boy without the proverbial sixpence made a fortune in a few years. It was a day of days for the young man who could see visions, who dared to fight for the realisation of his dreams. And some were already dreaming them true.

When George Williams arrived at Messrs. Hitchcock & Rogers's, Charles Kingsley was planning with all the vehemence of his impetuous nature a hundred and one schemes for the improvement of the material and moral conditions of the working classes. He had just published *Yeast*, wherein he had shown "what some at least of the young men in these days are really thinking and feeling." Charles Kingsley was among those who heard with awe and rejoicing a clashing among the dry bones. "Look around you," said Barnakill to Lancelot as they stood within a few yards of the place where George Williams was working, "and see what is the characteristic of your country, your generation, at this moment. What a yearning, what an expectation amid infinite falsehoods and confusions, of some nobler, more chivalrous, more godlike state! . . . What a chaos of noble materials is here — all confused, it is true, polarised, jarring, and chaotic; here bigotry, there self-will, superstition, sheer atheism often, but only waiting for the one inspiring Spirit to organise and unite and consecrate this chaos into the noblest polity the world ever saw realised."

Carlyle was issuing *Past and Present* — Carlyle was coming to his own, forcing men to think deep thoughts, to ask deep questions, to " begin to try." Ruskin was at work on *Modern Painters;* Tennyson and Dickens, in their several ways, were struggling to lighten the darkness; Lord Ashley was waging his magnificent warfare against oppression, tyranny, and injustice. On all sides voices were calling young men to come out from the world of cant and lies, to come out and dare.

In the religious world the Anglican revival was beginning, the Oxford movement was at the height of its power, Maurice was in the midst of his Christian Socialism campaign, Newman was making his great decision, and Chalmers was daring all for liberty.

Revolution, violent and horrible; revolution, peaceful, sometimes silent, but no less effective, — revolution was in the air. In politics, in arts, in religion, it was a time of upheaval. But the mass of the people still slept.

George Williams was not, it may be, consciously stirred by the mighty activities of the day, although Thomas Binney, that veteran watchman on the towers, was ever proclaiming the dawn and teaching young men to read the signs of the times. George Williams was of those whom poets despise but God honours, who see things to do, see them and do them. This young man was so absorbed in business, not only, or chiefly, for his own gain, but in business for his Master, that he seldom spared a moment for a sight of the world's horizon. Under his very hands there was so much to be done, so little time to do it. In any age his work would have prospered; but it was, without doubt, the splendid hope, the eager expectation of those days that secured for it such quick and enthusiastic recognition. Everywhere men were waiting for a leader. Everywhere men were launching out on glorious ventures of faith. The air was tingling with enterprise and progress.

To the sound of turmoil and strife, of revolutions, riots, and bitter controversies, Britain was fighting its way to religious and social liberty.

"And lo, in the East! Will the East unveil?
The East is unveiled, the East hath confessed
A flush; 't is dead; 't is alive; 't is dead, ere the West
Was aware of it: nay, 't is abiding, 't is unwithdrawn;
Have a care, sweet Heaven! 'T is dawn."

It was the day of the Young Man.

THE WORLD AND A YOUNG MAN

CHAPTER IV

THE WORLD AND A YOUNG MAN

IN order to appraise and understand a man's work you must know something not only of his environment but of his personality, of that inner life through which and in which the work first has its being. This young man from the country was chosen of God to start an unique and wonderful movement in the world. Three years after his arrival in the City the call came. He was ready. Some attempt must be made to picture the man as he was during these years of preparation; and this is not easily accomplished, especially when one is writing of days beyond recall of all but the few. In such circumstances it is safest to rely upon letters and private documents of various kinds which reveal the hidden things of the soul.

Unfortunately Sir George Williams left little material of this kind. During the latter years of his life he was often urged to put on record his reminiscences of things done and seen, but his invariable reply was that his life had been so uneventful that he had nothing to give to the world. Moreover, contrary to the accepted idea of the garrulity of old age, he was a man who seldom spoke of the past, seldom indulged in reviews of the years gone by — that favourite pastime of life's evening. Up to the last he lived in the future, for the future. It is no exaggeration to say that he died a young man.

Thus it is that I have before me but few papers of a personal nature. In his later years he kept a small pocket diary, but this contains only notes as to the time and place of the innumerable meetings at which he presided or in which he took some prominent part. To those who knew the man the reproduction of this diary of his daily engagements would mean much. It is the eloquent record of work that was never finished, of the daily life of one who, although often tired, was ever ready to serve the least of his brethren — His brethren. But it contains no revelation of the man's thoughts, of his innermost life. That must be gleaned for the most part from the acts of a nineteenth-century apostle.

There exist, however, three small books in his handwriting which are very precious. One is a manuscript volume of the sermons he heard during his early years in London. It is dated " January, 1841," the year of his arrival at the drapery establishment of Messrs. Hitchcock & Rogers. On the fly-leaf he has written: " February 5th, 1838 — Joined the Church at Bridgwater, and since that period proved an unworthy member. January 30th, 1839. Signed the teetotal pledge after hearing a convincing lecture from G. Pilkington, at the Friends' Meeting House, Bridgwater." I have already written of the services which he attended during these early years in the City, and of the men who did much to mould his religious beliefs. These transcriptions of sermons are interesting only as pointing to the preachers he most appreciated, and also because they contain, at the end of each sermon, a characteristic note, giving the names of the young fellows in the warehouse whom he persuaded to accompany him on each occasion. George Williams had the instincts of a missionary. If he could do nothing else, he could always discover some excuse for bringing men within the sound of the Gospel.

The diaries are of a much more intimate and personal character, and call for more detailed notice. They form the valuable autobiography of a Christian young man. Commonplace they may be — it is fortunate that men of twenty do not often write with an eye on posterity — but no excuse is needed for quoting some sentences from them, for, trivial as these may sound, they are at least full of self-revelation.

The world is so crowded with hypocrisy that in surveying the life of such a man as the founder of the Young Men's Christian Association, one naturally asks the question which so often discovers the giant's feet of clay: Did he practise what he preached?

He asked much of young men; no one, indeed, could ask more. He demanded of them a great sacrifice, the greatest of sacrifices. Did he deny himself? Easy enough for the man of years and honour, for whom success has made the pathway smooth, to talk of the Christian life a young man should lead in the City, of the beauty of holiness, of keeping one's self unspotted from the world. Easy enough for one raised above the press of care and throng of work to speak of the claims of Christ upon a young man's time and thought and money. What of the young man himself when he *was* young? Was he ever young? Or was he one of those unattractive phenomenons who are born old? Easy enough to talk of a young man's temptations from the serene heights of age and wealth, when the blood has cooled and desires have dulled, and a settled, certain comfort has rolled the roughness out of existence and softened its harsh conflicts. What of the young man himself, in the fierce heat of the fight, when he was making his way, forcing his way? What of the days when the tempter was a roaring lion, when passions flamed within him?

Did he, like so many, conveniently forget in after years the days of apprenticeship and struggle? Did he, like so many, build an imaginary past out of the desires of the present? Did he, greatly daring, preach a piety, a purity he had never practised?

Fair questions these; questions often asked, I

doubt not, of such men as Sir George Williams; questions to which he could never reply in his lifetime. Strange it is how many of life's questions can only be answered by death, how often a man's lips are sealed till his eyes are for ever closed. It is true that I might refer to the testimony of the few contemporaries of those early days who still survive him, but memories of such matters of the secret life are too often rose-tinted by time. Let me show how, in these days, as in the years that followed, his life never mocked his lips. As a man thinketh in his heart — these are his heart thoughts.

On the first day of the New Year, 1843, he writes: "Went to Woodbridge prayer meeting quarter after seven o'clock; attended our prayer meeting from nine to ten; heard Mr. Binney — ordinance day. Afternoon met various schools at Weigh House; closed about half-past four o'clock. Returned to Hitchcock's to tea. Attended our prayer meeting; went to chapel; heard Mr. Binney — a good day."

But, it will be said at once, this is a record of a Sunday, of the first Sunday of the year — the day of the new leaf in most lives — this is no fair test of a young man's religion. Many are the sneers at a one-day-in-the-week piety. But it may safely be said that you can gauge with some accuracy the fervour, if not necessarily the sincerity, of a busy man's faith by his life on Sunday. I know the arguments which may well be brought against a restless day of rest, a day crowded with work, as George Williams lived it through his career. I know, too, that in spite of the long and tedious hours of labour sixty years ago, the mental and moral strain of business was light judged by the standards of to-day, so that it would be unfair to reason that what was possible for a young man in the City in 1843, is equally possible, or, if possible, wise and justifiable, at the present time. Still, Sunday offered then, even more than it offers now, the one opportunity in the week for recreation, was then, even more than it is now, the one day of escape.

One of the secrets of George Williams's success in all his undertakings, religious as well as commercial, was his extraordinary capacity for work, his tireless energy of brain and body. It is a commonplace to speak of change of work as recreation, but that was the Sabbath rest as George Williams understood it. So far from the first Sunday being in any way an exception, it is one of the quietest recorded in these diaries. In addition to the Sunday School work at the Weigh House, which occupied him increasingly, he was soon visiting the slums on Sunday afternoon, and holding services in the darkest districts of London, whose darkness in those days was night indeed. Mr. Creese tells how the first day he spent in London he accompanied George Williams to the slums to visit absentee Sunday School children. "He ran up the almost perpendicular stairs with

THE FRIENDS' MEETING-HOUSE, BRIDGWATER.
Where, at the age of eighteen, George Williams signed the "Teetotal Pledge"

the lissomness of a cat, while I stumbled after him. On the top landing the voices of children were heard, and a rap at the door brought the mother, who cautiously opened it some six inches. George put his foot in to keep it from being closed, and asked if she had any children. After a little coaxing we were admitted, and my companion talked to mother and children and persuaded them to promise to be ready on the next Sunday when he would come and fetch them to school. Descending to the next landing, a gruff voice, ' Come in,' brought us into the presence of four Irishmen, who were playing cards. George Williams stood before them undaunted and, ignoring their protests that they had been to mass in the morning, denounced their conduct in such a terrific manner that we left them silent and evidently much impressed. He could be as tender as a mother with the children in the garret, but would meet the Sabbath breaker with the boldness of a lion."

A few Sundays later George Williams writes: "Got up at twenty minutes to seven, Scripture and prayer meeting in Room No. 2, heard Mr. Sherman on ' A Gracious Refuge.' Afternoon went to Darby Street School and visited Rag Fair. Another prayer meeting in No. 2. Heard, in the evening, Mr. Smith, of Brook Street Chapel." Then follows a list of the young fellows in the house whom he induced to accompany him to the various services, and the entry adds, " Quite enjoyed the day."

Early in the year he was appointed Secretary of the Sunday School at the Weigh House, and prays that "this office may not raise my vanity, but in every way may I be kept humble, in the valley, seeking His glory." In December he was visiting Duck Lane, Westminster, where he "sought out a congregation by candle-light, went into lodging-houses, and got them to come and listen to the Gospel," and soon he was too occupied with religious work of all kinds to attend regularly the services at Weigh House. By the end of the year he was addressing at least three services on Sunday — Mrs. Cutting's school in the morning, the little gathering of poor people at Husbord Street in the afternoon, and in the evening an open-air meeting at Duck Lane, besides attending several prayer meetings in the house of business, visiting various cottages round Paddington Green, and looking up children absent from the Sunday School.

A few months later he writes that he spent Sunday morning at Darby Street with the Sunday School, the afternoon at the Weigh House Sunday School, and the evening at Jurston Street Ragged School, and there can be no doubt that this young man of the cheery manner and unbounded enthusiasm was greatly in demand in a number of districts, especially in connection with work among children. In this way, while he had health and strength, his Sundays were always occupied. The work changed with the years. His Bible Class for young men, of which I shall have occasion to write later, gradually took the place of the afternoon Sunday School, and in its turn gave way to other gatherings of the Young Men's Christian Association. Heavy business responsibilities, marriage, a home of his own, a growing family — these were never allowed to interfere with his Sunday programme of work. As it was in the early days, so it continued. In this, as in most things, the young man of 1843 had settled and determined his life. George Williams kept young because he had no desire and no occasion to change his way of living when he was old.

The characteristic note of George Williams's religion in later life was its unfailing optimism, its sunniness. This was always the chief impression which those who met him casually took away from his presence. He seemed never to know what it was to be down-hearted or disappointed. When London was bound in fog, his office was radiant with sunshine. But one is glad to find that this was not the prevailing note of the early days — glad, because such serenity in a young man of twenty-three is unhealthy, and is almost invariably associated with smugness and self-complacency, that odious soul-sickness so sadly prevalent among young Christians. George Williams knew much of that divine discontent which humbles a man to the dust, which often digs the grave into which men are buried with Christ and from which they are raised up to walk in newness of life. He was, like most men of his age, decidedly introspective in religious matters. He had been taught by his fathers in Christ to examine himself, and he did this with his usual thoroughness. He was fond of tapping his spiritual barometer, and although the hand seldom fell to storm — in all his life you will see that storms generally passed him by — still there were times when the glass was low. Thus he writes: " Had a dark and gloomy spiritual week. Much to mourn over. Studied the predictions in the Old Testament and their fulfilment. A dark week." For several days afterwards he was " under a cloud," having " scarcely any enjoyment in prayer and not enjoying the happy feeling of unitedness to Christ. A week of much spiritual darkness and gloom." And again a little later: " A terrible week. Many things to mourn over. Much spiritual darkness. Done little for God. Cold in prayer. Oh, that the Lord would be pleased to revive His work in my heart! Oh, that God would pour out His Spirit, and cause this valley of dry bones to live!"

And then, as always, the gloom was dispelled by the gladness of more work for his Master. A day or two afterwards, he tells how " fourteen attended a prayer meeting in one of the bedrooms," and how he has much to encourage him, as " many young men have entered the business amongst whom we have been able to break the Bread of Life." with the result that "through the mercy of God I have enjoyed prayer a little more, and am feeling greater pleasure in glorifying Christ in all things." Again and again, after days of darkness and sorrow, we find him telling how he found happiness "in the service of Christ," and as a result of toil for others "found converse sweet with God." On most days he notes his meditation on special subjects. He writes, for instance, "Spiritually dwelt on humility. Had my mind much affected by the signs of the times. . . . Thought on the blessings pronounced on the meek. . . . Thought on the proper humility which is so attractive in the sight of God. . . . Studied meekness." At another time, "Thought on many who were blessed because they were hungering and thirsting after God." This prayer for humility is echoed from day to day, and who shall say that it was not abundantly answered in the years that followed, when a man who had more cause than most for pride, never lost the beauty of a simple spirit?

He writes much, too, of the loving kindness and mercy of God, which was always, I think, his favourite theme, the heart of his Gospel. "Oh, His great mercies in sparing me," he says at one time after he had been ill, "how ungrateful am I to Him! How few of His mercies do I appreciate. How kindly does He afflict. What do I deserve instead of gentle affliction? The rod, the frown, the trial. How great does His long-suffering abound toward

His sinful servant. How good is God in not sending me to hell. How plenteous in goodness and truth. . . . Oh, His love displayed in the atonement of Christ, how sweet to meditate on it."

It almost shocks us to find him mourning again and again his slothfulness in doing the Lord's business. Surely if ever a young man might have said, "I have been very jealous for the Lord," it was George Williams, but he was so filled with the ambition of God that he was ever conscious of failure to attain. "How much reason have I," he writes, "to be ashamed of myself, not only for not speaking to those I meet with on the all-important subject, but for exemplifying so much of the world in myself." He was but twenty-two years of age when he made this entry: "Hitherto the Lord hath brought me through many trials. Oh, my soul, how dull to spiritual things. How swift the time is passing, and ere long thou wilt leave all those near and dear to thee on earth. Make good use of thy time, like Whitefield did, in bringing souls to Christ."

Although it would appear that every spare moment during these years was occupied with religious work both inside and outside the house of business, it must not be imagined that he never went out into the world. Throughout his life he had a keen enjoyment of social functions, and there was not the slightest taint of the kill-joy about him.

He was fully alive to the interests of the life

beyond the warehouse. Politician he never was. He was never, indeed, a party man even in ecclesiastical matters, although at this time he was agitated by the Maynooth grant, and records several discussions as to Church and State with his friends. From the first he would tolerate no distinction of creed or party in Christian intercourse. In this connection Mr. Creese tells a characteristic story. He writes: " One Sunday evening four young men were standing talking outside Messrs. Hitchcock & Rogers's before separating each to go to his chosen place of worship. George Williams was one, I was another. It happened that four sections of the Christian Church were represented by us; but this was unnoticed by all excepting George, who, without a word, suddenly threw his arms around our necks, drawing us closely together, and said, ' Here we are Churchman, Baptist, Independent, Wesleyan — four creeds, one in Christ. Come along.'"

One of the first entries in the diaries refers to his decision to learn music, and it is interesting to note that he received his lessons at Exeter Hall. He evidently had some doubts as to the wisdom of this course, and it takes one back a long way to read that he decided in favour of music by lot. He evidently settled many difficult matters in the old Scriptural manner, for later he notes that he decided by lot not to attend one of Dr. Binney's teachers' teas. The music lessons took a good deal of time, and at one stage he wondered whether they were not interfering with his work, but he seems to have been encouraged by his progress, and writes with some gratification that he has "got beyond the Lark." Although he could never lay claim to any peculiar musical talent, George Williams always insisted upon the value and importance of music and singing, and he was certainly not a little grieved at the objections raised in after years by certain members of the Young Men's Christian Association against the sacred concerts held in Exeter Hall.

Later he joined an elocution class, and recited " a piece by Byron." "I hope," he says, " it will be the means of doing me good, so that I may be better able to work for Christ." He was fond, too, of walks in the country, especially when accompanied by his friends from the house — he was no lover of the life solitary — and when his relations came up from the country he would take them to Madame Tussaud's, and to the Polytechnic Institute, with its lectures, microscopes, and dissolving views, at that time one of the great show places of London, founded, as *Punch* stated in 1843, "for the exhibition of objects of art among its curiosities, and occasionally objects of nature among its visitors." He was, too, a regular attendant at lectures of all kinds. This was the period of the Mutual Improvement Societies. George Williams made good use of the opportunities they afforded of adding to a somewhat scanty education, though I do not think he, like so many self-made men, ever

THE BRIDGE ACROSS THE RIVER AT BRIDGWATER

At the end of the bridge now stands the George Williams Memorial Building of the Young Men's Christian Association
From an old drawing in the possession of George B. Sully, Esq.

put an absurdly high value on learning. Certainly he cared little for books, except in so far as they served him in his service for others.

During these first years in the City he spent his holidays with his family in Somerset, and the diaries contain references to two visits to his old home in 1843 and 1844. The religion of a Christian young man is often as severely tested by family as by business relationships, especially when the family does not display the most cordial sympathy with his aspirations. A man's home is still the hardest of mission fields. All the members of George Williams's family were constantly in his thoughts and prayers. He writes to them regularly, always putting in some plea for his Master. Hardly a day passes without a reference in the diary to a letter from his pen to some friend or relation in the country, and his unvarying practice of closing with an appeal on behalf of the things of the soul, was not the outcome of a habit of later times, but a part of his day's plan of work from the time that work began. Once more, here is proof of the way in which he modelled all his life on the lines of these early years. Again and again, in the sacred privacy of his diary, he goes over the loved names one by one, noting, for instance, that he has nearly one hundred relations, of whom he fears very few are saved; yearning over them, grieving for them, praying for each and all. He is greatly encouraged by their replies to his letters, and rejoices with unspeakable joy over the conversion of more than one.

It is evident that his mother, for whom he cherished the deepest affection, was in full accord with him, and on his return home she and one of his brothers used to accompany him to the meetings and services he attended almost every day. On Sunday they go together to hear the public examination of the children of Dulverton, the next day he has a "solemn conversation" with one of his uncles, on Wednesday he addresses the children at Dulverton; later in the week, in company with Mr. Poole, the Congregational minister of Dulverton, he goes to the outlying villages, distributes tracts, and again addresses children's services. On Saturday he visits his brother's home, and has "a little prayer meeting after tea." During the following week he assists at a farm sale, and has his soul "vexed with the lies and oaths of the auctioneer." "I talked with him," he writes, "but found him too far gone in drink to do any good, I fear. Oh, the curse of being too anxious for money!" On his return to London he makes the following entry in his diary: "Blessed be His holy name for all the goodness and mercy I have received. May this visit be of great good. Having sown the seed, I now pray for its growth." And later he records that one of his friends in Somerset had written to thank him "for being, through God, the unworthy instrument of leading her to Jesus." "Oh, Lord," he writes, "how long ere more of my own relatives will be brought to serve and glorify Thee on the earth? Is it not Thy will that all shall be saved? Oh, Thou Spirit, wilt Thou be pleased to exert Thy power on the hearts of my poor relatives that they may all be brought to Jesus?"

If the life of Sir George Williams has any message, if his life work, the Young Men's Christian Association, has any permanent message, both life and work must speak in no uncertain way of the possibility of practical religion. Of the genuineness and fervour of the religious spirit of this Christian young man there can be no doubt. But how did this spirit harmonise with the strenuous, strident call of the busy life? George Williams was a keen and successful man of business from the first. We have seen something of his enthusiasm for his trade when he was in his first situation at Bridgwater, and that he worked hard and ungrudgingly from the day of his entry into the London warehouse is abundantly evident from these pages. He took his work with the utmost seriousness, he felt strongly the ups and downs of his commercial experience. He notes "A good day"; "Business tolerable"; "Business pretty well"; and it is easy to see that he is quickly affected by the state of trade in his department. It is evident that he met with immediate success in no small measure, for in 1843 there is a note in the diary, "Took £32 in one day"; and a few weeks later he is entrusted with the buying of some things from the wholesale houses, and is much troubled to find how a trying day in the warehouse disturbs his mind for meditation and prayer.

The relationship between young George Williams and Mr. Hitchcock was of a much more intimate nature than would be possible in business nowadays, but sixty years ago the head of a firm was looked upon in the light of the father of the family, and, as such, was much more approachable than the present-day principal, guarded as he is from intrusion by serried ranks of clerks and office boys. It will come as a surprise to some to find that George Williams, at the age of twenty-two, notes that he had an interview with Mr. Hitchcock, and was "much delighted with good signs of life," and that later, having a sore throat, he went to ask Mr. Hitchcock's advice, and "had a delightful hour's conversation with him."

On his return from Somerset he was put into the "Cashmeres," and was much pleased at being "exalted to occasional shopwalker." The hours were long and the work arduous, for he notes that in November, 1843, the business closed for the first time at seven P. M., and several times afterwards he speaks of special work keeping him until after ten P. M. In November his salary was advanced by Mr. Hitchcock, and he writes, "Oh, that I may be faithful with it and spend it to the glory of God, and not on my own indulgence! Mr. Hitchcock expressed to me a feeling of great attachment. Oh, that I may ever be found faithful!"

I believe I am right in saying that at this time he was giving away regularly two-thirds of his income.

In July of the following year he made a great stride in business, and the entries are so typical of the young man's attitude of mind, that they are worthy of somewhat full quotation. He writes: "Mr. Hitchcock asked me, or rather offered for my consideration, the drapery department as a buyer. And now, oh, Lord, another department of Thy vineyard opens to my view. Thou hast brought me here and supported me up to this time, and now, oh, my God, I ask Thy direction. If it is Thy will wilt Thou cause Mr. Hitchcock so to appoint, but, if otherwise, may his mind be set against it. I ask not honour, nor wealth, nor luxuries, only to glorify Thy name. Oh, God, now let my cry come unto Thee. I plead it in the name of Jesus. Lord, enable my ears to hear a word behind me saying, 'This is the way, walk ye in it.' Oh, my God, if it be not in accordance with Thy will, may something prevent it, wilt Thou influence his mind, but if it be in accordance with Thy mind, then bring it to pass, and enable me, Holy Father, to feel I am in the path where Thou wouldst have me to go." In his diary he sums up the difficulties that are sure to beset him in such a new position, and writes of the special business qualifications necessary to make the department a success — " manlike decision, judgment, taste, knowledge of the stock." On the following day he is much perturbed to find that Mr. Hitchcock has not decided definitely in his favour, and it is noteworthy that he is encouraged by the hearty co-operation of " all the brethren in the house," and feels that by their prayers he will surely succeed. " Yea," he writes, " with the wisdom which cometh down from above I *cannot* fail."

One likes to think of his popularity among his associates, though they must have had much cause to envy him his outstanding success, and must have watched and criticised him unsparingly. But although in some things he kept himself apart, he was ever willing and anxious to help any and all of his fellow assistants. One of those who was with him in the early days says that he remembers distinctly how, when any one was behindhand and hard pressed with work, George Williams was always the first to assist, and gave his aid ungrudgingly and with the utmost cheeriness. He was never too busy, too weary, to be of service, and if ever a man were in a scrape it was to George Williams that he appealed. There is something uncommonly attractive about a Christian young man, who is at the same time a successful business young man, and whose genuineness and righteousness have so impressed themselves upon his companions, that, in spite of his religion and in spite of his success, every one wishes him well. That is one of the finest of all tributes that can be rendered to practical Christianity.

On July 18th he was called into Mr. Hitchcock's counting-house, and appointed drapery buyer. "This day," he writes, "is a day of worldly exaltation." The next morning he goes into the markets for the first time, and says he finds his mind much occupied by business, and laments that it is so difficult to call away his attention from it.

"What is my aim?" he writes. "Is it money, honour, dignity, luxuries, ease? What is there in money that will satisfy thee, oh, my soul? What honour can there be compared to the honour I already possess of being a child of God, and having a title to an inheritance incorruptible? What dignity so ennobling as what I already possess? What greatness equal to being a child of God, a joint-heir with Christ? Luxuries, what are they? Pleasing to the flesh, but not half so pleasing as the smiles of His countenance. Ease, what is that? Do I require it? No, not whilst souls are going to hell."

Gradually, as the responsibility increases, he finds trials abound more and more and temptations growing in severity. He is most fearful of falling a prey to "colouring and exaggeration." "Oh, Lord," he writes, "wilt Thou keep me from it, and preserve me to the end. Strengthen my memory and bless me in all I do. May I in business act as though

Mr. Hitchcock were standing by. Oh, my Father, help me to be conscientious in all I do. Oh, Lord, by Thy wisdom and strength all will become right, but help me to be more humble and patient; guide my judgment and keep me in the right way."

He seems at this time to have been troubled by his healthy appetite, and writes of "eating" as another besetting sin. On one occasion he gives in detail an exact *menu* for the day — so many pieces of bread and butter at each meal, with an exception at dinner "on pudding days" — and promises to fine himself sixpence for the benefit of the Missionary Society each time he exceeds the allotted amount. His notes as to the stock in his department, and his anxiety on account of certain parts of it which he marks "heavy," prove him to have been particularly anxious to make a good showing at the end of the business year. The diaries are full of the details of trade, which would be of no interest to the general reader; but from all one gathers proof, if proof were necessary in view of the success and prosperity which were his in the following years, that this Christian young man, whose religion was the most potent force in his life, was not therefore a poor hand at a bargain. He records in 1845, that in six months he has done £3,800 more business than the previous year. Christianity, as he understood it, never blunted his keenness, never weakened his capacity for work. He was not one of those who find a comforting refuge in religion when they have failed in everything else, — men who adopt piety as a last resort, the final excuse for existence; above all, not one of those who find it in their hearts to curse that " Sabbathless Satan,"

> "Who first invented work, and bound the free
>   And holiday-rejoicing spirit down
> To the ever-haunting importunity
>   Of business, in the green fields, and the town —
> To plough, loom, anvil, spade — and, oh! most sad,
>   To that dry drudgery at the desk's dry wood?"

That he was conscious of the conflict between the gods of this world and the God whom he served, is evident enough from the extracts I have quoted — often he writes that he finds Satan, " that old foe," very busy, and prays for strength against him — but I have failed to find any suggestion that he doubted for one single moment the possibility of living the life as he knew it in Christ, while at the same time doing everything that in him lay to produce a satisfactory balance sheet. He was proud, too, of his work, finding nothing in the dignity of business incompatible with the humblest service for Christ. And more than that he realised quickly the possibilities of the social side of such service. He was from the first an ardent supporter of every kind of reform in matters of trade. Although his name is generally associated with active evangelistic work, it must not be forgotten that Sir George Williams was one of the leaders in the fight for improved conditions of labour. The success of the early-closing movement owes much not only to the support he gave, but also to the example he afterwards set as an employer. As a young man he went with his friend Valentine to the first great public meeting held in support of early closing in the drapery trade. He knew what it was to be "tired in body and lifeless in spirit" at the end of the day's work, knew that this weariness of soul was due in large measure to physical causes. He did not forget when success had earned for him a measure of independence. He never made the mistake of some of those who subsequently laboured with him, of belittling work for the improvement of the social and physical life of young men. He remembered how hard and cramped and degraded were the circumstances of his early business experiences, realised that health of body made for health of soul.

I could wish, then, that this message from his life might ring out clear to those who, in the cruel strife of trade, fear to remember God, lest the memory should mean the failure of earthly hopes and ambitions. Helped by no trick of favour or chance of birth, suffering no taint of hypocrisy, and seeking first in all things the Kingdom of God, this young man of the single life, the life modelled on the letter of Scripture, at an age when most men are only beginning to form ambitions, attained a position of responsibility and prospective wealth. I could wish that this confession and creed of the Christian young man, who was also a successful young man of business, might reach a thousand baffled and troubled hearts.

"What," he writes, "is my duty in business? To be righteous. To do right things between man and man. To buy honestly. Not to deceive or falsely represent or colour.

"What is my duty to those under me? To be kind, patient, winning, and respectful. When I see a fault, to call the party aside and talk to him rather than rebuke him before others.

Oh, my soul, do all under me think I am sincere? Where is the difference in my daily actions from another man's? Am I more kind, more forbearing? Do the wicked glorify God on my behalf?

"What ought I to do? Constantly repose on God. He tells me to be careful for nothing, but in everything by prayer and supplication make my requests known unto Him.

"How short of that have I lived. How ought I rather to have felt that He who placed me in this situation will give me wisdom and strength to glorify Him in its midst. Oh, for a stronger faith in God. What have I to doubt or fear? Yea, by His help I will not. I would be righteous and holy in business, doing it as for Christ.

Oh, Lord, Thou hast given me money. Give me a

92   SIR GEORGE WILLIAMS

heart to do Thy will with it. May I use it for Thee and seek to get wisdom from Thee to use it aright."

George Williams did not attempt to serve God and mammon.

He served God, and made mammon serve him.

THE UPPER ROOM IN ST. PAUL'S CHURCHYARD

CHAPTER V

THE UPPER ROOM IN ST. PAUL'S CHURCHYARD

"SIR," said a friend to John Wesley, "you wish to serve God and go to heaven. Remember you cannot serve Him alone; you must, therefore, find companions or make them. The Bible knows nothing of solitary religion."

When George Williams joined the firm of Hitchcock & Rogers, his first concern was to find or to make companions of the Christian way. There were in the house some 140 assistants, of whom he wrote: "I found no means of grace of any kind. My heart was very warm — I was little over twenty at that time — and I asked myself, 'What can I do for these young men? There were five or six of us in a bedroom, and the conduct of my companions was altogether different from anything you can form an idea of. In an inner room which opened out of this bedroom there were four or five young men, one of whom was a Christian, and one was a good moral character, although unconverted." Through the efforts of this Christian young man the two obtained the privilege of meeting in his bedroom for prayer, the other assistants being persuaded to stay away for a short time, and not to interfere with them. Here is George Williams's summary of these early beginnings: "We met, our numbers grew, and the room was soon crammed. In answer to prayer, the Spirit of God was present, and we had conversion after conversion."

Let it never be forgotten that the foundations of the Young Men's Christian Association were laid in a prayer meeting in an upper room, in the fervent, effectual prayers of two young men.

Immediately upon his arrival in London, George Williams singled out one after another from among the assistants in the drapery establishment and pled for them individually at the Throne of Grace. Mr. William Creese, a survivor of the twelve original members of the Young Men's Christian Association, remembers having once seen George Williams throw himself on his bed in a passion of weeping, so great was his agony of spirit over some prodigal in a far country. "Without blood, there is no" — nothing effectual in work of body, mind, or spirit, certainly no effectual prayer. George Williams poured out of his life-blood in the tremendous battle to win a single soul for Christ. That is the only certain way of victory.

His diaries contain many references to these early wrestlings. "In (room) No. 14," he writes at one

SIR GEORGE WILLIAMS AS A YOUNG MAN
From a photograph taken soon after the start of the Young Men's Christian Association

SIR GEORGE WILLIAMS AT 80 YEARS OF AGE
From a photograph taken soon after the start of the Young
Men's Christian Association

time, "the Lord having closed me in, I was enabled to plead, and I believe the Lord has given me ——" Here follow the names of three assistants. "Oh, Lord, now come down and let me plead with Thee until I prevail." On the next day another name is added, and every week the list grows. At the end of the year he enters the names of nine friends for whom he has made special supplication, all of whom "have received Christ." In one case the answer came within two days. His belief in the power of prayer seldom faltered. His was the assurance of faith that works miracles. "I believe," he writes, "that T—— will feel his sins this day and turn to Jesus. Oh, Lord, hear and answer my prayer." Two months later there is an entry which proves that the prayer was abundantly answered. On December 23, 1844, he mentions a number of men for whom he is praying, and on the 1st January of the following year, six of these are "under conviction and give evidence of the work of grace." Surely never young man had quicker or more abundant harvest. No wonder that he adds: "Oh, that we could sufficiently praise God for His goodness and wonderful works to the children of men."

The meetings grew rapidly in numbers and in influence; for while he notes that on Friday, June 30, 1843, a prayer meeting from half-past six to half-past seven was established in No. 1 bedroom, a month later there are twenty present at an early morning prayer meeting, and in September about twenty-five at the Bible meeting conducted in No. 2 bedroom by Christopher Smith, one of the ablest of the young men, a student and a scholar. Room after room was requisitioned as the attendance increased, and at the end of the year there were on one occasion twenty-seven present at the prayer meeting in Room No. 13.

To these young men George Williams introduced the two books by Charles Finney to which reference has already been made, and as a result of the discussion of the ways and means of revival, they banded themselves together to enter upon a systematic campaign. A kind of informal home missionary society was formed, one of the plans of which was that in due course every one in the house should be spoken to about his soul. At each meeting certain names were brought forward of those for whom special and united prayer was suggested, and in this manner man after man was marked out, and no opportunity was lost of speaking with him. In almost every case their faith and their works were rewarded, and almost daily there were added unto them such as should be saved. Never was revival started on such business-like, matter-of-fact lines, but behind all the planning there was the fire of tremendous faith and earnestness. George Williams was possessed also of that extraordinarily rare virtue in a young man — tact. He was wont to say, when asked as to the means he suggested for tackling a young man, "Don't argue, take him to supper," and in more than one instance he carried out his suggestion literally. In reviewing these early days, George Williams used to tell the story of how they won over to their side one of the young fellows in the house who was most active in his opposition, and whose conduct was a terrible ordeal for their faith. He held a good position in the business, and as George Williams relates, "we could not get near him in any way. When any young fellow gave his heart to Christ, he would pounce upon him and say, 'We'll soon take all that nonsense out of you!'" This young man was the organiser and chairman of the "free-and-easy" held on Saturday evening at the adjoining public-house, "The Goose and Gridiron," and largely frequented by Hitchcock & Rogers's assistants. In a short time he had promoted a very active and vigorous campaign against these young men of the upper room, and naturally he was at once marked out by them for special and particular prayer. For many weeks they waited in vain for sign of change. His hostility increased in vehemence and bitterness.

The best part of one evening's meeting was devoted to a discussion as to the most likely means of getting into touch with this most unsympathetic young man.

"Can any one tell me," said George Williams, "if there is anything he is specially fond of which we could give him? Can we do anything that will overcome his dislike for us?" One of those present suggested with a touch of humour that he had a passion for oysters. "Let's give him an oyster supper then," said George Williams. "Who is the best man to invite him?" They selected one who was on comparatively friendly terms with the chairman of the "free-and-easy," and in due course he was casually informed that a number of the young fellows were going to join in a big oyster supper, and would be glad if he would accompany them. The idea of these Christian young men indulging in such frivolity amused him immensely, and in a spirit of bravado he accepted their invitation. It was a lively evening for all concerned, and all enjoyed it, for George Williams had given strict instructions that no attempt at proselytising was to be made on that occasion. Their avowed enemy, finding himself in such pleasant company, came to the conclusion that these young men were not so black as he had painted them. As a return for their hospitality, he consented later on to attend one of their meetings. The sequel is best told in an extract from the diary of George Williams's friend, Edward Valentine, who writes in May, 1844: "In the course of the day George Williams came to me and said he believed something particular was going to happen to-day, inasmuch as the Spirit's operation seemed visible in our midst. A young man by the name of Rogers was seriously impressed about his soul's salvation.

G(eorge) W(illiams) spoke to him after we had arranged to have a prayer meeting in the evening, and whilst engaged packing up a parcel Rogers came to me and told me that he was thinking very seriously about his immortal soul." The next morning Rogers was still more concerned, and William Creese noticing his attitude, said to George Williams, "George, what is up with Rogers?" "I do not know," he replied, "but I feel I cannot pray for him any longer. I was praying for him this morning until it seemed as if I heard a voice from heaven saying to me 'Yes,' and I knew he would be converted." Shortly afterwards Rogers definitely threw in his lot with the little band of the upper room. His name is to be found among the first twelve members of the Association, and by a curious coincidence his is the only one of the twelve cards of membership which has been preserved. It is reproduced on another page.

The intense earnestness of young George Williams was an abiding memory to all who met him at this period, and while it was an inspiration and delight to those who shared his zeal, it was, I doubt not, a constant embarrassment to those who wished at all costs to avoid him. Going to bed at night was an undertaking calling for much careful scouting on the part of those who had attracted his attention, and they would carefully examine the passages leading to their bedrooms to make sure of the coast being clear, for their zealous comrade was often lying in ambush, and, given the opportunity, would not be denied.

Strange to say, however, his importunity never offended. He had, as was often said, a way with him. It was impossible to resent his cheery, unaffected sincerity, his manly directness, his courageous simplicity. And all in the house respected him, for he was admitted to be one of the best salesmen in the City.

At one of the earliest meetings these young fellows determined to join in special prayer for the head of the firm, Mr. George Hitchcock, who, at that time, although one of the most enlightened and kindly principals in the City, made no open profession of religion. The movement which was literally turning his establishment upside-down soon came to his ears, although he was unaware at the time of the special mark set upon him, and contrary to general expectation he took the greatest interest in it, and went out of his way to encourage the leaders. Note has already been made of the entries in George Williams's diary, in which he writes of having many earnest conversations with Mr. Hitchcock, and there can be no doubt that, as a definite result of these meetings and talks, the head of the firm came out strongly on the side of Christ. In the autumn of 1843 he expressed concern for the spiritual welfare of the young men in his employ, and provided a chaplain to conduct morning worship. After many months of constant prayer on his behalf the little band was rewarded by the announcement that he had accepted the presidency of their Young Men's Missionary Society, and would support it with his presence and his purse. On November 1, 1843, at a special meeting convened and held in the cloak-room, they presented a Bible, for which £20 had been collected, to Mr. Hitchcock as an expression of their gratitude to him for the interest he had shown in Christian work among his employees. As showing how whole-heartedly he entered into the work and how seriously he regarded his responsibilities as an employer, the following extract from a letter engaging an assistant may be quoted. Writing early in 1843, he says: " I conclude from your letters that your earnest desire is to *live to God*, and this moves me to engage you. Be much in prayer, then, that God may make you useful in my establishment. Come in a spirit of prayer and God *will* bless you."

George Williams and the two or three who had stood almost alone in 1841, found themselves in 1843 the respected leaders of a movement that had affected the whole house from the head of the firm to the youngest apprentice. A Mutual Improvement Society and a Young Men's Missionary Society, with frequent Bible classes and prayer meetings, were visible signs of an altered condition of things.

Much of George Williams's spare time was devoted

to obtaining subscriptions for the Missionary Society, for, while he was always himself a generous giver, he was also from the beginning a very successful "beggar"—and that, too, he continued to the end. In June, 1843, he had collected in the house over £8, and later on the sum was raised to more than £20 a year, and this at a time when salaries were certainly not on too generous a scale. The missionary meeting in the house, at which, in 1843, about seventy were present, has been held each year in Messrs. Hitchcock, Williams & Co.'s establishment without a break to the present day. George Williams was a regular attendant at the meetings of the London Missionary Society in Exeter Hall, and his visit to the *John Williams* missionary ship made a deep impression upon him. It was at this period that he was much inclined to offer himself for work in the mission field. His friend, Mr. Cutting, who kept open house for young men from the business establishments of the City, and whose wife had a Sunday School at which George Williams often taught, dissuaded him, however, by pointing out the vaster field of work that lay before him as a business man. Mr. Cutting never figured prominently in the work of the Young Men's Christian Association, and his name has never been honoured at its gatherings. Let this, then, be a tribute to his wisdom, to his faith. He builded better than he knew. It was after this interview that George Williams came away from a Home Missionary

Meeting in 1843 "convinced of our duty to make more strenuous efforts to spread the Gospel among our own countrymen," and although he was always ready to support every effort put forth on behalf of foreign missionary enterprise, particularly in later years in connection with the British and Foreign Bible Society, it was the home mission field that from this time held the first place in his heart. George Williams's religion began in his own home, in his own business circle, and ended — in infinity.

On May 24, 1843, a missionary meeting was held in No. 1 sitting-room, to consider whether or not it was the duty of these young men to give up half of the amount they collected to home missions and half to foreign missions. The result was delightfully characteristic of the spirit of these early days. Mr. Valentine — "My friend Val," as George Williams called him, an ardent co-worker in the beginning, as in the years that followed — stated that he had been giving twopence a week to the Missionary Society, and would hereafter give fourpence. This example fired the others, so that on the next Saturday night George Williams collected 10s. 5d., being, as he says, "much larger than anything previous." It is interesting to note that one of the speakers at the meeting urged, as a special reason for supporting home missions, the hurtful effects of Puseyism.

Up to this time the work had been confined entirely to the one establishment. In their own place of business its success was assured. Could it be spread outside with equally encouraging results? That was the question that throbbed within the heart of George Williams. "If," said he, "God has so blessed us in this house, why should He not give such a blessing in every house in London? The answer to that question was the formation of the Young Men's Christian Association.

The actual birthplace of the Young Men's Christian Association was an upper room, the bedroom where the young men gathered together for prayer and Bible reading. It was in George Williams's own bedroom that the first meeting was held. But the scheme which had been forming in vague outline in his mind first took definite shape in a spot as eloquent of the greatness of the need as was the upper room of the means of grace which would meet such need.

It was upon old Blackfriars Bridge that the words were spoken which called the Young Men's Christian Association into being. No more appropriate scene could have been chosen, for, in the year 1844, even more than to-day, Blackfriars Bridge focussed the life and struggle of the City. In the early hours of every week-day, or again as the warehouses are closed in the evening, you may watch on that bridge the tragic panorama of anxiety and care that is the life of London. Men who, during the hours of business, keep a brave front and a stiff upper lip to the world, for the City has no use for cowards and weaklings, relax the tension when outside the office, and you may read on many faces the story of weariness and struggle and pain and sometimes of despair. On Blackfriars Bridge you may see the cruel aftermath of the day's battle. I confess that the sight moves me as deeply as any display of ragged poverty or sweated industries. George Williams was one of the first to realise that there is a distinct class, a great race of workers, untouched by any agency of philanthropy, whose need is as deep as any in London. These men of the middle class, of shop and warehouse, of stool and counter, make no loud appeal for help, scorn to advertise their wrongs, suffer silently and in loneliness, for such is the way of "respectability."

But George Williams was one of them, one with them. And he knew.

It was as he crossed Blackfriars Bridge on his way from St. Paul's Churchyard to Surrey Chapel that George Williams first mentioned to another his desire to extend the benefits of the Young Men's Society at Mr. Hitchcock's establishment to every drapery establishment throughout London. His confidant was Edward Beaumont, who had joined the place of business in the early spring of 1843, and been converted as a result of the extraordinary efforts already described. In a letter to Sir George Williams written some years ago he recalled the incident:—

"On one Sunday evening in the latter end of May, 1844, you accompanied me to Surrey Chapel. After walking a few minutes in silence you said, pressing my arm and addressing me familiarly, as you were in the habit of doing, 'Teddy, are you prepared to make a sacrifice for Christ?' I replied, 'If called upon to do so, I hope and trust I can.' You then told me that you had been deeply impressed with the importance of introducing religious services, such as we enjoyed, into every large establishment in London, and that you thought that if a few earnest, devoted, and self-denying men could be found to unite themselves together for this purpose, that with earnest prayer God would smile upon the effort, and much good might be done. I need not say that I heartily concurred, and said that I would gladly do what I could to assist you. You told me at the same time that I was the only person to whom you had mentioned it.

"This conversation was resumed the following week, and collecting together three or four, or it may be more, of the religious young men of the establishment, the matter was gone more fully into, and, if I mistake not, this took place one evening after our prayer meeting and Bible class, when a few of the religious young men remained behind for conversation.

"We then resolved to call a meeting of all the religious young men of the establishment, to meet on Thursday, June 6, 1844, to consider the importance and practicability of establishing such an association."

It should be said here that the movement begun at the St. Paul's Churchyard house had already spread to another quarter. Mr. Hitchcock, who had become so intimately interested in the young men's meetings, one day described with enthusiasm the work going on in his establishment to his friend, Mr.

THE UPPER ROOM

W. D. Owen, the principal of a large drapery business in the West End. Mr. Owen mentioned the matter to his principal assistant, Mr. James Smith, and both of them being earnest Christians, they commenced similar meetings amongst their own young men.

It would seem that the idea of further extending the movement occurred to George Williams and James Smith almost at the same time, for on May 31, 1844, the latter wrote to the former:—

"I have been truly rejoiced to hear that the Lord is doing a great work in your house, and I hope that the leaven thus set will go on increasing abundantly. I am engaged here in the same work, but stand almost alone, and from what I have heard am induced to say, 'Come over and help us.' We have a prayer meeting this evening at half-past eight o'clock. Mr. Branch, a City missionary, will be with us. Will you favour us with your company, and if you can bring a praying brother with you, do. If you could, by any possibility, be here at eight o'clock, I should be glad, as I want to advise with you on another subject in reference to our trade, *viz., whether anything can be done in other houses.*"

By the time George Williams received this letter, he had already explained his idea at the informal meeting mentioned by Edward Beaumont, and accordingly James Smith was invited to be present at the now historical meeting of June 6, 1844. This was held in "the little upper room" in which George Williams slept, and there and then the Young Men's Christian Association was founded.

This memorable gathering consisted of twelve young men, all of whom took an active part in building up the Association, many of them continuing to support it heartily to the end of their lives. The twelve whose names surely deserve to be written in letters of gold wherever young men congregate, were George Williams, C. W. Smith, Norton Smith, Edward Valentine, Edward Beaumont, M. Glasson, William Creese, Francis John Cockett, E. Rogers, John Harvey, John C. Symons, with James Smith from Mr. William Owen's establishment. These formed the first committee, electing as their officers, James Smith, Chairman; Edward Valentine, Treasurer; with John C. Symons and William Creese as Secretaries.

With the exception of James Smith, all were members of Mr. Hitchcock's establishment, while more than half of them owed their conversion to the revival initiated by George Williams, to his personal efforts and example.

It is entirely in accordance with the modesty of the man that George Williams's own diary contains no actual reference to this gathering, and that at this very period he was much troubled by his "ingratitude and want of love to God." One would have imagined this to be a time of great uplifting, but how much more attractive it is to find that within two days of the successful formation of the Society, he is praying that God may help him to tear up the fallow ground of his own heart and summing up his soul's indebtedness to grace. He writes of his want of love to God, of how he has listened to self-indulgence rather than to God's voice, of how, when there has been a battle between the man of sin and the voice of God, the man of sin has often gained the ascendancy. He bemoans, too, his neglect of the Bible, the many hours spent in bed, "which ought to have been given up to reading and studying God's word." He speaks of his unbelief, of the times he has prayed for individuals and not expected a blessing to descend — even of his neglect of prayer, and a want of seriousness. "What indifference," he exclaims, "in His presence! Shame, shame! I have been a member of a Christian Church for six and a half years, and what little good have I done? How many days have passed away when no apparent word has been said for God? How often have I been more inclined to scold the ungodly rather than to feel for them and weep over them and plead for them?"

No detailed account exists of this first meeting. We know that a sum of thirteen shillings was collected towards immediate expenses, that it was arranged that another meeting should be held on June 13th. Failing other records the minutes may be said to exist in the following entry in the diary of George Williams's friend, Edward Valentine: —

"Thursday, June 6, 1844, met in G. Williams's room for the purpose of forming a society, the object of which is to influence religious young men to spread the Redeemer's Kingdom amongst those by whom they are surrounded. Mr. Smith, of Coram Street, President; Self, Treasurer, *pro tem.*; Creese and Symons, Secretaries. Committee, those there present belonging to us."

A second meeting at which twenty were present was duly held " for the purpose of carrying into effect the system of introducing religious services into drapery establishments throughout the Metropolis," and thus was started a series of weekly gatherings held regularly throughout the early days of the Association.

It was felt that in view of the proposed extension of the work to other business houses, it would be desirable to hold the meetings on some more neutral ground than the first committee room, George Williams's bedroom, and the increase in numbers also made a move necessary. A room which held about twenty was accordingly engaged at St. Martin's Coffee House, in a court on the south side of Ludgate Hill, at half a crown a week.

This was the Association's first outlay for rent. To-day it owns property valued at many millions in all parts of the civilised world.

One of the first steps taken by the Committee in carrying out their programme was the issue of a carefully drafted circular to most of the large establishments in London, especially those in the drapery trade, and it was in this coffee-house that

WILLIAM CREESE   JOHN C. SYMONDS
The first Secretaries of the Young Men's Christian Association

EDWARD VALENTINE   EDWARD BEAUMONT
"My friend Val," First Treasurer   To whom the idea of the Association was
of the Association   first mentioned by George Williams

the important document was discussed and finally composed.

The cost of printing this letter caused some hesitation on the part of the Committee, for it must be remembered that the members were young drapers' assistants, earning for the most part very small salaries, while definite promises of outside support were not yet forthcoming. But while they were discussing its advisability, George Williams brought his closed fist with a crash on the table, and exclaimed, "If this is of God, the money will come!" His words carried the day, and one of the most critical moments in the history of the Association was passed.

This circular was sent out in July, 1844, dated from 72, St. Paul's Churchyard, and signed by the two secretaries. As the original manifesto of a movement that has now become world-wide, it is of special interest and importance and may be given in full: —

"DEAR FRIENDS, — Suffer us to bring before your notice some important considerations, to which, for some time, our minds have been directed, and which intimately concern the eternal welfare of a large class of our fellow mortals.

"We have looked with deep concern and anxiety upon the almost totally neglected spiritual condition of the mass of young men engaged in the pursuits of business, especially those connected with our trade, and feel desirous, by the assistance of God, to make some effort in order to improve it; and as we regard it to be a sacred duty, binding upon every child of God, to use all the means in his power, and to direct all his energies, in and out of season, towards the promotion of the Saviour's Kingdom and the salvation of souls, we earnestly solicit your assistance in the great and important undertaking we now lay before you.

"We have seriously and carefully consulted as to the best means by which to accomplish so great a work; and we have come to the decision — we trust by the direction of the Holy Spirit — that there is nothing so calculated to discountenance immorality and vice, and to promote a spirit of serious inquiry among the class in which our lot is cast, as the introduction of some religious service among them, which they shall be invited to attend; and as of the various means in use for the salvation of souls, among the Church and people of God, prayer has been of all others the most honoured, we would suggest that the service thus introduced should largely, if not entirely, consist of prayer.

"We shall not be surprised if such a proposal as this be reckoned by some a Utopian scheme. And we expect that from many who name the name of Christ we shall meet with considerable opposition. We are likewise aware of the numerous difficulties which in many places will present themselves, and the obloquy and contempt which such a procedure will bring down upon the promoters and supporters of such an attempt, from the irreligious members of some of our large establishments. We have calculated upon all these difficulties and shall not be surprised or discouraged if we behold them increase, but we hope that these things, instead of discouraging us in the great work we have commenced, will only induce us to increase and redouble our efforts. Shall it be said that the followers of the Lamb are afraid to incur the frown and censure of the world? Shall it be said that the ridicule of the world prevented the use of the means such as those to which we have adverted? Shall persecution —

for we shall doubtless be called upon to suffer it — keep us back from attempting the salvation of souls? We believe that every true Christian will answer — 'No.'

"A society is now formed, the object of which is the promotion of the spiritual welfare of young men engaged in the drapery and other trades, by the introduction of religious services among them. We earnestly entreat your Christian co-operation in this great work; and in order to lay before you fully the plans and views of the society on whose behalf we address you, a deputation from the Committee, prepared to give you all the requisite information, will wait upon you at your earliest convenience, when we hope to hear of your hearty concurrence in our plans. We shall feel obliged by your informing us, as early as you can, the time and place at which the deputation shall wait upon you.

"(*Signed*)

"JOHN SYMONS,
"WILLIAM CREESE."

Before the issue of the circular news of the proposed Association had been spread by letter, so that when a meeting of what had been called, for want of a better name, The Drapers' Evangelical Association was held at St. Martin's Coffee House on June 24th, George Williams, who presided, was able to report that an encouraging response had already been received from several establishments, while a sum of thirty shillings was paid to the Treasurer towards expenses.

The fifth meeting on July 4th was largely given up to the discussion of a suitable name for the society,

C. W. Smith, who had been requested by the Committee to find a name, having suggested three: —

The Berean Association.[1]

The Christian Young Men's Society.

The Young Men's Christian Association.

On July 12th George Williams's diary contains the entry "Our Young Men's Religious Association getting on nicely," and it is evident that the movement was rapidly spreading among other houses, for those who took the chair at the four meetings in July were all from outside drapery establishments. It should be noted that until then George Williams had presided at nearly all the meetings. Edward Valentine's diary makes it clear that Mr. Smith, of Great Coram Street, was absent from many of these earlier gatherings, and that George Williams, by general consent, took the chair in his stead. From the first there appears to have been no doubt as to his actual initiation and leadership of the movement, although as an obscure shop assistant he naturally gave way to better known and more influential men when they were present. It was George Williams who personally invited each of the twelve to the first meeting, and it was in George Williams's bedroom that that first meeting was held. This should be clearly stated, for some misunderstanding has arisen due to the prominence given in early

[1] In reference to the men of Berea (Acts xvii. 11 and 12), who "received the Word with all readiness of mind, and searched the Scriptures daily, whether these things were so." A sect of this name was founded in Scotland in 1773 by the Rev. John Barclay.

reports to men who held higher positions in the business world and accordingly took precedence at the meetings they attended.

In a few weeks the movement had prospered to such an extent that another move became necessary, and in October George Williams and Edward Beaumont were deputed to obtain more convenient premises. After some little trouble, for most of the possible meeting-places were not available for gatherings on temperance lines, a large room was secured at Radley's Hotel, in Bridge Street, Blackfriars, opposite the site of the present Ludgate Hill Station. The cost of this room was seven shillings and sixpence a week, an increased expenditure which seemed to many almost too daring a venture. It was let to the society on the strict condition that they did not sing, a restriction which probably weighed heavily on the young enthusiasts. Despite this drawback Radley's Hotel became the headquarters of the Association for the next five years, and until it was demolished an annual breakfast was given there by George Williams so that the members of the Association might fitly commemorate its humble beginnings and give thanks for its wonderful extension.

The first home of the Young Men's Christian Association was the coffee-house and the tavern, placed amid surroundings which suggested to all the too "free-and-easy" entertainments with which young men beguiled their spare hours. In 1844 the only accommodation for such meetings as these was to be found in the tavern, a state of things which the Association with its splendid buildings, its institutes, its club and class-rooms, has done so much to remedy.

A word may in this place be said of the societies for young men started in 1824 by the revered David Nasmith, the founder of the London City Mission, which some have confused with the Young Men's Christian Association, while one or two misinformed persons have gone so far as to state that George Williams's work was in reality only an imitation of that started by David Nasmith in Glasgow. Such assertions have from time to time been brought into prominence, and as they have caused some pain to the friends of the Young Men's Christian Association it is as well that they should be answered definitely once for all.

It has never been suggested that there was anything original in the scheme for a society of Christian young men. Such associations date from about the year 1678, when, according to the account given by the "pious" Robert Nelson, the eighteenth-century precursor of the Earl of Shaftesbury, a few young men belonging to the middle station of life began to feel their need of spiritual intercourse and of mutual encouragement in the practices of piety. It is of peculiar interest to note that these societies had to contend with precisely the same "prejudice and suspicion" which beset the early path of the Young

Men's Christian Association. Their promoters were charged by men of " duller sensibility in religion " with setting up a Church within a Church, with using their associations for party purposes, and with forming " sects and schisms "; but in *A Companion for the Festivals and Fasts of the Church of England*, Robert Nelson defends them against such accusations, and writes of them as doing much to " revive that true spirit of Christianity which was so much the glory of the primitive times." These particular societies came to a melancholy end during the decay of religion under the Georges, and at one of their last annual meetings at Bow Church in 1738 a special sermon was addressed to the members warning them against being led astray by the irregularities of Whitefield. But others of a different character took their place, and among them Whitefield and Wesley found many of their most earnest fellow-workers.

And, as far as can be ascertained, none of the twelve first members was acquainted with the societies established by David Nasmith. In the year 1839 David Nasmith had stated that he had resolved to start no more of his young men's societies, and had predicted the speedy termination of those in existence. He had organised them on a broad basis that " he might enclose within the fold the youth of all conditions and of every phase of faith," believing that the " association even of the worldly-minded and unbelieving with the earnest few would be beneficial," but with sorrow he was forced to admit that the work had been marred by the disorders which had arisen among the members, by "the unseemly violence of opinion, the exhibition of un-Christian temper, and the alarming influence of improper persons at the meetings," so that he much feared for "the stability of even good young men under such trying circumstances."

That these Nasmith Societies had no connection, and indeed little in common with the Association started in the upper room in St. Paul's Churchyard, can be abundantly proved from their official organ, for in the *Young Men's Magazine and Monthly Record* for January, 1845, there is a long extract from the first report of the Young Men's Christian Association, which is commended to the serious consideration of its readers. In the April issue it is distinctly stated that "beyond what we borrowed from that report we were then unacquainted with the plans and views of the Association," and that now, having paid some attention to its proceedings, "we should be failing in our duty did we not give it our cordial support, and use whatever influence we may possess towards attaining its all-important object," an object it should be noted which the writer clearly understands to be different from that of the Young Men's Societies which he is addressing. He goes on to lament, indeed, that up to that time "no adequate effort" had been made towards the improvement of the *spiritual* condition of young men, that the best attempts hitherto made had met with but little success. Finally, he promises to keep the readers of the magazine " acquainted with the progress of an Association which has *entered upon a field* of more than ordinary promise."

At this date the magazine contains particulars of some twenty-five meetings of the Young Men's Societies to be held in London during the month, but when it is noted that according to the rules laid down in the official list at the end of the paper " the society shall consist of men of good moral character, not professing opinions subversive of evangelical religion," and that the chief work at the meetings is the reading of essays, it will be clear to all that these societies, whatever the original intention of David Nasmith, were little differentiated from the multitude of Mutual Improvement Societies which abounded at that time, and had little but the name in common with the definite religious association founded by George Williams.

THE EARLY DAYS OF THE
YOUNG MEN'S CHRISTIAN
ASSOCIATION

CHAPTER VI

THE EARLY DAYS OF THE YOUNG MEN'S CHRISTIAN ASSOCIATION

IT has been well said that the three great factors which combined in the genesis of the Young Men's Christian Association were: Personal contact, united prayer, and the study of the Bible. From the single association in the single house of business, there grew an association of associations as the young men of the separate houses came together in a common bond of fellowship and union, co-operating to widen and further their interests and influence.

The records of the early work of the Association are full of encouraging reports of the way in which, as the result of the personal contact of each of the members of the first Committee, this work was spreading from young man to young man and from business to business. George Williams himself was one of the most assiduous visitors to other establishments. Naturally, he met with many rebuffs, even from those interested in matters of religion, for while a number of the young men in the drapery establishments were willing enough to join in the house prayer meetings and Bible classes, many were reluctant to identify themselves with anything in the form of a public religious association.

As one writer, reviewing the history of the work, remarks, the causes for this reluctance were obvious. These young men had been brought up in different religious persuasions, some of them in the Church of England, many in various Nonconformist communions, and it was not easy, even in so broad a movement as that which George Williams originated, to induce Church and Chapel to shake hands, in spite of the fact that the whole plan of the organisation, even to its name, was designed to meet such a difficulty. Moreover, there was a certain prejudice on the part of the employers to be overcome, for some pretended to see in the success of such an association of young men a strengthening of the movement for the earlier closing of places of business, which at that time was regarded by many with suspicion. It was publicly contended, indeed, that the Young Men's Christian Association was merely an offshoot of the Metropolitan Drapers' Association, then in the forefront of the fight for shorter hours. It was in meeting such objections as these that George Williams's invariable good humour, his sense of fun, his quickness of repartee, stood him in excellent stead. From the very beginning the winning personality of this young man was one of the great mainstays of the Association, and this it remained for more than sixty years.

One might find himself unable to agree with George Williams's methods or suggestions, but there could never be the least trace of bitterness or rancour in such opposition, for it was only on the rarest occasions that George Williams allowed anything to cloud the sunniness of his temper, and his undimmed, inexhaustible enthusiasm for what he believed, was, in itself, the most forceful of arguments.

This personal contact, the corner stone of the Association, was supported and strengthened on every side by the study of the Bible and by united prayer. The practice of singling out certain individuals for peculiar intercession was adopted by the Association with the same wonderful results as had been obtained when the two or three had first met together for prayer in the upper room. Mr. Creese writes: "The plan adopted in our house was this. The number of young men thought to be unconverted was taken, and these were apportioned among the members of the Association, averaging about five to each of them. No formal resolution was taken, but it was felt by every member that a solemn engagement had been entered into to embrace every suitable opportunity of speaking a loving word to these young men, of praying earnestly for their conversion, of trying to prevail on them to attend the prayer meetings and Bible classes, and to accompany us to our places of worship on the Lord's Day.

The first months of the Association's existence were

marked by many signs of steady progress. Religious services were established in fourteen other houses of business, while weekly meetings were held at Radley's Hotel, "from which gatherings the members of the Association separated to their various places of business strengthened and cheered by such fellowship for the difficult task of keeping their flag flying in dormitory, shop, and warehouse." The members were increasing constantly, and fresh conversions were announced at every meeting. At this time, certainly, no attempt was made to appeal to what is known as the popular taste. Apart from friendly social conversation over tea and seed-cake, which George Williams always considered the best preliminary to a successful gathering of any kind, the meetings were of a strictly "spiritual" nature, and none but members of a Christian Church were admitted to fellowship. That there was nothing narrowly sectarian about the Association is proved by the fact that of the first twelve members three were Episcopalians, three Congregationalists, three Baptists, and three Methodists. It must not be forgotten that the work started as an association of Christian young men, young men full, it is true, of missionary zeal, but anxious, first of all, so to strengthen each other by this bond of companionship that they might, by their united stand, show a bold front against the forces of evil which threatened to overcome the weaker brethren.

72, St. Paul's Church Yard.

Dear Friend

Suffer us to bring before your notice some important considerations; to which, for some time past, our minds have been directed, and which intimately concern the eternal welfare of a large class of our fellow immortals.

We have looked with deep concern and anxiety upon the almost totally-neglected spiritual condition of the mass of young men engaged in the pursuits of business,—especially those connected with our own trade,—and feel desirous, by the assistance of God, to make some effort in order to improve it; and, as we regard it to be a sacred duty, binding upon every child of God, to use all the means in his power, and to direct all his energies, in and out of season, towards the promotion of the Saviour's Kingdom, and the salvation of souls, we earnestly solicit your assistance in the great and important undertaking we now lay before you.

We have seriously and carefully consulted as to the best means by which to accomplish so great a work; and we have come to the decision—we trust by the direction of the Holy Spirit—that there is nothing so calculated to discountenance immorality and vice, and to promote a spirit of serious enquiry among the class in which our lot is cast, as the introduction of some religious service among them, which they shall be invited to attend; and, as of the various means in use for the salvation of souls, among the church and people of God, prayer has been of all others the most honoured, we would suggest that the service thus introduced should largely, if not entirely, consist of prayer.

We shall not be at all surprised if such a proposal as this be reckoned by some as an Utopian scheme, and we expect that from many who name the name of Christ we shall meet with considerable opposition. We are likewise aware of the numerous difficulties which in many places will present themselves, and the obloquy and contempt which such a course of procedure will inevitably bring upon the promoters and supporters of such an attempt from the irreligious members of some of our large Establishments. We have calculated upon all these difficulties, and shall not be surprised or discouraged if we behold them increase; but we hope that these things, instead of discouraging us in in the great work we have commenced, will only induce us to increase and redouble our efforts. Shall it be said that the followers of the Lamb are afraid to incur the frown and censure of the world? Shall it be said that the ridicule of the world prevented the use of means such as those to which we have adverted? Shall persecution—for we shall doubtless be called to suffer it—keep us back from attempting the salvation of souls? We believe that every true Christian will answer—No!

A Society is now formed, the object of which is, the promotion of the spiritual welfare of Young Men engaged in the Drapery and other Trades, by the introduction of religious services among them. We earnestly intreat your Christian co-operation in this great work; and in order fully to lay before you the plans and views of the Society on whose behalf we address you, a deputation from the Committee prepared to give you all the requisite information, will wait upon you at your earliest convenience, when we hope to hear of your hearty concurrence in our plans. We shall feel obliged by your informing us as early as convenient, the time and place at which the deputation shall wait upon you.

Signed on behalf of the Committee,

John C. Symons
William Creese
} Secretaries.

A FACSIMILE OF THE LETTER ANNOUNCING THE FORMATION OF THE
YOUNG MEN'S CHRISTIAN ASSOCIATION

EARLY DAYS OF THE ASSOCIATION

The Association was at first self-protective, a Christian union against a Satanic tyranny. As the need for this mutual protection grew less with the years, largely on account of the growth of such associations, the Young Men's Christian Association extended its aims and plans, but the fundamental idea in George Williams's mind was to introduce such a union as had been formed in his own place of business into other drapery establishments, so that no Christian young man should feel alone and forsaken, and in his loneliness and despair hold out a flag of truce to the enemy. From the moment the Young Men's Christian Association was founded, from the moment its name meant something definite and tangible, that danger of isolation, a real and terrible one as George Williams knew from his own experience, was greatly lessened, and with the years has ceased almost to exist.

In a short time the Committee found it expedient to add to its original plan by the formation of Mutual Improvement Societies and courses of lectures, and later admitted as associates those who had not as yet become members of a Christian Church. In the first two reports one of the rules was that the object of the Association should be "the improvement of the spiritual condition of young men." In the third report the significant words "and mental culture" are added. This forward policy undoubtedly owed much to George Williams himself, who throughout the years stood undaunted, and at times against considerable opposition, for the broadest and most progressive policy, so long as that policy did not interfere with the central idea of the Association. He was one of those men who seem to catch the spirit of the coming days, in religious as well as in business affairs, one of those rarely gifted mortals who have the power to see ahead and to prepare to-day for the needs of the day after to-morrow.

A landmark in the early history of the Association was reached on Friday, November 8, 1844, when a tea meeting was held at Radley's Hotel, and the first report read. The chairman was Mr. W. D. Owen, whose name has already been mentioned as one of those outside the business of Messrs. Hitchcock & Rogers who gave cordial support to the scheme of the Association when it was first suggested to him by George Williams. At this meeting there were present 161 young men, the majority of whom were already enrolled as members, a most encouraging state of affairs when it is remembered that the movement was then only five months old. The report contained the twelve rules, which defined both the aims of the Association and the lines upon which it was to be continued. The following may be quoted as showing the scope of the work at this early date:—

"That the object of this Association be the improvement of the spiritual condition of young men engaged in the drapery and other trades, by the introduction of religious services among them."

EARLY DAYS OF THE ASSOCIATION 131

"That two social tea meetings be held in the year (the time of such meetings to be left to the discretion of the Committee) at which a report of the society's proceedings shall be read."

"That a general meeting be held once a fortnight (or oftener if required) for the purpose of hearing reports from members of the progress of the work of God in the various establishments, and for such and other purposes as the Committee shall see fit to determine; and that all meetings shall be opened for members, and those friends whom they may consider proper persons to bring, and to those who shall receive invitations from the Committee."

"That no person shall be considered a member of this Association unless he be a member of a Christian Church, or there be sufficient evidence of his being a converted character."

"That all persons desirous of becoming members shall be proposed at a general meeting, and a deputation be appointed to inquire into their moral character, upon whose report the Committee shall decide whether they be eligible or not."

"That each person be expected on becoming a member to pay the sum of sixpence, and to contribute sixpence quarterly to the general funds."

On the 20th of January of the following year George Williams notes in his diary that a very important meeting was held in connection with the Young Men's Christian Association, at which he and other members of a special committee examined the candidates for the secretaryship of the Society. "Oh, Lord," he writes, "direct us to a man who shall be useful in Thy work, and be very instrumental in leading to Christ the young men of London and the world in connection with my trade."

In spite of the way in which the work was going forward on all sides and of the wonderful results already attained, the founder himself was at this time in a far from happy frame of mind. It was one of the most critical periods in his business career, and he felt the fierceness of the struggle, felt a sense of disappointment that there was progress everywhere but in his own heart. Oh, Lord," he writes, " revive Thy work in my heart. The world with its influence has had much claim upon me, and Satan has taken the advantage. Whilst the body has been busy Satan has suggested ease and indulgence, which, alas! I have given way to. Oh, Lord, be not angry for ever, but come again and revive Thy work, that Thy dust may be useful and desirous of glorifying Thee and feel the power of Thy Holy Spirit. The deep spirit of prayer and piety seems lessening. Oh, Lord, come again, come now and revive true piety in our hearts. Pour upon us the power of the spirit of prayer. How many there are among us, moral characters, almost converted, yet yielding to the world."

The second social gathering held at Radley's Hotel on March 6, 1845, was evidently regarded as a most important function, for George Williams formed one of a special sub-committee to invite the Hon. and Rev. Baptist Noel to preside, and a number of clergymen and ministers of different denominations to attend.

EARLY DAYS OF THE ASSOCIATION

About 300 people in all sat down to tea, and the report showed that the Association then had 160 members. Its fortnightly meetings were steadily increasing in numbers, and a West End branch had already been opened. The outstanding event of the year was the employment of a salaried Secretary and Missionary. Already £60 had been promised towards the creation of such an office; to this Mr. George Hitchcock gave ten guineas, Mr. Owen two guineas, and Mr. Thomas Gurney one pound. The matter was fully discussed, and, as a result of the recommendation of the special committee, the appointment of Mr. T. H. Tarlton as first paid Secretary was shortly announced.

Mr. Tarlton was a City missionary who first came into contact with George Williams when taking the morning services at Messrs. Hitchcock & Rogers's. Hearing of the work among the young men of the house, he became one of the earliest members of their Association. When, after the rejection of a candidate who had presented himself in answer to the advertisement, and had been examined and found unsuitable, Mr. Tarlton suddenly offered himself for the post, the Committee was surprised beyond measure, for it was felt at once that the Association could not afford to offer anything like adequate remuneration for his services. But this young man was prepared to make considerable sacrifice if by so doing he could further the work, and stated at once that he was quite willing to accept any payment the Committee thought proper. Thus it was that from the start the most important work of Organising and Missionary Secretary was undertaken by one who was a contemporary and companion of the founder, and who understood and appreciated in the fullest manner the aims and ambitions of the first Committee. A forceful speaker, a really manly young man, an enthusiastic organiser and worker, Mr. Tarlton was from this time one of the great forces in the progress of the Association. George Williams found in him a devoted and most loyal friend, and it was through the Secretary that George Williams's influence was persistently brought to bear upon all phases of the work. Travelling together in all parts of the country, and for a period living together in London, these two worked as one, George Williams supplying most of the ideas, suggesting most of the improvements in organisation and methods, the Secretary carrying them into effect by the persuasion of his tact and eloquence.

A few days after the announcement of Mr. Tarlton's appointment there enters into George Williams's diary one of the few expressions of real exultation. "Go on, Thou mighty God," he writes. "Go on, Thou Prince of Peace, and thou, my soul, magnify Him who has thus listened unto the cry of His servant. Happy art thou, oh, my soul. Praise the Lord, oh, praise Him, sing of His great loving kindness, exult in His great name. Oh, my soul, ask what thou wilt, thou canst not be too bold."

In April he writes to "my dear old Brother Creese" that he has had a very delightful meeting with the "Young Christians" in his room, and that they are thinking of starting "something like a class meeting at which they might relate any particular trial or temptation which beset them." He speaks of the "hallowed and stirring time" he enjoyed during a recent visit to his home. "Oh, shout!" he writes, "God is at work. I saw numbers under concern and asking the way to Zion. Oh, Creese! cry aloud to the people where you dwell."

Later in the year new offices for the Association were secured in Serjeant's Inn, Fleet Street. This enlargement was made possible by the generous contributions of Mr. Hitchcock. "He was," writes George Williams, "the instrument chosen by the Lord for us. Oh, that he may feel the blessing in his own heart!" It would seem, however, that things were not going altogether smoothly in the organisation of the work, for George Williams notes in his diary that he has been giving much anxious consideration to the Association, and that he formed one of those who had entirely remodelled the Committee.

At this time he was considering the possibility of residing at Serjeant's Inn with Mr. Tarlton, the Secretary. He writes: "If Thou wishest me to go there, incline the hearts of those who have the arrangements. Only send me not hence if Thy rich and blessed Spirit go not with me. Oh, this city! Wilt Thou not bless these thousands of young men and make us happy in God!"

What is known as the First Annual Report of the Association was presented at the next half-yearly tea meeting at Radley's on November 6, 1845. It contained a list of twenty-two clerical vice-presidents, including many of the most distinguished preachers of the day. The Chairman of the Committee was Mr. R. C. L. Bevan, an honoured name which has always been connected with the work of the Association. Mr. George Hitchcock was then Treasurer, and another name on the Committee, which for years figures prominently in the reports, is that of Mr. John Morley. Mr. Bevan was in the chair at the meeting, and gave an account of his early struggles, saying, writes George Williams, that he had tried the world — hunting, shooting, sporting, dancing — but found these did not yield either joy or happiness. Then he had tried reading and study, and found even these left a void. Now he could bear his testimony that " piety and holiness were the only things that could make life all he could wish for." Mr. Binney made one of his straightforward, hard-hitting speeches, in which he emphasised the importance of a fine manly character that would spurn any low, mean action, and that, in view of their profession, it was of the utmost importance that these young

EARLY DAYS OF THE ASSOCIATION 137

men should be very jealous for their characters. He announced that one of the members of the Association had decided to study for the ministry, but, very characteristically, he did not encourage such a choice, adding that an honourable, upright, intelligent man of business, moving in the world among men and exercising the influence of his high character, might be as useful as any minister. The Hon. and Rev. Baptist Noel also spoke, and it is pleasing to note that at one of the earliest meetings of the Association its undenominational character was emphasised by the presence of representatives from Church and Nonconformity, while the speakers included that prince of City merchants, Mr. Samuel Morley.

It was at this meeting that the first mention was made of the movement towards placing the Association on a wider basis. " Since your last meeting," it was stated, " your Committee have added to their plans the formation of Mutual Improvement Societies, as in many large houses containing upwards of eighty to a hundred young men, no Christian young man is found, or, if there be one, his position is so isolated that he is prevented from carrying out the other part of our plan. Now, many unconverted young men would assist and feel interested in a Mutual Improvement Society. So would principals of houses, and we shall deem it no unimportant result if we can lead to the library and useful knowledge rather than to cards and billiards, the cigar divan and concert room, the theatre, and the seducting and polluting retreat."

It is almost amusing to notice that George Williams was at this time forming other schemes for carrying on similar work in different directions. Only two days after this public meeting in connection with the Young Men's Christian Association he writes: "Oh, Lord, what can be done now for the young ladies of London? Wilt Thou help us. Give us wisdom in this matter, that we may be able to do something for Thy honour amongst them," and there is reason to believe that a circular discovered among his papers after his death, in which reference is made to the starting of a "Young Ladies' Christian Association," was sent out broadcast about this time, and was the result of a scheme which he then formulated, and which anticipated by some years the Young Women's Christian Association.

It has always been admitted that this work among young women was suggested by the Association founded by George Williams, but it is not generally known that he made such definite attempts so early in his career to organise a companion movement.

In December of 1845, George Williams writes: "On Sunday last we met for the first time at Serjeant's Inn. Found the Lord with us, and I hope had a very profitable time." It was at Serjeant's Inn that Mr. Tarlton started the first of his exceedingly successful Bible classes, which soon became an important feature in every branch. These classes, according to a statement in the Association's *Occasional Papers, No. 1*, " are for young men who are not members of Churches and form a directly evangelistic effort. There are no members of the Association present, save those who are engaged in the conduct of the necessary arrangements, it being the object of the Association and the desire of the Committee and of the members that all who, through grace, have believed should at once take part in Sunday School or Ragged School teaching, or in some of those varied instrumentalities by which the Gospel is carried to the destitute and perishing on the Lord's Day." This statement was issued to clear away a misapprehension as to the object of the Bible class, many believing that it served to draw young men away from the places of worship they had hitherto attended.

The beginning of these gatherings was small indeed, for, according to Mr. Shipton in his report to a later Paris Conference, " chairs round a small table sufficed to serve the company. But," he continues, " God was there, His blessing filled the place, and the manifestations of His power and grace have never since been wanting. Of how many souls renewed, of how many backsliders reclaimed, of how much evil prevented, of how many on the verge of destruction saved and restored to virtue and to peace, of how many weak brethren strengthened, of how many who were poor and sorrowful relieved and gladdened by brotherly kindness and love, of how many happy friendships formed to last through eternal ages, of how many equipped for the battle of life, of how many mothers' hearts gladdened and how many fathers made to rejoice over the return of prodigals given up for lost, time would fail us to speak."

This Bible class was shortly afterwards placed under the control of George Williams, who from the first presided at the overflow meeting from Mr. Tarlton's class, and took the place in his scheme of work hitherto occupied by the Sunday School and the Sunday visiting to which he had given so much time. Once more tea and seed-cake, for a long time provided by Mr. George Hitchcock, played their important part. One of those who regularly attended George Williams's Bible class in Serjeant's Inn writes that to this day seed-cake is never absent from his table on Sunday afternoon — " Sunday would not be the same without ' seedy ' cake as we used to call it in those days of the Bible class in Serjeant's Inn " — while as showing the extraordinary attraction of George Williams's personality Mr. Walter Hitchcock, another member of his Bible class, writes that he walked eight miles every Sunday to be present. The address was a simple study of the Word of God, questions were freely encouraged, but I have been unable to discover that there was any particular attraction in the originality or eloquence of the speaker. It was the man himself who drew these

EARLY DAYS OF THE ASSOCIATION 141

young men. "I picture him," writes one who belonged to his class, "as a sort of Apostle John as he engaged us in wise and loving talk and would then pair us off to hear some great preacher of the day such as Baptist Noel or Mr. Reeve of Portman Chapel." There was something in this young man, something undefinable, which radiated from his very presence, something in his manner of gripping the hand, something in the cordiality of his welcome, something in the geniality of his presence, something in the brightness of his face, that made irresistible appeal to young men.

In this connection it may be recalled that throughout his connection with the Association George Williams unceasingly urged the importance of the Bible class as one of the most valuable features of the work. Speaking at a conference some years after he undertook the work at Serjeant's Inn, he advised the conductors of such classes to form committees of young men who would come to the class thoroughly acquainted with the subject for discussion. Immediately the conductor had opened the lesson some one, "without a moment's loss of time," should deal with it; he would then be followed by others prepared in a similar way, and so the interest would be maintained, and long, uncomfortable pauses avoided. He also urged the necessity of making proper provision for watching the strangers who attended the classes. There was, he truly remarked, something known in

London of the results of a hearty shake of the hand, and everywhere it should be some one's definite business to watch for the newcomer, " to find out who he was and where he came from, to invite him to tea and get him to come again. I would have it," he continued, " a treat to attend a Bible class. I do not think the prayer meetings of the ordinary kind are satisfactory. Young men want something quicker, brighter, more lively. The tunes, hymns, and exhortations should all be chosen in this spirit, and the conductors of the Bible class should not make the mistake of restricting themselves too much to prayer."

During the following year, writes Mr. G. J. Stevenson in his *Early Records*, quite a new form of popularising instruction and information was adopted, which came upon young men of the Metropolis with a combination of surprise and delight. This was the inception of the famous Exeter Hall Lectures, which probably did more than anything else to commend the Association to a wider circle of young men. The idea originated with a few gentlemen interested in religious and intellectual matters, prominent among them being the beloved Dr. James Hamilton, of the National Scottish Church, Regent's Square, and the Committee of the Association took up their suggestion with great heartiness. It was carried into practical effect in a most successful manner by Mr. Tarlton and his Associate Secretary, Mr. Shipton. The first of the lectures was given on

December 9, 1845, at the Wesleyan Centenary Hall, by one of the most popular and cultured divines of the day, the Rev. Dr. Stoughton, the subject being "The Connection of Science and Religion." History, science, and archæology, considered in their relation to and bearing upon the Scriptures, formed the subject of the twelve lectures that constituted the first winter course. Their popularity was immense; the cheapness of the tickets, one shilling for the course, or twopence for a single lecture, undoubtedly contributing to their success. Tickets were soon at a premium, and, as a result of the general interest in these lectures, they were continued for twenty years during the months of December, January, and February. Although they were popularly known as the Exeter Hall Lectures, they did not become associated with that famous building until 1848. For the first year they were delivered alternately at the Wesleyan Centenary Hall in the City, and in a room in the West End of London — in 1846 at the Leicester Square Institute, and in 1847 at the Hanover Square Rooms. At last they became so popular, and made such an extraordinary demand on the accommodation of the various meeting places, that it became necessary to incur the expense of securing the large Exeter Hall, which from that date gave them their title. The lectures were of such uniform excellence and attracted such wide attention that it was decided to print them in pamphlet form. The publication was undertaken by Mr. James Watson, of Messrs. Nisbet & Co., who had been one of the original promoters of the scheme, and during the first four years some 36,000 copies were sold.

One important result of the publication of these lectures in book form and their subsequent large circulation was the high reputation that the Association gained among thinking men of the day, and no difficulty was afterwards encountered in securing leading orators for the Young Men's Christian Association platform.

It would serve no purpose to give a detailed list of the lectures delivered during these twenty years; but some idea of their importance may be formed from the names of lecturers which included such famous men as Archbishop Whately, Bishop Bickersteth, Dean Alford, Dean Alexander, Dean Stanley, John Angell James, Dr. Dale of Birmingham, Morley Punshon, C. H. Spurgeon, Dr. Stoughton, "A. K. H. B.," Prof. Richard Owen, James Hamilton, Thomas Binney, Dr. Alexander Duff, Hugh Miller, Earl Russell, Hugh Stowell Brown, Luke Wiseman, and J. B. Gough, while the subjects ranged from the Tabernacle of Israel to the Mythology of the Greeks, from Renan to Hogarth, and from Christian Evidences to Popular Amusements. Perhaps the most extraordinary scene witnessed at these meetings was when, in 1854, Morley Punshon delivered his first great lecture, "The Prophet of Horeb," to nearly

C. W. SMITH
Who gave the name to the Association

EDWARD ROGERS
One of the twelve original members of the Association

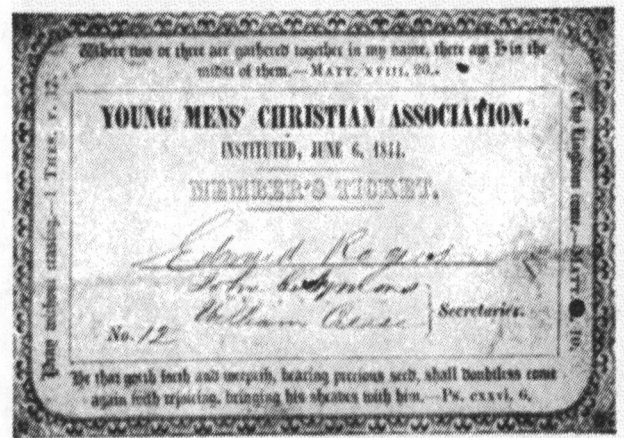

THE ORIGINAL CARD OF MEMBERSHIP OF THE YOUNG MEN'S CHRISTIAN ASSOCIATION

C. D. SHAW
Who gave the house to the Association

DOYLAN HUGHES
One of the early Pilgrim members

EARLY DAYS OF THE ASSOCIATION 145

three thousand people, raising his audience to a pitch of enthusiasm which has never been surpassed, and seldom ever approached under such conditions.

The year 1846 saw a notable definite forward movement. Several additions were made to the Metropolitan branches, and meetings for prayer and Bible study started at Islington, Pimlico, Southwark, and Whitechapel. It was about this time that George Williams began his deputation work with Mr. Tarlton. Together they visited a number of prominent towns and cities in the provinces, separating for a few days while George Williams made a short stay at his old home, finding time on the way to start an association at Taunton, and then meeting again at Bath, where they held a large meeting in the Town Hall, and secured some thirty new members for the Association. This was the way, indeed, in which George Williams took his holidays, not only in these early days, but throughout his life. His family would laughingly say that it was his habit not to consult his own or their wishes in the selection of a suitable place for a holiday, but to consult the records of the society, to note a district which did not as yet contain a Young Men's Christian Association, and to settle there with his family and start branches throughout the neighbourhood.

This record of the early growth of the Young Men's Christian Association may fitly close with a quotation taken from George Williams's diary on

Wednesday evening, August 19, 1847: "I do solemnly declare from this evening to give myself unreservedly to this Association, to live for the prosperity of the Young Men's Christian Association. I do praise God for having called me by His grace and so blessed me temporally. I do desire to be very low at His feet for all His mercies. I thank Him for the determination of so living as to be useful among the young men of the world. And now, oh, Lord, I pray Thee to give me from this hour a double portion of Thy Spirit that I may so labour and work in this Thy cause that very many souls may be converted and saved."

THE WORLD-WIDE GROWTH OF THE YOUNG MEN'S CHRISTIAN ASSOCIATION

CHAPTER VII

THE WORLD-WIDE GROWTH OF THE YOUNG MEN'S CHRISTIAN ASSOCIATION

FROM this time forward the public life of Sir George Williams is written in the reports of the Young Men's Christian Association, with occasional footnotes in the records and subscription lists of many other societies with which he became more or less closely connected. Of his intimate inner life we get fewer glimpses as the years pass. It must be remembered that this young man had attained to a maturity of mind and an assurance of belief that come to few at such an age. The years that followed varied little in worldly experience, except in so far as they were marked by ever-increasing honour and success. George Williams rapidly broadened his commercial outlook and grew in such favour with his employer, Mr. Hitchcock, that the head of the firm came to regard him not only as his most successful buyer and assistant, but of so great importance to the business that he was entitled to a share in its control and profits.

The life of George Williams now enters upon the years of almost unbroken prosperity of soul and body. The story of unceasing work would be monotonous and colourless if recounted in detail. He was most actively engaged and most intensely interested in his business, and the struggle must have been severe, for success even in those days of the nation's prosperity came only as a result of much thought and toil, but anything like a minute description of the ways and means of commercial progress can be of no great interest to the general public. And although it is true that the Young Men's Christian Association was the life of his life, that he was intimately bound up in all its growing activities, that behind and through all he was guiding, helping, giving with full heart and hand of his time and substance, it would be outside the scheme of this book to attempt any full and formal history of the Young Men's Christian Association. I must content myself with noting some of the occasions when his influence upon the work of the Association was peculiarly apparent during its years of world-wide growth.

It was one of the triumphs of George Williams's career that he was able to induce men who, as a rule, were not to be seen on such a platform as Exeter Hall to take a prominent part in public meetings of the Association. George Williams knew the value, the attraction, of a big name. The Lord Mayor of London, the Earl of Harrowby, Lord Ebury, George Moore, Samuel Morley, and other heads of the great City houses, are constantly mentioned in the records of the annual meetings. It is no exaggeration to say that the platform at the yearly gatherings of the Young Men's Christian Association, especially during these middle years, was occupied by more notable men from all sections of society than were to be found at any other public gathering of a religious nature. George Williams believed in doing a big work in a big manner. The Young Men's Christian Association was a great work, and the world had to be told so. He knew that the best way — the only way — to impress the great public, to prove that the Association was not a narrow or circumscribed movement, but one which any young man would consider it an honour to join, was to place at its head men whom the world, from worldly motives, was bound to have in respect.

The most noble of all names connected with the Association will ever remain that of the heroic philanthropist and statesman, Lord Shaftesbury. It was in 1848 when, as Lord Ashley, he had reached the height of his power in the House of Commons, and had added to the long list of his political and social triumphs the Public Health Act and the emigration grant of £1,500 for the Ragged School children, that he first came into close personal touch with George Williams. From that time forward their intercourse was of the most intimate character. The complete story of their friendship will never be told. George Williams would not have wished the details

of such a relationship to be made public, and silence
is the golden tribute to both men. It is enough to
say that one of the finest, strongest characters of
these latter days spoke of Sir George Williams as
his "best friend," and asked repeatedly for him as
he lay waiting for Death. Throughout the years
that followed Lord Shaftesbury was a warm supporter of any movement with which George Williams
was identified, while, when riches increased, George
Williams, reserving himself as he always did prin-
cipally for one work, was ever ready to give generous
financial aid to the multitudinous schemes set on foot
by his friend for the betterment of men. In matters
of religion the two men had much in common, and
in later years Lord Shaftesbury was known to say
that he took no important step without consulting
his "best friend." For nearly thirty-five years the
heroic figure of the friend of the poor, "the good
old Earl," was seldom absent from any important
gathering of the Association held in England, and
one of the last public acts of his life was to accompany, a few days before his eighty-third birthday,
"that dear man George Williams" to the opening
of the Young Men's Christian Association at Brighton
— "that valuable institution," as he writes in his
diary, "set for the glory of God and the good of
men."

In 1849, when for the first time the annual meeting was held in Exeter Hall, which, thirty years later,

GROWTH OF THE ASSOCIATION 153

became the property of the Association and its central home, Lord Ashley had consented to take the chair, but was prevented at the last moment by illness. From the following year till his death he presided at every annual meeting save two or three.

In the same year the headquarters of the Association were removed to new and much larger premises in Gresham Street, City, and it was then that George Williams urged the wisdom of admitting to the library, reading-rooms, and class-rooms those who were not available for membership in the Association, while the additional accommodation enabled the Committee to introduce evening classes for young men, the Association thus taking its place among the pioneers of this department of educational work. This suggestion of enlarging the usefulness of the library and reading-rooms was strenuously opposed by certain members of the Committee, but, after a discussion, which at times became heated, the Committee decided " that without in the slightest degree interfering with the distinctive character and design of membership in the Association, the value of which every year brought additional proof, many young men of moral character and regular habits might be provided for by the Association upon the simple terms of a money subscription, and by this means in widening the sphere of its influence the Association would fulfil its aims and by God's help promote more largely the spiritual improvement of young men."

The acquisition of the rooms in Gresham Street proved most successful. In accordance with the earnest desire and expectation of the more liberal members of the Committee, many who first attended merely for the sake of the library, reading, and class rooms, in due course joined the Bible classes and devotional meetings of their own free will, and many who could not otherwise have been reached were thus brought under the influence of the Association and led to make a definite profession of faith. It would be foolish to deny that certain influential members of the Committee at this time were of the narrowest disposition, and one of the most important works that George Williams accomplished in the Association was in smoothing over the thousand and one difficulties in matters of religious organisation which naturally presented themselves as a result of the rapid growth in all parts of the country. The local secretaries looked to the Central Committee in London for guidance in solving all troublous problems, and if it had not been for the presence and wise counsel of George Williams there can be no question that the work of the Association would again and again have been confined and narrowed by the prejudices of the few. It was owing in great measure to his tact and good humour that the opposition of those who were most fearful of broadening the basis of the work, and whose alienation from the Society would have meant, in more than one instance, most serious loss, was in the end overcome. George Williams met such men on their own ground. He was in full sympathy with their religious views; in a large degree he shared them; but his unanswerable argument was that as long as the fundamental doctrines of the Association were not jeopardised they were entitled, compelled rather, to use all means to save some.

Lest I should be charged with endeavouring to minimise the narrowness which, it must be admitted, characterised even the Central Association, let me quote two amazing extracts from its official organ of about this date, not in any spirit of criticism or condemnation, but only as additional proof that had it not been for the presence and influence of one who, in spite of his own strict Puritanism, steadfastly set himself against the bigotry of many of his dearest friends, the Association would hardly have survived the years of early manhood.

Writing as late as the early sixties, the Secretary, in answer to a correspondent, says: "We have no hesitation in saying that a Christian young man had better not compete in a swimming match, or indeed in a match of any kind. The desire of distinction will in itself be a snare, while if he should win in the strife, passions of envy, jealousy, or disappointment may be engendered in his competitors"; and a few days later a severe rebuke is administered in the same organ to Archbishop Trench and Dr. Dale of Birmingham, who had "trailed their Christian priesthood in the dust to offer homage at the shrine of a dead playwright" at the Shakespeare tercentenary celebrations. "We see," the editorial article continues, "that Archbishop Trench closed his discourse at Stratford Church by referring to the correctness of Shakespeare's views on the corruptness of human nature and on the atoning sacrifice of the Lord Jesus Christ. Did he think such matters were of much account to those who were about to join in idle pageants, theatrical fooleries, and above all that oratorio of the *Messiah*, wherein, as John Newton once said roughly but pointedly, 'the Redeemer's agonies are illustrated on catgut.' Masquerade and sermon, pageant and oratorio!— it is very mournful."

The men responsible for such statements as these had undoubtedly their excuse if not their justification. They had been brought up in a day when even the most innocent amusement seemed tainted by the association of licence and vice, and had been taught, and believed, that most forms of recreation were therefore vicious. Narrowness was the almost inevitable outcome of an age of extremes. The wonderful thing is that an association for young men should have survived the almost inconceivably bigoted attentions of some of its friends and officials. This was certainly due first to its Christian character and spiritual basis, and then in large measure to the in-

GROWTH OF THE ASSOCIATION 157

fluence of George Williams, who, it is very noticeable, never joined in these discussions, nor lent himself to the narrow definition of conduct which some were anxious to introduce into the work of the Association. Often he broke into these arguments with the question which he spent all his life in answering, "What shall we do to *win* young men?" He had unbounded confidence in the good sense of young men, and his sole object was to lead them to Christ. It was well for the world that he compelled those in charge of the Association to remember that this was its great and abiding work.

The month of May was then, as now, the great time for religious anniversaries, and in 1850 the opportunity afforded by this gathering together of men of all denominations from every corner of the kingdom was seized to interest a wider circle in the work. As the annual meeting of the Association was, during its early years, held in the winter months, George Williams, always a believer in the social gathering, suggested the inauguration of a public May meeting breakfast, which soon became one of the most popular of all the "May meetings." The first breakfast was given under the presidency of the Hon. Arthur F. Kinnaird, the father of the present Lord Kinnaird, now president of the National Council of the Young Men's Christian Association, and it may be remarked in passing that one of the most interesting features in Young Men's Christian Association work has been the way in which, in so many instances, the sons have in due time taken up the fathers' work, so that such names as Morley, Bevan, Tritton, and Kinnaird have always been in the forefront of its supporters.

It was at this kind of social gathering that George Williams looked and felt happiest. Whatever calls came upon his time it was only on account of severe illness that once or twice, in all the years, he failed to be present at the May meeting breakfast and at the Christmas breakfast, organised some time later "for the benefit of the hundreds of shop assistants who live at their place of business, and whose homes are at too great a distance to make the Christmas journey." George Williams had the happy knack on such occasions of making everybody feel at home. He had the magic faculty of convincing every young man present that upon him rested the vast responsibility of making the meeting, and even the Association itself, a success. And when you have filled a young man with the belief that so much depends upon his strength and faithfulness, you have gone a good way towards making him a hero, or, if need be, a martyr.

George Williams did not confine these social gatherings to the central building. The early reports are full of short accounts of *soirées* and teas "kindly given by Mr. George Williams" at branches in various parts of the Metropolis, and throughout the country. It was personal contact that George Williams believed in and practised with all his might. During the earliest years these are practically the only occasions upon which his name is prominent, so careful was he to keep himself in the background.

The many social meetings and breakfasts inaugurated by George Williams are so typical of his work in the Association that they merit more than a passing notice. "Christopher Crayon," writing some years later, said that a ride along roads almost impassable on account of the snow, a tramp along the dark and silent streets of London, was well compensated for as soon as he arrived in the genial atmosphere of Gresham Street, where by half-past eight some two hundred members met for their annual Christmas morning breakfast, for "Mr. Williams and Mr. Shipton always carried sunshine with them." "What," he asks, "is the secret of the success of such a gathering as this on one of the most disagreeable mornings imaginable? I answer: The family nature of the gathering. Mr. Williams seems the friend of every one present." George Williams had known the loneliness of London shop life, and he knew how to show sympathy with those who "at the season of joyful reunion were left behind in the great city," at holiday times one of the most desolate spots on earth. It was his delight to make these breakfasts real family reunions, and at them he gave many of his happiest and heartiest little addresses. There sounded through them all the ring of welcome, of encouragement, of great joy. "My heart," he said on one occasion, "is full of sincere gratitude this Christmas morning, full of hope and encouragement. Personal reasons make this a very happy Christmas morning. It is the time for taking stock — for counting up our riches. Oh, what a stock of riches we have in Christ!" Truly he could say at one of the later Christmas meetings, that though he feared grey hairs were to be seen among them, their hearts were still young, and "through God's grace we mean to keep young in love, in joy, and in work for the Lord."

This seems a convenient place to make mention of the other great social gathering at which George Williams presided to the end of his life. Radley's, the quiet old hotel in Blackfriars, suggestive to most Londoners only of Masonic dinners, Christmas balls, meetings of insurance societies, and an occasional wedding breakfast, held a place in the affection of the founder and of the earlier members of the Association, which later comers could hardly realise and appreciate. The two rooms in the old City hotel were crowded with sacred memories. "There are some of us," wrote one of the members when the society was twenty-five years old, "who go up to Radley's meeting with feelings akin to those of the ancient Israelites as they went to their sacred feasts." When after

J. H. TARLTON

First Paid Secretary of the Young Men's Christian Association

W. EDWYN SHIPTON

Mr. Tarlton's successor and one of the great organizers of Association Work

the move to Gresham Street the association with the hotel was severed, George Williams, as has already been stated, decided to perpetuate the old memories by holding at Radley's an annual social gathering consisting of the members of the Committee of the Parent Association and its various Metropolitan branches. This was accordingly done each year until the demolition of the hotel, when the gathering was transferred to the Freemasons' Hall, in Great Queen Street, where, however, it still preserved the name of Radley's meeting.

The meeting was preceded by a reception at which the founder of the Association welcomed his friends in the hearty manner for which he was famous, and which gained so much from his remarkable memory for faces and the personal nature of each individual greeting. After an hour's social intercourse over "seedy" cake and a cup of tea taken, as some one once explained, in peripatetic fashion — for many of those present only met thus once a year — the meeting settled down in a circle round the host's table to hear reports and personal testimonies. Afterwards it was George Williams's custom to suggest some topic of conversation or discussion in connection with the advancement of the society, such as "The special difficulties encountered in the work for young men," "Lessons to be learnt from developments in America," or "The duty of members to the Association." It was in connection with this last subject that, at a

Radley's meeting held in 1870, George Williams urged that the claims of every class, every section of society, might, in future, be provided for in the organisation. He calculated that of the 250,000 young men in the City at that time, at least 150,000 might be ranked as inferior in social station to those employed in warehouses and shops, such as then constituted the staple of the members of the Association. He was strongly of opinion that members should use the advantage which they derived from the Association Bible classes " in order to instruct young men of the artisan class whom it might not be convenient or desirable to introduce into existing meetings, and for whom rooms in suitable localities might be provided."

It is to be feared that this forward policy has not been carried out in Britain with the enthusiasm it deserves, but it should be noted that the general idea of adapting the Association work to suit class needs which has been taken up with such amazing results in America was formulated more than thirty-five years ago by the founder.

There was nothing formal or precise in the discussions at Radley's, the host calling upon one after another to speak of their special work and vigorously wielding his hammer to enforce observance to his ruling that no speaker should occupy more than five minutes. It was delightful, for example, to hear the chairman's spirited address followed by a speech in broadest Northern dialect by a young man who said he had for years longed to be a member of the Committee of the Association so that he might have the opportunity of telling at "Radley's" what he owed to one of its members. He then proceeded to relate how, many years before, he had entered London and stood, wayworn, friendless, and poor, under Highgate Archway. A young man spoke kindly to him and, learning that he was friendless in the City, turned back to the house of a tradesman of his acquaintance with whom he procured for this stranger immediate employment, or, as the narrator pithily said, "put him to bread," within an hour of his entrance upon the life of London.

He had never seen his benefactor since, but he had never forgotten, and when he recalled that this service had been rendered him by one who had announced his membership in the Association as the reason for his friendly conduct to a friendless stranger, he felt intense love for the work, and a great desire that all the members should be encouraged by hearing what comfort and blessing to himself had resulted from a chance meeting with an Association young man. He had found, at the same moment, protection from want, and the temptations by which poverty and isolation in London are too often accompanied.

This is but one instance of hundreds which might be recounted of how the Association was daily fulfilling the hopes of those who started it in the Upper Room, of how their belief in the power of personal contact had influenced the whole work. The Association, started by twelve enthusiasts who in their daily calling came into contact with some one hundred and fifty others, had in four years increased its membership to nearly one thousand who, it was calculated, were in a position to exert a daily influence over at least six thousand young men.

When the Great Exhibition was held in London in 1851, peculiar efforts were put forth to interest the visitors from all parts of the world in the Young Men's Christian Association, and the story of the work was thus carried into many lands. It was a year of enthusiasm and activity and high hopes in all directions. Everything that was best in the forties, all the ideals and aspirations of the period, found in this Exhibition their splendid climax. Men saw, indeed, a new heaven and a new earth, and there were those who seriously expected that men who had once been prevailed upon to meet together in friendly and peaceful rivalry would never again join in the fierce rivalry of battle and conflict.

If the Young Men's Christian Association entered upon the year of the Exhibition with the high hopes that marked the country generally, it did not suffer the severe disappointments that came to those who had expected so much in other directions. On the contrary, however high George Williams and the Committee of the Association had set their ambitions, they

GROWTH OF THE ASSOCIATION 165

could hardly have dreamed of the wonderful effects that this International gathering was to have on their work.

As they had taken advantage of the May meetings to explain their plans and methods to representatives from all parts of the United Kingdom, so they now sought to influence the nations of the world in the cause of the Christian union of young men.

At Exeter Hall, special lectures were given on religious topics, illustrated by the Great Exhibition and its wonderful gatherings. The members of the Association carried out a vast plan of tract distribution, and presented no less than 362,000 leaflets and booklets to those who had come to London to see the sights. Not only did these tracts bring many newcomers to the Bible classes, but they fell into the hands of visitors from the Continent, from the Colonies, and from America, and thus led to the formation of branches abroad and in reality were largely instrumental in starting the International aspect of the work. It was with grateful hearts that the Committee, in issuing their report, stated that " during the year the Association had held over 550 public meetings of young men, for prayer and the communication of religious truth, and that more than a thousand others had been conducted by its members in commercial establishments, while probably over a million young men have been reached by the tracts and addresses which have been distributed."

In the following year during a business visit to Paris, where he bought at that time a large quantity of the dress goods sold in his establishment, George Williams found himself one Sunday morning in the Methodist Chapel, and entering into conversation with a young man, asked his usual question, "Have you a Young Men's Christian Association in this city?" On being told that none existed, and that such an organisation would scarcely be feasible in their city of pleasure, George Williams, nothing daunted, called together a number of prominent religious leaders, and after explaining the nature and scope of the work in London, invited them to form a similar Association in Paris, meeting successfully the many objections which were raised. It was agreed to call on a number of pastors in Paris to obtain their advice and, if possible, their approval; and, at the close of the meeting, George Williams, as was his custom, headed the subscription list with a substantial gift towards the first expenses of the proposed Association. A few weeks later, with the cordial support of Pasteurs Monod and Pressensé, an Association was formed, the first and chief of the many branches which are to be found throughout France to-day. A commercial traveller who was present at the first meeting in Paris, introduced the work to Holland, and thence the Association spread to other countries, so that it may be said with truth that George Williams was more than nominally the founder of the Associations on the

GROWTH OF THE ASSOCIATION 167

Continent of Europe, the work in Paris having been set on foot entirely through his initiative.

In the same year a young man from a business house in London, laid the foundation of a flourishing Association in Adelaide, and shortly afterwards branches were also started in Calcutta, in Montreal, in Boston, and other cities in the United States.

Space will not allow of any adequate review of the growth of the Associations in foreign parts, of how the societies which quickly circled the globe were united and knit together by the creation of a great International Committee, while to the chapter dealing with the Jubilee of the American Association, must be reserved the story of the wonderful work on the Continent of America. It is only right, however, at this point to make mention of the "devoted and self-sacrificing men" who led in the inception of the American Associations. They were inexperienced and obscure, with very limited financial resources, and with little public support and confidence in their plans, but they possessed keen sympathy with their fellows, and a "deep-seated desire to lead them to the truth as it is in Jesus," and multitudes were speedily attracted to them. The work grew with too startling rapidity, so that a decided reaction occurred after a few years, and it was not till 1864 that there appeared the signs of renewed life, and of that strenuous endeavour which has made the American Association a power in the land, and indeed throughout the world.

While it was so rapidly spreading its influence in other lands, its growth throughout Great Britain was equally encouraging. In London it had within ten years outgrown building after building, and in 1854 it was decided to purchase the lease of new premises at 156, Aldersgate Street, formerly occupied by the City of London Literary and Scientific Institute. This new move involved altogether an expenditure of over £3,000. On the occasion of the opening meetings in the new premises, it was estimated that upwards of six thousand young men had joined the Bible classes since their commencement in Serjeant's Inn, while over 500,000 had attended the lectures, the reports of which had sold to the amazing number of above 650,000 copies. The Aldersgate Street building was in size and equipment a notable advance on anything hitherto attempted by the Association, and to this day it continues one of its most active and prosperous branches. With it George Williams was always most intimately connected. Never a week passed when George Williams was in London without at least one visit to its noonday prayer meeting. To him and to those who could recall the early meetings of the Association it represented the work they had originally planned, the Association for the young business men of the City. Within its walls still linger memories of the pioneer days in Radley's Hotel, Serjeant's Inn, and Gresham Street. While, in time, Exeter Hall became the central headquarters of the Young Men's Christian Association, Aldersgate held its position as its home in the heart of the City.

In August of 1855 George Williams was one of the fifteen English delegates at the first general Conference of the Young Men's Christian Associations held in Paris, when the delegates arrived at the important decision that the affiliated societies in all parts of the world should be "one in principle and one in operation, preserving independence of organisation and modes of action."

This Conference marks the beginning of the Association as a world-wide organisation. Reports were received from all the countries in which the Association had started branches. The Swiss Associations were spoken of as "the younger brothers of those in Germany and England," although at Bâle the members traced their descent from the Junglingsverein founded in 1787. Here the organisers of the work had to struggle against the peculiar difficulties of Arianism and Socinianism which had ravaged the Churches, and the struggle had put them under the reproach of dogmatic exclusiveness, for they had been compelled to deny membership to many of "unfixed and speculative views" who denied that Christ was "God manifest in the flesh." In Holland, the Alliance of Young Men's Christian Associations was formed in 1853, one Association at Rotterdam having since ceased to exist, for it "had not wished to break with the world." In connection with the report from Holland some regret was expressed at the exclusiveness which ruled in the Dutch Associations, and at the maintenance of class and social distinctions which, said one speaker, "no longer exist in the Christian brotherhood," but which, as a matter of fact, exist to this day, and have compelled the most progressive Associations to recognise that, while, as one of the defenders of the Dutch Associations stated at this early date, "real affection and fraternal sympathy exist between the branches, young artisans, mechanics, and labourers who gladly come to the classes in rough blouses will not join with the other classes of society represented at other gatherings." It was stated at the time by George Williams that in London "the lawyer, the artist, the man of letters and of science, and the working man, were seen associating with those engaged in commerce in the same Association," but it is now generally recognised that the most promising work of future years lies in the direction of definite class associations.

The report from Germany was of a most encouraging nature, there being at that time some six thousand members, the highest authorities, civil and ecclesiastical, having expressed their sympathy with the work in many ways; while that from France spoke of the members of the Association as standing "alone in their desire to live in God by the faith

GROWTH OF THE ASSOCIATION 171

of the Gospel in the midst of a generation sceptical and immoral." Mr. Edwyn Shipton, the Corresponding Secretary, read an exhaustive report on the history and development of the London Association, in which it is interesting to note that no direct mention is made of the name of George Williams. He is referred to only as "the originator of the first meeting."

From America came a long account of the rise and growth of the work "kindled from an English shrine," to which further reference will be made in a later chapter. But the Conference had a more practical outcome than the reception of gratifying reports. It inaugurated the "bond of union" between different Associations, which was to impart mutual strength, and to express the "inestimable truth" of the sacred unity of the Church of Christ — that alliance of Young Men's Christian Associations, one in principle and in operation, which recognised the unity existing among the Associations, while preserving for each and all complete independence in organisation and modes of action. How George Williams must have rejoiced in that day, when representatives of all the important Associations in Europe and America united upon that common and permanent basis set forth in the words of the Conference Resolution: —

"*The Young Men's Christian Associations seek to unite those young men who, regarding Jesus Christ as their God and Saviour according to the Holy Scrip-*

tures, desire to be His disciples in their doctrine and in their life, and to associate their efforts for the extension of His Kingdom among young men."

The message from the upper room had conquered the world.

THE CRITICAL YEARS OF THE YOUNG MEN'S CHRISTIAN ASSOCIATION

CHAPTER VIII

THE CRITICAL YEARS OF THE YOUNG MEN'S CHRISTIAN ASSOCIATION

THE Conference of 1855 marked the beginning of the most critical period of the history of the Association. As a more or less localised and comparatively unambitious work it had been eminently successful. It had now to undertake world-wide responsibilities, to meet which many changes were needed in the organisation, and there was no small danger that in grasping all it might lose all. Success, as the Secretary of the Association publicly stated, was at that moment their greatest danger. There was the danger, too, of thinking too much of the organisation of the Association, of looking upon it as an end and not as a means, of looking to the agencies " to accomplish themselves those results which we can only have by the influence and gift of the Holy Spirit."

One of the first results of the Paris Conference was the starting of a General Correspondence of the Young Men's Christian Association, which should be the means of keeping in touch with the progress of the work in all parts of the world, and it is noticeable that, at first, difficulty was experienced in inducing certain branches, notably at Dublin and Bristol, to join in the Confederation. These Associations feared that their rules of membership would be compromised by their adoption of the Paris Basis and Resolutions. This misunderstanding arose from the fact that sufficient emphasis had not been laid upon the preamble of the Basis in which it was expressly stated that "a complete independence as to their particular organisation and modes of action" is to be preserved by each Association. This difficulty was only overcome by the exercise of much tact and consideration, and George Williams was kept busy writing to explain the advantages of a confederation which should strengthen all the societies, while leaving them liberty of individual action.

From December, 1855, the minute books of the Central Committee are available, and it is at once noticeable what a prominent part George Williams took in the remodelling of the work, often presiding at meetings and speaking as the chosen representative of the Committee on many important occasions, particularly when it had to consider the question of the retirement of Mr. Tarlton, who was about to join the ministry of the Church, and the appointment of his successor, Mr. Edwyn Shipton.

It is difficult to do justice to the part played by these first Secretaries in the building up of the Young

Helen Hitchcock (Lady Williams)   Sir George Williams at the age of 32
From photographs taken at the time of their marriage

THE CRITICAL YEARS 177

Men's Christian Association. Two more devoted and, in their several ways, more brilliant men than Mr. Tarlton and Mr. Shipton it would have been impossible to find. The first was the enthusiast, the orator; the second the statesman and the organiser. Mr. Shipton would have succeeded in any walk of life. He relinquished a promising business in order to give himself wholly to the work for young men, and he brought into that work all the ability and fertility of resource of a successful merchant. His tact, his quickness, his grasp of detail, his breadth of mind, his power of work, and his tremendous energy were of the utmost service to the Association. It was in a large measure owing to him that the work so triumphantly won through its most critical years.

It was at this time that George Williams composed a set of rules for his daily life, which afford some idea of the strenuous way in which he practised what he preached. Among the few papers found in his private drawer after his death was one dated January 6, 1856, and it is easy to see that it had often been consulted during the years that followed. It runs:—

The Lord be pleased to help me to form resolutions and then give me grace to keep them.

That I determine to get an alarum and when it goes off that I am out of bed before it has finished.

That I read and meditate upon a portion of God's Word every morning and spend some time in prayer.

That I strive to live more in the spirit of prayer.

That I do not parley but resist at once the various temptations which beset me.

That I resist the Devil at once, however he may come to me.

That I pray more for my dear relatives and strive for their conversion.

That I spend some time in praying for the young men at St. Paul's.

That I have certain days and times for certain things and strive to be regular and punctual.

That I strive to gain a better knowledge of the Scriptures and have Bible readings with dear Helen.

That I read these resolutions over before every ordinance day.

In 1857 we find the first mention of a Committee meeting at George Williams's house in Woburn Square, and from that time forth meetings of the Committee "for social and brotherly intercourse" were frequent in his home. It was in this year, too, that the question of a Youths' Bible class came up for consideration, and received the warm support of George Williams, who from that time took a peculiar interest in the "Youths' Section," now one of the most encouraging and useful branches of the work.

In the following year the tact and broadness of George Williams were well illustrated in the way in which he dealt with the very difficult questions of creeds, religious and political, which from time to time agitated the Association. It was reported, for instance, that the Secretary had received several communications expressing surprise and some measure of distress on hearing that the Committee contemplated inviting Mr. Spurgeon to take part in the next course of lectures, and it had been suggested that, as a consequence of such an invitation, the society would "be placed in some difficulty with the other gentlemen, especially certain dignitaries of the Church of England." George Williams, however, took a strong line on the absolutely undenominational basis of the Association. He was then, it should be noted, a regular worshipper at Portman Chapel, which he had joined soon after his marriage with Miss Hitchcock, whose family were all members of the Church of England.

It was at this time also that some attempts were made to use the influence of the society at an election, but George Williams made a point of disassociating himself from politics, and wisely insisted upon the same absolute neutrality in all the officials of the Association. By upbringing he was a Tory of the old school, and all his days he was by nature conservative in outlook and temperament, but only on one occasion was he tempted to take any active part in the struggle of politics. That exception was during one of Bradlaugh's famous campaigns, when he was urged by certain members of the Association to allow himself to be nominated as a Christian candidate against the professedly atheist member. For a time he was inclined seriously to consider the proposal, but after consultation with a number of influential friends he was dissuaded from taking any part in what must certainly have proved a most disastrous campaign. He took the wise view that his defeat at the hands of Mr. Bradlaugh — and against such an antagonist victory was out of the question — would have been of more than political significance, would have been advertised by the opponents of Christianity as a triumph of secularism. Although of an intensely patriotic nature, he took but slight interest in questions of party government. He was sternly opposed to any State support for Roman Catholicism, and was disturbed by the growth of ritualistic practices, but from most questions of debate and discussion he deliberately kept apart, assured by the early threatenings of 1859 that in a very short time the strife and bitterness of politics might ruin the Christian work of years. For the same reason, although he was a life-long abstainer and in full sympathy with the Temperance and Lord's Day Observance movements, he always opposed the attempts which were made more than once to affiliate the Young Men's Christian Association with temperance or other societies. He had but one work, one aim, he would often say. The whole purpose and desire of his soul was to strengthen the religious, the Christian, lives of young men, and from this single work for the conversion, the improvement, the elevation of young men — to him the grandest work in the world — he would not be diverted to any side issue.

In 1863 the Committee of the Association put on record their belief in the great importance of all means by which the minds of those "engaged in the active duties of life could be fitly informed, cultured, and disciplined." "But," continues the manifesto, "this provision of nobler engagements, while useful in contrast to the pleasures of the world, these agencies of educational character, the lectures on topics of general interest, the library, filled with works of value in every department of literature, these merely embody and express Christian sympathy. The one great aim of the Association is to win young men for the Saviour." Mutual Improvement Societies might come and go, Young Men's Societies of every class and degree might serve their time, but the social needs change with the years, and a society for social reform signs its own death warrant the moment that reform is achieved. One thing stands clearly forth as we survey the history of work for young men, not merely of our own times, but of the years that are past. It is this: No society for young men however necessary, however useful in its day and generation, has endured, or shall endure, for more than a comparatively limited period unless it keep steadfastly in view the "one great aim" set forth in this statement of the Committee.

In 1857 the finances of the Association began to

give George Williams serious cause for uneasiness. The work had grown beyond its resources. There were now in London alone well over 1,200 members, and it was part of George Williams's work in the years that followed to interest in the Association those who were able to give largely and liberally. In this he achieved remarkable success. In one instance about this time a debt of over £1,500 was wiped out within the year.

For George Williams personally these were years of peculiar anxiety. He had only recently been made a partner in the firm, and business and family affairs made increasing demands upon his time and thought, while the illness of his father-in-law and partner added greatly to his responsibilities.

It was at this juncture that the society lost the support of one who had served it most devotedly from the beginning, and whose experience and capacity would have been of peculiar value in view of the rapid extension of the work. Mr. George Hitchcock died in 1863. In the history of the Young Men's Christian Association insufficient importance has perhaps been attached to the part played by Mr. Hitchcock, for although the idea originated with George Williams it was to the head of the business in which he was employed that the means of carrying the idea into practical effect was largely due. In a sense Mr. Hitchcock was the first fruits of the meeting in the upper room, for he always took delight in testifying that it was owing to the prayers and to the conduct of these young men in the house that he came out strongly on the side of Christ. Into his Christian work he put the enthusiasm and strenuous endeavour which had made him such a successful man of business. It is interesting to remember that George Williams's habit of speaking words of warning and entreaty to all those who sought employment in his business was a continuation of the custom of his former master, of whom it has been said that it was " in his house of business, in the connections to which commercial engagements introduced him, in the hundreds of persons of every rank and condition who came to him for counsel and aid, that he found his mission for Christ." To all who came to Mr. Hitchcock in search of work the inquiry, " What department do you know? " was followed by the sharp, incisive question, " Do you know Christ? " a question generally followed by prayer and by the gift of some suitable book. Leaving none unwarned, none without an earnest plea for consecration to the Master's service, fearlessly reproving sin and unbelief, steadfastly contending for the faith, jealously watching against the introduction of opinions which might lead men from the simplicity of faith in Jesus, he had during the twenty years of his active Christian career worked without ceasing to win souls to Christ. At the opening of the new Association buildings in Aldersgate Street, Mr. Hitchcock spoke of his work in St. Paul's Churchyard: "I conceive it is my duty," he said, "as God gives me grace to do it, to sanctify everything in the Lord, to buy and sell, to engage young men, to pay them their salaries, to give them social comforts, all as to the Lord. If God has brought these young men under my influence, I believe that to be a talent from God, which I am to use for His glory." "His solicitous efforts and prayers," it was written at the time of his death, "were concentrated on the immediate spheres of service opened to him in the providence of God; first his family, then his household, then those who served him in business, then the members of the same trade, the commercial community to which he belonged, then the poor and degraded inhabitants of the City in which he lived. Beyond these regions of immediate concern, the missionary cause in all its branches shared his generous regard. He gave to the latter of his substance; to the former he gave himself." The fact that there were at one time no less than seven men who had been in his employ preparing for the ministry speaks for the success which attended his efforts.

His liberality towards the Association and to kindred works was open-handed to a degree. From the first he undertook the difficult position of Treasurer of the Association. Not only was his financial support of the greatest service, but the fact that, from the very commencement, a large employer of labour identified himself so closely with the work was of supreme moment. The presence of Mr. George Hitchcock was an excellent reply to the suggestion that this association of young employees was aimed against those in authority, and at the same time the hearty co-operation of a successful merchant did much to secure for the Young Men's Christian Association the serious consideration of other employers.

His later years were clouded by grievous sufferings, which left him unequal to the cares and anxieties of business, and it accordingly fell to the lot of his devoted son-in-law to undertake the control of his public and private affairs. Mr. Hitchcock's death added greatly to George Williams's burden of work both in St. Paul's Churchyard and in the Young Men's Christian Association. He was now in sole control of a great business, and at the same time in response to the urgent call of the Association he undertook the very arduous and troublous position of treasurer of the Association.

How little he sought publicity in connection with his work is shown in his answer to Mr. Bevan, who conveyed to him the wish of the Committee that he should accept the position of Treasurer of the Association. He writes: "After mature and prayerful consideration I confess to some reluctance in accepting the invitation, as my name is so little known to the general public, and I fear the Committee have been more influenced by personal regard to myself

than to what is best for the Association. I do not
hesitate to undertake the responsibility, but I think
the Committee would act more wisely in selecting for
their future treasurer a gentleman whose name would
be at once an ornament and a tower of strength."

From that time forward, as his prosperity increased, George Williams became the chief financial
stay of the Association. His donations from first
to last must have reached great figures. " When an
Association was in debt," says one of his chief helpers,
" I have often heard him say, ' Now, Mr. Hind Smith,
I will divide this cake. I will *give* half if you will
get the other half.' Very often before a meeting
broke up we had cleared the Association of its burden."

It is impossible to give any idea of the extent of
his generosity to the Association. He would have
rejoiced that this is so, for he gave on old-fashioned
lines, delighting to keep his left hand in ignorance
of his right hand's doings. In the records of the
Society one is constantly coming across references to
his munificent donations to branches in all parts of
the world, to the way in which, in times of financial
stress, he was always ready, not only to give largely
himself, but to stimulate others to do the same.

Mention is often made of gifts of prizes at the
Association classes, and presents of books — both
for prizes and as additions to libraries — are frequently referred to, while as early as 1872 we find him
offering to the Committee a sum of £200 towards

wiping out the debt, which "has long impeded the work of the London Association," as a practical way of "showing our gratitude that God has mercifully delivered us from the dire calamities which have distressed our neighbours."

Many of his letters to provincial secretaries have come into my hands, and it is delightful to notice the unostentatious way in which the help is given, the almost apologetic tone in which his contribution towards the funds is mentioned casually in a postscript.

It was in the year 1864 that what may well be termed the turning-point of the Association was reached. The time had come for a critical review of the work of past years, in order that the lines of future progress might be exactly considered and laid down. The Exeter Hall Lectures had ceased to be a marked success, and had, indeed, caused friction among the members on account of certain statements of some of the speakers. Other means of forwarding the work had to be devised, and it was of the utmost importance that the Basis adopted at the Paris Conference of 1855 should be universally recognised and upheld with enthusiasm, and that the general unity of the work should be acknowledged by all, especially in view of the fact that several Associations had lately shown signs of departing from first principles, while others were in a more or less moribund condition, or had become institutions existing merely for the advancement of education and good fellowship. A meeting of delegates from most of the Associations in Great Britain was held at Edinburgh in July of this year, and into the work of this Conference George Williams threw himself heart and soul. His attitude was that of a general reviewing the battalions before the battle.

The first burning question that came up for settlement was the attitude of the Association to the Church. This had been a difficulty from the first, but lately it had become acute, and George Williams took at once the strong line that the work he had founded had always been intended as an auxiliary to the Church; that, in fact, it had proved a great gain to the Church. It was contended that the movement had taken away certain Sunday School teachers, but even if that were the case the Church had been repaid tenfold. "With the grain taken from the heap," he told his hearers, "it has reaped many more." No encouragement was given to young men to remain "learners in the Lord's vineyard." The message of the Association was, "Get to work! Do something for Christ!" At the same time it was rightly pointed out that many young men could only be reached by an organisation which was willing to sink denominational lines of distinction, which had for its chief object the winning of young men to Christ, and, after they had been won, sought to ally them to whatever section of the Church they might favour. However much might still be done inside the pale of any one section of the Church, there remained, it was contended, a still vaster field outside, and much of this work could be most effectually accomplished by such an organisation as the Young Men's Christian Association.

It was inevitable that in such a discussion as this the whole question of sectarianism should arise. The example of the Association had led to the formation in many towns of denominational Associations, and there could be no doubt that, in certain quarters, ministers of various denominations were inclined to look upon a central, unsectarian association with a jealous, if not an unfriendly, eye. The dangers of allowing the work to take on any semblance of denominationalism were well illustrated by the example of a large city in which an excellently intentioned Baptist minister endeavoured to start an Association, but neglected to invite to the first meeting representatives from other Churches. The society thus formed was dead within six weeks. In another case a flourishing Association was rapidly killed by the simple expedient of moving its Sunday Bible class from the Town Hall to a Wesleyan schoolroom, and in a third society sectarian feeling was aroused by the invitation given to the vicar to preside over the gatherings, with the result that the attendance at the Bible class and devotional meeting soon suffered.

It was suggested at the time that the Young Men's Christian Association might serve its best purpose by becoming a kind of "feeder" for these newly formed denominational societies, but it is well that such a scheme met with the most determined and immediate opposition. The difficulty of keeping denominational associations for young men in anything approaching a flourishing condition — especially in small towns — had already become sufficiently evident, and has been felt increasingly with the years, and proof was given again and again at this Conference that by leaving the choice open to young men, while always insisting upon the importance of membership in some Christian Church and never regarding membership of the Young Men's Christian Association as a substitute for Church membership, the best ends of religious activity were served. As a matter of practical experience it was found that one of the chief values of the Association lay in the fact that it formed a neutral meeting ground for members of all sects and denominations, and it would have been nothing less than disastrous if anything had been done to interfere with this admirable freedom of Christian intercourse.

As an example of the catholicity of the work it was stated that at an Association meeting held about this time, it was discovered that among those engaged in a most amicable and profitable discussion upon "Christ fulfilling the Law," were a hyper-Calvinist, a Broad Churchman, a Plymouth brother, a fierce Millenarian, an Irvingite, and a Swedenborgian.

There were then, as there are still, those ardent sectarians who share in the opinion of a certain clergyman, that the connection of young men of his Church "with persons of different views took something out of them and disqualified them from being as useful as they ought to be," or of an anonymous correspondent, to whom the Rev. Dr. Miller referred at the annual meeting of 1860, who protested against his attendance at " an essentially Dissenting Society." The answer given at that time might well serve as long as the Association lasts. "We have not found that the association of believing men for active efforts in the service of the Redeemer has tended to diminish their piety or disqualify them for usefulness." Such results as those feared by this clergyman, and by the anonymous correspondent, could never be possible as long as the Associations were doing their proper work. "Any young man," wrote the Secretary — and it is clear that he had the whole Committee, and particularly George Williams, at his back when he made the reply, for he stated that " an attached member of the Church of England " was guiding his pen — " Any young man who uses or seeks to use his position among us to bring others to his opinions and to advance the interests of his own sect is a traitor to our principles, and if the fact were proved against him he would be excluded from our fellowship. The only work we have to do is to win young men from sin to holiness, to instruct those who are ignorant, and to guide and uphold those who desire to walk in the paths of virtue and truth. If our members are doing this work, they will have no time and they will certainly acquire no disposition to enter into matters of ecclesiastical strife. If members of different sections of the Church of Christ think they can best serve their Lord and aid young men by forming denominational societies, our best wishes will go with them, but we must protest against their using our Catholic designation. A Church of England Young Men's Society, or a Nonconformist Young Men's Union, are understandable things as conveying the idea of fellowship among those of one class, but the term Association was selected by us specially to indicate the union of Christian young men of different Churches, and we hope that truth and fairness will prevent the name of the Young Men's Christian Association being adopted for any party or sectarian ends."

It is of importance to remember, in view of the suggestion that this was a Dissenting Society, that, according to the advice of the London Committee about this time, the secretary of a new Association should, " other things being equal, be a Churchman, to avoid all appearance of proselytism."

Another matter discussed was the value of the Bible class as a part of the work of the Association,

SIR GEORGE WILLIAMS
From a photograph taken about 1870

Sir Rowland Williams.
From a photograph taken about 1870.

a subject very near George Williams's heart, while a paper was read on "Prayer as Essential to Christian Usefulness," in connection with which George Williams mentioned several instances — already referred to in the story of the Upper Room — of the spirit of prayer which animated the first members of the Association. "In prayer for ourselves and others whom we desire to be brought to Jesus," he said, "is our strength. We may commit no end of blunders, we may be as weak as nothing, but if we will only pray we may be as strong as the omnipotent strength of God can make us."

During the following days addresses were delivered on "The Condition and Means of Usefulness," those present comparing experiences of the value of various agencies, of devotional meetings and tract distribution campaigns, and other methods of stimulating work among individual members. One of the most important events of the Conference was the long and, at times, heated discussion on the use of amusements in the Young Men's Christian Association, at which the theory, hitherto accepted by many of the workers, that "young men should be left to find their amusements for themselves," was vigorously attacked as one of the gravest dangers in the work. Speeches in defence of making the Young Men's Christian Association "a place of resort for young men," were delivered by many of the delegates, while several of the secretaries bore their testimony that the news-room, the library, and the introduction of amusements had helped rather than hindered the great fundamental purpose for which the society existed. These speakers laid stress upon the missionary character of Association work as defined in its original rules, and in view of such a definition felt that anything in the way of harmless recreation which would attract young men to the buildings of the Association would be of benefit, and would thus bring them under the influence of the Gospel.

At the same time it must be admitted that this was not always the interpretation of the scope of the work favoured by the London Committee, with which George Williams was most closely connected, and which came into somewhat unpleasant prominence a few years later in connection with what became known as the *Punch* incident. It appears that a question was raised in a meeting of the Dover Association, as to the retention of *Punch* in the reading-room, and certain persons present, according to the record in the Association's *Quarterly Messenger*, " pressed for its continuance on grounds altogether wide of the Young Men's Christian Association, while others better instructed as to the Association resisted it on grounds which we think equally untenable as regards the publication in question." It was on this occasion that the Rev. Hugh Price Hughes first came into conflict with a certain section of the Committee, and although throughout his life he never forgot the incident, or completely forgave the Association, he was more than once in later years a welcome speaker at its public meetings. *Punch* was excluded from the Dover reading-rooms as a publication "contemptuous of religious influences, if not absolutely hostile to them." The matter was taken up in the most scornful manner by the press throughout the country. Mr. Hugh Price Hughes and others lost no time in calling a special meeting to reconsider the question. The picture in question was "triumphantly produced" by one of the Dover members from a back number of *Punch*, and contained a humorous illustration of an old lady imparting to a sympathetic friend the fact, that although she permitted Susan ("It's true she's a Dissenter!") to go to chapel three times a Sunday since she had been with her, she didn't cook a bit better than she did the first day! This, argued the member, was a sneer at religion, but as *Punch* on May 25, 1871, in a biting article entitled "Dolts at Dover," asserted, the meaning of the picture was the exact reverse of that imagined. Mr. Hughes, as his daughter recounts, " laboured with the greatest courtesy and understanding, quoting Elijah and the other prophets to prove to the narrow-minded and prejudiced the fact that the prophets themselves indulged in humour, and the Saviour Himself in satire." He carried the day by four votes, and *Punch* presented him with his "royal thanks" in the next issue. The matter was referred to the London Committee, and it is not difficult to trace the influence of George Williams in the reply of the Secretary, which is worth quoting as showing how he regarded the work of the Association, and how his outlook and sympathies broadened in the years that followed.

"With the provision of opportunities for religious culture and of education under religious sanctions, our engagements," writes the Secretary, "with young men are fulfilled. We have never proposed to ourselves, or in any manner undertaken, to cater for the recreation of young men, even in directions which are both lawful and expedient. The provision of recreative literature would stand on the same ground as the provision of physical recreations or other lawful amusements. It should not be looked for in connection with the arrangements for the Young Men's Christian Association."

It was on this ground, and on this ground alone, that the Committee advised the Association, "steadfastly to resist the admission of *Punch* into the reading-room." At the same time the Secretary was quite unable to concur with the views expressed by certain members as to the contents of *Punch*, which, he contended, were not shared by religious people generally. "We all know," he writes, "that *Punch* is largely read in religious families, and is sometimes quoted admiringly even in the columns of the *Record*, the religious journal most tenacious in matters of this

SIR GEORGE WILLIAMS IN 1876
From a photograph taken during his visit to America

THE CRITICAL YEARS

kind." *Punch*, indeed, was praised as having taken a common-sense view of matters relating to religion brought under public discussion, and while, as in the case of most journals, "the watchful eye of the editor may not always catch turns of expression which may give pain to devout persons," the Dover members were advised to remember how much there was of good in the publication, rather than to be over-sensitive, when it pointed out the weaknesses "which belong to a great many religious persons, and of which, possibly, we ourselves have only too large a share."

As showing how carefully the Central Committee guarded the absolute neutrality of the Association in matters of discussion between Church and Dissent, one further paragraph deserves quotation: —

"I do not like," writes the Secretary, "to be a mere critic of men with whose religious sentiments I concur, but it would seem to me that your President exhibited a great want of tact in producing the 'Jemima'[1] illustration, since it appears to have afforded to a minister of religion present an occasion for violating the neutrality of your Association by introducing a sneer at what he was pleased to call the State Establishment."

The Edinburgh Conference was the first of a long series held every few years in different cities and dif-

[1] As a matter of fact it was "Susan," not "Jemima."

ferent countries, and although George Williams was present at most of these, little would be gained by any attempt to review the topics raised and discussed at such gatherings. The Conference of 1864 merits, however, special notice, for it established the work on the firmest foundation, it faced the growing difficulties boldly and in a thoroughly businesslike manner, while reaffirming the Association's adherence to the principles underlying the work at its commencement. It must not be forgotten, in justice to those whose views may now appear almost absurdly narrow, whose idea of the work seems almost petty and pitifully circumscribed, that it was as a result of minimising the importance of the definite religious basis of the Association that so many societies at this time came to grief. Certain Young Men's Christian Associations had so far departed from " first principles " that they admitted to membership any young men who " professed to believe in the Evangelical doctrines of Christianity," but in a few years their work was undermined, the Bible class and devotional meetings abandoned, and they passed into oblivion. It may be said that, without exception, those who departed from the original lines laid down by the rules were marked for failure.

The Conference of 1864, while insisting with the deepest earnestness upon the necessity of what appeared to some as a narrow definition of eligibility for membership — " decided evidence of conversion " — yet opened the way for a wonderful extension of the Association in all directions, and laid the foundation for its ultimate, far-reaching success.

THE YEARS OF PROGRESS

CHAPTER IX

THE YEARS OF PROGRESS

THE Conference of 1864 marks the end of the critical years, and the beginning of established and certain success. The Association had come of age, had passed triumphantly through the testing days of early manhood, and entered now on a period of ever-widening influence. It does not belong to the plan of this book to trace in anything like detail the work of the thirty years, which culminated in the Jubilee of the Association in 1894. Nor would I burden this biography with analyses of reports and statistical records. I propose in this chapter to note certain landmarks in the years of progress, landmarks which tell of the way George Williams and his friends had been led, and of the means they employed to ensure and increase the prosperity of the work of their hands.

One might dwell on the wonderful annual meetings of such years as 1868, when there stood side by side with George Williams, on the platform of Exeter Hall, the noble figures of the Earl of Shaftesbury and Mr. Spurgeon, both racked with pain, both full of unbounded faith and enthusiasm, both received with acclamation by the vast crowds of young men; or upon that moving scene at the annual meeting of 1872, when the Earl of Shaftesbury, his voice trembling with emotion, spoke of the misgivings he had harboured that the Young Men's Christian Association might become tainted " with the abominable leprosy that is abroad — that opposition to the retention of the Word of God in the elementary schools, to be established by the school boards." There must still be many who can remember how his voice rang out as he said, " This I will say, that we must stand steadfastly by the great principle of holding the Word of God to be indispensable as the basis, the middle, and the end of all our education. If, in the least degree, to the extent of a hair's breadth you depart from that principle, you may remove me out of this chair, and find some other man to sit in it, for whilst I draw my feeble breath never shall you see me in your presence again." One might, indeed, write at length of anniversary after anniversary, for this annual meeting of the Association — bringing together on one platform, as it has always done and will continue to do, many of the most striking figures in the Christian Church — will ever be one of the religious events of the year.

At each of the gatherings during the thirty years, there was abundant evidence of increasing power and usefulness, and an important landmark is the statement hidden away in one of the reports, that the young men in the employment of the great firm of Messrs. I. & R. Morley had so developed their "missionary" society, that many of the men in the house were now actively engaged in Sunday and Ragged schools, in organising banking and clothing clubs, evening classes, mothers' meetings, temperance societies, and Sunday and week-night services in the Mission Hall at Golden Lane. This was the splendid way in which the idea of the Association was taken up in various parts of the City and adapted to varying needs. There were, for instance, in George Williams's own house of business, a Young Men's Missionary Society, the object of which was "to supply and sustain spiritual influences among the members of the establishment, to enlist sympathy on behalf of the spiritual destitution in the vast Metropolis, and in the still more vast and destitute regions in foreign countries," various Bible and prayer meetings, collections for the support of missions at home and abroad, a definite mission carried on in connection with night schools and lectures in a densely populated district in the neighbourhood of St. Paul's. In the famous firm of Messrs. Copestake, Moore & Co., many excellent lecturers were provided, chiefly under the auspices of that great merchant and philanthropist, Mr. George Moore, while similar associations had been formed in a number of other important houses of business. These meetings were all under the supervision of members of the Young Men's Christian Association, and the Committee of the Association was constantly exercising its influence upon each of these local assemblies, the officers attending from time to time and assisting in various ways in their management. Owing, undoubtedly, to the influence of the Association, and in particular to George Williams's example, the provisions made by many of the largest employers in the drapery business for the comfort of their assistants were greatly improved, while in connection with many of the houses Mutual Improvement and similar societies were introduced with great success.

The London report of 1869 affords a good survey of the attainments and scope of Association work during these middle years. Special attention is drawn to the number of largely attended Bible classes, the object of which was to assist those who were preparing for religious work, and from which the Ragged and Sunday schools of the Metropolis were constantly supplied with teachers. The attendance at these classes was recruited by the systematic distribution of tracts and papers among young men by an organised band of recruiting agents. Such work was proof of the fact that the Society, in the words of one of its manifestoes, "does not exist as an agency in competition with other agencies on a similar field. It occupies its own ground, goes where others cannot go, and having done its best to train its members to the love and the exemplification of the things that are honest, just, pure, lovely, and of good report, brings all the result of its work into the service of the Christian Church, pressing upon every young man who is won to the acceptance of religion and the service of Christ, the duty of Christian fellowship in connection with some section of Christ's holy, Catholic Church." Mention is also made of many devotional meetings, and of addresses at social gatherings, at which the Committee provided hospitality for a large company of young men gathered from the commercial houses of the City to the number of from six hundred to seven hundred on each occasion. These social evenings were generally presided over by one of the leading merchants of the City, while the addresses were given by ministers of various denominations.

Another feature of the London Association was the daily noon prayer meeting at Aldersgate Street which " became the resort of many earnest and faithful servants of God, and was regarded by them as an important aid to the due prosecution of the engagements of business as well as a means of strength and solace amidst trials and difficulties." As has already been stated, George Williams attended the noon prayer meeting, whenever he was in the City, presiding each Thursday, when the special subject for prayer was always " The Conversion of the Children of Godly Parents." Side by side with the purely religious work, the Association was increasing its

educational work, and a number of classes met each
week at Aldersgate Street. Meetings in French and
German for foreign members of the Association in
London were also held, and in 1869 certain friends
of the Association raised a fund for the employment
of a travelling agent to reorganise Associations which
had become inefficient, and to form new societies. This
move was due entirely to the way in which George
Williams had impressed upon the Committee "the
duty and importance of seeking to extend the work
of the Association to the great towns of the country."
In reviewing the work in the provinces he had been
struck by the small number of Associations in com-
parison with the need and the opportunity, with the
weakness of much of the organisation in country districts, and had applied personally to some friends of
the work for assistance in starting this special fund.
He himself headed the list with £100, and obtained
promises for a similar sum from Mr. R. C. L. Bevan,
Mr. Samuel Morley, and Mr. J. D. Allcroft. There
were two special grounds for the employment of
a travelling representative. Many Associations in
reality connected with particular Churches had been
formed throughout the country, and had taken the
title of the Young Men's Christian Association, thus
compromising its catholicity and missionary character.
On the other hand many societies " offering to young
men the advantages of literary culture and social
intercourse and making good moral character a con-

Sir George Williams in 1898

Sir George Williams at the Age of Sixty

dition of membership" had taken upon themselves to use the name of "Christian" Association. It was not, said the Secretary in supporting George Williams's plan, possible to make any effectual protest against these assumptions except by the provision of the "real thing." As a result of one year's work by the new Travelling Secretary, one Association was thoroughly remodelled, and ten of the older societies were visited and assisted to adjust and improve their methods, while new Associations were formed at twenty different centres. In the following year special work was started among Sunday excursionists at Paddington Station. On Sunday evenings similar efforts were put forth among the crowds in Hyde Park, where the members of the Association were among the first to commence open-air preaching when the parks were thrown open for the purpose a few years previously. In several of the low lodging houses services were held on Sunday evenings, while on Saturday evenings members were stationed at the doors of music halls and theatres to invite those entering to come to the services of the Association, and "to endeavour by personal influence and conversation to lead them to reflect upon their course." On one occasion at a social meeting given at a Branch Association by Mr. Bevan, no less than forty of the young men present had received their invitations on entering some place of amusement the previous Saturday evening.

A detailed account of the activities of members

of the Association in various houses of business is to be found in one of their periodicals about this time, and affords eloquent testimony to the far-reaching effects of the work. This was not confined to the cities, for we read of a nine-years-old village Association, consisting at the beginning of ten members, which had entirely changed the religious life of the community and had started a spirit of revival which had wakened the whole district.

In 1873 mention is first made of the visits and addresses of Mr. D. L. Moody, and although his work was not directly connected with the Association, it owed much of its success of organisation to George Williams and his friends, who worked night and day to forward Moody's campaign. It was largely due, indeed, to George Williams's personal efforts that Mr. Moody came to London, and the two became on terms of intimate acquaintanceship. Mr. Moody was a great believer in the Young Men's Christian Association, declaring that in his preparation for spiritual work, he owed more to the Association than to any other human agency, and while in London he addressed a series of special meetings for young men at the Association's headquarters in Aldersgate Street. When an effort was being made in Liverpool to raise funds for a new building, Mr. Moody, in the course of a passionate appeal, said that he believed there was no Christian work in England or America which was so little understood, and for which there was so little sympathy as this Association. The reason was that not one man out of a hundred took pains to inquire into its objects. They had an idea that because such Associations did not exist in the days of their fathers, they were unnecessary now. But other times, other manners. Fifty years ago when young men came to the cities their employers took a fatherly interest in them. "I contend," he said with growing vehemence, "that they do not do so now. In those days an employer felt himself responsible for a young man in his employ. To-day he does not. Who is there to look after him? If he is not a Christian young man and does not introduce himself to the minister of a Christian Church, the Church leaves him alone. Since I have been in Liverpool, there is hardly a night when I do not meet in walking from this hall to my hotel a number of young men rolling through the streets. They may be your sons. Bear in mind, they are somebody's sons and they are worth saving. A good, warm grasp of the hand, a kindly word and a smile, will do more for a young man who comes for the first time to the City than ten thousand of the most eloquent sermons ever heard. These young men want some one to take an interest in them. I contend that no one can do this so well as a Young Men's Christian Association."

It was some months later that Mr. Moody, under the auspices of the Association, addressed a mighty meeting of business young men in the Agricultural

Hall, pleading in his inimitable, heart-searching manner with the prodigals — " sons who are breaking their mothers' hearts " — denouncing in an outburst of terrific passion the vices of the day, and crowding the after-meeting until well beyond midnight with anxious, inquiring souls. Wherever Messrs. Moody and Sankey went during their tours throughout the kingdom, they stimulated and helped the work of the Associations, and the revival of these years among young men was in a large measure due to their campaign. Mr. Moody's name has never been officially connected with the most striking development of the work which culminated in the purchase of Exeter Hall, but there are many who consider that it was the enthusiasm he aroused for the Association in all parts of the kingdom which, in great measure, made possible such a daring forward movement a few years later.

Behind and through all these varied agencies of the Young Men's Christian Association George Williams worked steadily and steadfastly. He was, in reality, the power behind the machine, no mere figurehead but a force whose influence was felt throughout all the ramifications of the work. Those who knew him only from seeing him on public platforms have been inclined to speak lightly of his judgment, as if kindness and Christian sympathy were his only characteristics. No greater mistake could be made. George Williams was a strong man, keen and resourceful: he could be very stern, he was occasionally very angry; he was always deliberate, sometimes obstinate. He was the last person in the world to be persuaded against his better judgment or to act from feelings of mere sentiment. The National Secretary recalls an occasion when a certain case was put before George Williams, and a strong attempt made to obtain his decision in accordance with what — in the judgment of the Secretaries — would be the wisest and best course to pursue. A deputation of senior officers waited upon him, and a careful plan was made for the presentation of the case. The first speaker had scarcely opened the subject when there came that gentle shake of the head which always meant so much. It had come to be realised that once his mind was made up — and this was often indicated by the slightest possible movement of the head — nothing could change him. In this case the second senior officer added his remarks and made them as persuasive as possible. Before the third officer's turn came it was realised that it would be useless to pursue the matter further, and the officers made their exit, admiring the courage and strength of will of their President, feeling they were baffled, but withal in so kind a way, that they could scarcely restrain laughter at their own defeat.

George Williams's one recreation at this time was the attendance at various Association Conferences held in different parts of the country. He often presided, delivering his bright little speeches, cheering all present by his geniality and enthusiasm and leaving behind a substantial cheque and a memory of encouragement more valuable than gold. He believed that such meetings were quickening and refreshing to the heart, and certainly he did everything in his power to make them so. He had a firm belief in the good work done by these meetings of delegates, in spite of the criticism of certain excellent but impatient people who declared that the members of the Association were better at talking than at doing. It was at the second Conference of delegates in London that he delivered a notable defence of such gatherings, at which, said he, " by the blessing of God our hearts will melt, and flow out in love and kindness to each other, and we shall return to our respective homes better, happier, and more useful men. To my own mind they bring back the remembrance of ascending great mountains, where high as you go one range after another meets the eye, ranges stretching far out into the infinite. Is there not something like this in the work we are doing for young men? Thousands of them are being rescued for a future of glory, honour, and immortality, the grandeur of which eye cannot see, nor heart conceive. There are other advantages too. We see what our work is, and see better how to do it. At the Darlington Conference held recently one of the delegates stated that some years ago he was in London attending a Conference. He returned home with new zeal animating him, and during a few months five young men were brought to the Lord. All of them are now ministers of the Gospel, and it is interesting in connection with this fact to note that one of these young men is now a Church of England clergyman, two are Baptist ministers, one an Independent minister, and one a Methodist."

George Williams could never lay claim to being an orator, but he had the happy knack in his speeches of saying just the right things in a few words. I have before me as I write a collection of notes of addresses delivered during these years at meetings and Conferences throughout the country. Contrary to general belief his speeches were prepared with great pains. It was his habit to paste in a commonplace book any cuttings from newspapers which he thought might be useful, and the apt and timely illustrations of which he made such excellent use and his neat turns of phrase were not, as many have imagined, extemporary efforts, but most carefully written down and committed to memory. Such speeches as these do not bear lengthy quotation. They depended entirely for their effect upon the manner of delivery, which, while it was not in any way ambitious, was admirably suited to the matter and the audience. What George Williams had to say was always eminently practical, and he had a practical way of saying it. He liked to hang his remarks on some such catchwords as, " Aim high. Fight shy.

Keep high." Short, sharp sentences were jerked out as he raised himself on tiptoe and brought down his fist with a great swing of the arm. He had the remarkable gift of relieving the many meetings in which he took part of any taint of tedium or dulness. There was a sparkle and vivacity about him altogether contagious. He was one of those small-built men who, when they speak in public, seem compact of energy. According to recent testimony he was the best chairman of a religious meeting of his time. Only once in all his long career did he allow an audience over which he presided to get out of hand, and that was owing to a misunderstanding. George Williams was always strict in keeping speakers to their allotted time, and on this occasion one of the most popular preachers of the day thought his coat-tail had been pulled in consequence of his enthusiastic reference to a prominent statesman, and sat down without completing his sentence, obviously in high dudgeon, whereas the explanation was simply that he had already disregarded a similar but less emphatic warning that his " time was up! " The audience had been worked up to a high pitch of excitement, for these were passionate days, and refused to hear any one else, and neither George Williams nor the organist could silence their demands.

Here are a few characteristic quotations from his speeches during this period.

At the Conference of delegates in 1871, speaking

of the means of increasing the success of the Association, he advised his hearers to "get to know the names of young men. Take one at a time. Write a letter to him. Give him a shake of the hand. Ask him to have a friendly cup of tea. Talk kindly, naturally, with him. Take him for a walk. Show him a little kindness and you will get hold of him. Get one to come, and others of his class will follow like a flock of sheep. Have warm hearts, loving, big souls. By God's blessing there will be no failure. By using these means every difficulty will be surmounted."

Some years later, in the course of a speech to Conference delegates, he said:—

"Oh, let us be men of one idea! We have — I know I have myself — too many irons in the fire, and our energies are scattered and worth nothing. If this Conference would result in inspiring us to keep to our one work, it would prove a blessing indeed. . . . We ought to comprehend in our regard and prayerful sympathies every young man in the kingdom, from the Prince of Wales down to the lowest beggar, every young man from fourteen to forty. In England at the present time great power is being given to the working classes. How is it to be turned to the best account? Is Bradlaugh to be allowed to have his say to the working classes, and are there to be no young men amongst us able to meet his attacks on revealed religion?"

He loved to dwell on the possibilities of good in every young man, and liked to recount such possibilities in detail. Writing to one of the Secretaries, he said: "Please remember that one youth brought to know and love and follow the Saviour is a good year's work. That youth may become a joy and support to his parents and friends. He may become a Sunday School teacher, a member of a Christian Church, an active worker for, and contributor to, home and foreign missions, a churchwarden, deacon, elder, or class leader. He may become an active member of the Association, and be the means of leading many young men and young women to Christ. He may become a member of a Committee of the Association, and rise to be a large employer and promoter of virtue and happiness, and leave behind him a family devoted to the Lord's work."

At many of the Conferences this review of a young man's future was the burden of his presidential address. "Why," he asks on one occasion, "all this to-do about young men? Why should there be a separate Association for young men at all? I will answer by showing what a young man can do. He can injure his health, he can undermine his constitution, he can destroy his moral character, he can lose his situation, he can become a drunkard, he can break his mother's heart, he can lead other young men and women astray, and surround himself to all eternity with lost spirits who will look upon him as the means

THE YEARS OF PROGRESS 219

of their perdition. But, thank God, he can do something else. He can become an associate of the Young Men's Christian Association — I am glad we have active and associate members — he can repent of his sins, he can believe in the Gospel, he can give his whole heart to Christ, he can take care of his life, he can gain the esteem of and become a great help to his employer, he can help his father and become a great joy to his mother and sisters, he can become a Sunday and Ragged school teacher, he can contribute to and become a zealous advocate of foreign missions, he can become an abstainer and persuade hundreds of others to abstain, he can become an *active* member of the Young Men's Christian Association, and by his life and zeal for the souls of young men and women become instrumental in leading many to the Saviour, who, instead of accusing him of being the cause of their ruin, shall be a joy to him throughout the countless ages of eternity."

In 1873 another landmark in the work of George Williams was reached by the opening of Hazelwood House, Ryde, as a holiday home for young men. Such was the success of Hazelwood House that a few years later another young men's home was established at Margate. These homes, to which more particular reference is made in a later chapter, owe their existence almost entirely to the initiative and munificence of George Williams, who determined to wipe away the reproach of a sceptical young man who once said to him, " All that your religion does for me is to offer me a farthing tract."

It is noticeable, in reading the reports of the many meetings of the Association, that the founder and treasurer seldom appeared in any prominent manner before the public. He contented himself for the most part with moving votes of thanks, and presiding at social gatherings of all kinds, and, with the modesty which was such an attractive feature in his character, always took a place in the background, seldom allowing any particular account of the work he had done for the Association during the year to appear in its official records. In 1878 it was felt that the time had arrived for the development of a general organisation for the Continental work, and it was in great measure the outcome of his generous support that the work of the International Committee of the World's Alliance was established at Geneva in that year. From that date this Committee has exercised a remarkable influence throughout Europe, while members from forty different countries are represented on its board of management. At the time of writing there are over three thousand separate Associations on the continent of Europe alone, and nearly eight thousand in all are embraced in the World's Alliance.

In 1880 several changes were made in the organisation of the London Association. Mr. Shipton, the successor of Mr. Tarlton, of whose tact and geniality and organising power mention has already been made, retired from his position, and was followed by Mr. W. Hind Smith, who had been one of the most active of the provincial Secretaries since he joined the Association at the time of the Edinburgh Conference. Mr. Hind Smith's indefatigable zeal and work have counted for much in the progress of the later years, and it is a pleasure to pay a tribute, at this place, to one who has worked nobly in the cause of the Association.

In 1880 the East Central London Branch of the Young Men's Christian Association was opened in King William Street, when the chair was occupied by Mr. J. Herbert Tritton, of the great firm of Messrs. Barclay, Bevan, Tritton & Co., whose partner, Mr. R. C. L. Bevan, presided at the first annual meeting of the Association thirty-four years previously.

It was this year, too, that saw the beginnings of the greatest ambition of George Williams's life — the purchase of Exeter Hall for the Young Men's Christian Association. Speaking at the annual meeting of the Association in 1880, he said: "Your old and excellent friend, Mr. R. C. L. Bevan, has referred to the commencement of this Association, when it was but a very small gathering of young men. You remember, when the sapling was planted, what a poor, sickly thing it appeared. But it has grown, it has spread out its branches, it has covered nearly the whole of Europe, America, and many of the British provinces, and we hope ere we come to the end of the chapter, that it will cover the whole of the world. We have, indeed, grown out of our home in Aldersgate Street. We do not know what to do with the multitude of young men coming to us. We want a larger place. And we must have a larger place. I hope it may be our great pleasure to have our President in the chair when, at no distant date, we shall have a much larger place for the Young Men's Christian Association in this great Metropolis of the world."

The history of Exeter Hall is bound up in the religious and social history of the last century. It was originally built in 1831 to provide a place of meeting for philanthropic and religious societies, which, up to that time, had been compelled to make use of the tavern and hotel. It was here that the Prince Consort made his first appearance in June, 1840, on behalf of the abolition of the Slave Trade; here that the first Temperance Meeting in London was held in June, 1831, and that J. B. Gough delivered his wonderful temperance orations; here that Morley Punshon swayed multitudes; here that Mendelssohn's "Elijah" was first performed in its present form; here that Jenny Lind's famous concerts took place. But after fifty years it was decided to sell the building, for the enterprise had not proved successful as a business speculation. There was some talk of a music-hall syndicate purchasing the premises with a view to turning Exeter Hall into a place of amusement, but there was a clause in the deeds requiring that before it was disposed of for any other purpose, it should be first offered to some religious society.

George Williams, like all successful men, loved big things, and immediately he heard of the proposed sale of Exeter Hall he determined to make a great attempt to purchase the leasehold of the building for the Young Men's Christian Association. The idea of acquiring the hall for the benefit of certain religious societies originated, it should be stated, with Mr. T. A. Denny, who approached the shareholders with a proposition, but, at the time, failed in his negotiations. When George Williams conceived the plan of making it the headquarters of the Association, Mr. Denny and his brother readily entered into the scheme, in spite of the fact that it was at first almost ridiculed by many of the Association's firmest friends. When it was seriously discussed, it met with most strenuous opposition. It was contended that, even under existing conditions, it was not easy to keep the Association, with its rapidly growing work, free from debt — that special appeals had frequently to be made to clear off outstanding liabilities. But as Mr. Hind Smith, who perhaps more than any one else was in George Williams's confidence in Association work, recounts, the stronger the opposition the stronger became George Williams's determination to attempt the purchase of the building. At last one afternoon, as they sat talking together of the proposal, George Williams, after meeting objection after objection, threw himself back in his chair, rubbing his hand across the back of his head, a habit he had when much perturbed, and almost groaned out, "Mr. Hind Smith, I think I should die happy if we had Exeter Hall for the headquarters of the Young Men's Christian Association." "I saw he was absolutely determined to make the attempt," says Mr. Hind Smith, "and I answered, 'Very well then, we *will* have it.'" Ways and means for raising the required sum were then immediately discussed. It was agreed that probably the only way was to get five gentlemen to give £5,000 each. George Williams was at first startled by such an idea, but after thinking it over agreed to try, adding that he would, of course, be one of the five. An appointment was made for the next morning with Mr. Samuel Morley, who, after considering the proposal in his quick, shrewd manner, at once promised to be the second of the five. Within two days the whole sum was secured, Mr. R. C. L. Bevan, Messrs. T. A. and E. M. Denny, and Mr. J. D. Allcroft each giving £5,000. George Williams did not meet with a single refusal.

This opportunity may be taken of acknowledging in the warmest manner the way in which, throughout

EXETER HALL
Opened as the headquarters of the Young Men's Christian
Association on March 29, 1881

THE YEARS OF PROGRESS 225

his career as a Christian philanthropist, George Williams was supported by a noble band of men whose generosity, whose business ability, and whose wholehearted co-operation were of incalculable service to the Association he founded. The Young Men's Christian Association, as it exists to-day, was not the work of one man, but of a splendid and devoted company. In such a book as this which attempts to tell the life-story of a man rather than of an institution, I have written chiefly of the work as it was influenced by the central figure. Let this, however, be a passing tribute to the "men who helped," to the men, indeed, who have made the Association possible in its present form and have worked so untiringly and with so much self-sacrifice for the honour of the cause, some of whom will, in the days to come, lead it to still more glorious conquests.

A few weeks later Exeter Hall was purchased privately for the use of the Young Men's Christian Association. To complete the building in a fitting manner, many extensive alterations and improvements were indispensable, and immediately the preliminary details were settled, an appeal was issued by the Committee and resulted in a few months in subscriptions to the amount of nearly £20,000. Shortly after the purchase, on March 29, 1881, exactly fifty years after the original opening, Exeter Hall was reopened as the headquarters of the Young Men's Christian Association.

The reopening, according to Earl Cairns, marked not only an epoch in the history of London, but of the country at large. The gathering at the evening meeting was magnificent. Every corner of the great building was full, and the audience, as one of the writers of the day said, was precisely of the kind which the ardent promoters of the new undertaking must have been delighted to welcome. It was, indeed, " a gathering upon which none but a hopeless cynic could have gazed without some emotion." As the Earl of Shaftesbury appeared on the platform, the audience grew wild with delight, but it was George Williams who received the proudest ovation of the day. Lord Shaftesbury was accompanied by the Archbishop of Canterbury, who delivered one of his stately and sympathetic addresses, by members of the noblest families in the land, by the Lord Mayor, and the most prominent ministers of all denominations. It was the Archbishop who proposed the first resolution, in which deep thankfulness was expressed " for the enlarged sphere of usefulness presented to the Young Men's Christian Association," and the building " dedicated to the praise and glory of our Lord Jesus Christ." Earl Cairns followed the Primate, and Mr. Samuel Morley was particularly happy in his testimony as a business man that not a shilling had been wasted on the building. Speeches were delivered by Canon Fleming and by Dr. Oswald Dykes, and then the Lord Mayor proposed a vote of thanks on behalf

THE YEARS OF PROGRESS 227

of the Young Men's Christian Association and of the Christian community at large, to the gentlemen through whose munificence Exeter Hall had been preserved for the purposes originally contemplated by the founders. George Williams, whose rising was the signal for a tremendous outburst of enthusiasm, was almost overcome with gratitude and rejoicing. He found it difficult to voice his heart's thankfulness. He said simply: " I thank you all, dear friends, for your sympathy, your kind co-operation, and for your most ready gifts, for I am sure that in visiting you in your own homes, as I have had the privilege of doing, I have been rejoiced and made glad with the freedom, happiness, and cheerfulness with which you have given your gold and silver for this most blessed work." And as he ended, the vast audience rose again and cheered and cheered. It was Mr. Herbert Tritton who had the privilege of expressing, in the name of all, their gratitude to the one who "conceived the idea of making Exeter Hall the headquarters of the Young Men's Christian Associations throughout the world, and who carried that idea into such successful effect." " The conception of the idea and the carrying out of its completion is," he said, " due and the praise is to be given under God, for we recognise His hand in all, to your Treasurer, Mr. George Williams."

Just one month afterwards the thirty-sixth annual meeting of the Association was held, and it was no wonder that a jubilant note was sounded in the year's report. "Other societies," we read, "may have entered into larger possessions of silver and gold, but we reckon ourselves rich indeed, for we possess not only the results of munificent gifts, but we have to-day, and hope we may long have in our midst, the generous donors themselves, and we record the fact with heartfelt gratitude that they have given, not only money, but have also laboured and prayed for the work with an earnest and unfaltering zeal."

In the following year there was held at Exeter Hall the ninth International Conference of the Young Men's Christian Associations, attended by three hundred and thirty-eight delegates from sixteen different countries. Needless to say George Williams was prominent throughout the meetings. It was during this year, too, that a National Committee was formed with George Williams as chairman, composed of the district Secretaries in England and Wales, and other representative members, the design of which was to seek the "best means of more systematically and uniformly developing and carrying on the work of the Association." With the spread of the Associations throughout the country the need of a supervising agency was increasingly felt. Up till now the necessary oversight of the work had been undertaken by the parent society in London, but a feeling had developed amongst some of the largest centres that a more representative organisation was needed. George Williams threw himself heartily into plans formulated by Mr. J. Herbert Tritton, who had recently taken an active part in the work, and, conjointly with Mr. Samuel Morley and Mr. R. C. L. Bevan and others, guaranteed the financial help required. It was to the work of the National Council which " linked together " the Associations of the country " for mutual advice, counsel, and extension " that, from this time onward, the founder of the Association gave special attention, presiding at all its important meetings, his intuitive understanding and appreciation of the multitude of issues which came before the Council proving of immense value. No worker in the Association had a keener appreciation of the difficulties of individual members or associations, or was more ready to appreciate the importance of measures proposed and to obviate and overcome difficulties in their realisation.

The fears expressed by many that Exeter Hall would not prove a success as a centre of work, were soon proved to be groundless. The spirit stirred by the acquisition of this new building had been felt from end to end of the country, and had infused new life and energy into the work in all directions. In the whole history of the Association the following years were, perhaps, the most remarkable of all in their rapid and successful progress. The work marched forward everywhere, the public meetings were marked by almost unprecedented enthusiasm, the various Conferences were attended by greater numbers than ever before. In 1884 George Williams took a prominent place in the reception given by the Lord Mayor when the Freedom of the City was presented to the Earl of Shaftesbury, who, on this occasion — at the end of his career — bore his testimony to the work of the Association. " The Young Men's Christian Association is one of the greatest inventions of modern times. It has been the means of providing comfort and encouragement and protection to hundreds of thousands of young men who are to be the future merchants of this country, and upon whom this country will rest for its character and even for its safety."

In the same year George Williams was one of the ninety British delegates at the International Conference held in Berlin, when a letter of welcome was read from the Emperor. During this period a determined attempt was made by certain of the associates of the Young Men's Christian Association to introduce a more secular element into the work at Exeter Hall, and it became necessary to state once again in the most definite terms the high purpose for which the work had been founded, and to emphasise the fundamental rules of the society. The work, however, was being carried on in no narrow spirit, and it is interesting to note that the Rev. Hugh Price Hughes, at a meeting held in the same year, testified to " the fact

THE YEARS OF PROGRESS 231

that the strong and hearty character represented by the Associations had no objection to any kind of learning or science."

It was two years later that, upon the death of that noble friend of the Association, the Earl of Shaftesbury, the Exeter Hall Committee, on the 18th of April, 1886, unanimously elected George Williams President of the Association. In the course of his first presidential speech at the annual meeting held the following month, he said: —

"I am greatly indebted to the Central Association, and to all the friends of the Association, for the great honour conferred upon me, in placing me in the position of President of this great institution. I do confess to have taken a great interest in the movement from its very commencement. I do humbly thank God that I have been permitted and spared, not only to co-operate in the work in England, but to see its wonderful growth on the Continent and throughout America. No one, I think, can well estimate the enormous advantage which the Association has been to a very large class of the community — in the United States and Canada as well as in Australia, and in various other parts of the world. Now we are met together under very new circumstances. Our great Moses has been taken up. We thank God for his life. It was a life lived for the welfare of the United Kingdom of Great Britain and Ireland. The results of what he did must be abiding, must continue; and I do hope and pray that now he has been taken up, God will raise up hundreds of Joshuas to carry on the various and multifarious associations in which he took such a lively interest.

"Now it is a very great pleasure and satisfaction to me, that this Association is in no way narrow or sectarian. It is as broad and large-hearted and catholic as any Association can be, and we are constantly saying, that if we find a man proselytising we put him out of the synagogue. We meet, belonging to different denominations, and agreeing to differ on minor points in the presence of the great object before us — that of putting young men into the path that leads to eternal life."

It was at this meeting that Samuel Morley rendered his last service to the Association he, too, had loved so well. Ever since 1845 when he supported a resolution at its first annual meeting he had proved himself one of the staunchest supporters of the work. Not only did he contribute in his princely manner to all branches of the Association and in times of commercial depression entrust large sums to the Secretaries to assist anonymously various cases of need, but he was from the beginning one of the leading members of the Executive Committee, and was particularly interested in the welfare of the Aldersgate Street branch, with which, as a great employer, he felt himself specially identified, and which, as he said in his last speech, "had done its work nobly in the past, was doing it nobly now, and had ample scope for doing even better things in the future."

In the following year George Williams opened the Association building named after him in Bridgwater, the spiritual homeland of his youth. In his speech he referred to those present who remembered him " when he was a boy with a chubby face and dressed in a little round jacket." It was at Bridgwater, he said, that while engaged in toiling at his business, he had gained the knowledge of those elements of commercial life which had stood him in good stead throughout his career; here, too, that the fountain sprang up " which had flowed all over the world."

This visit to Bridgwater in October, 1887, was made the occasion of quite a public ovation. The town was decorated, the Mayor attended in state, and many journeyed long distances to be present at the " festivities," as George Williams called them, on that " happy and glorious day." The handsome building was opened by George Williams as a " memorial of the power of the grace of God in the human heart, designed to give expression to the work of the Lord, through the means of the Young Men's Christian Association."

It was one of the most pleasing traits in his character that he never forgot his old friends in the West Country. On one of his rare visits to Dulverton, he asked the vicar of the parish if there was anything he could do to beautify the church he had attended as a boy, and under whose shadow his father was buried. It was suggested that the building stood much in need of some new windows, and a short time afterwards he presented to the church a costly set of stained glass windows, giving much thought to the choice of the texts. He also contributed regularly some £40 a year, in support of a special colporteur for the district.

And so throughout these years of progress George Williams journeyed to and fro in the interests of the Association, reviving old societies and starting new ones, never losing heart, always resourceful, always stimulating, always finding fresh encouragement.

The inspiration of his presence was as remarkable as his unfailing liberality. However desperate a case might appear, whether by reason of debt or weakness of organisation, he always refused to be convinced that the branch should be closed. One of his favourite methods of revival was the holding of drawing-room meetings at which his charm and geniality always did wonders in rekindling interest in the work. On one occasion such a gathering was held in a town where the Association was in an almost moribund condition. Only twenty-five persons were present, and when it was stated that the only way to ensure any progress was to purchase or erect a properly equipped building, the situation appeared hopeless. George Williams, however, started the subscription with £250, and such were his powers of persuasion that before the meeting of twenty-five broke up he had secured promises of nearly £1,500 towards the erection of a new Association building.

At the annual meeting of 1889 he spoke of the manner in which, at the World's Conference at Stockholm, men had witnessed how God was gathering young men for His work from all parts of the world. In countless ways the members of the Association were branching out into new spheres. Many were entering the ministry, and in England alone nearly fifty had, in a single year, gone into the mission field.

And this marks the climax of the thirty years, for, with the appointment of a Travelling Foreign Secretary, the Young Men's Christian Association entered upon a new and greater work, the results of which are only now beginning to be realised. The initiative was taken by America, but in 1892 two foreign missionary secretaries were sent out from England, and since that time the pioneer work of the Association in foreign lands has never looked back.

The last of the thirty years of progress was, indeed, the most progressive of them all.

THE RELIGION OF A SUCCESSFUL MERCHANT

CHAPTER X

THE RELIGION OF A SUCCESSFUL MERCHANT

THE previous chapters have been devoted, almost exclusively, to a review of the public life of Sir George Williams and of his work in connection with the Young Men's Christian Association. This work was, as has already been noted, carried on simultaneously with all that is entailed in the daily round of a successful merchant; indeed, the scope and responsibility of both activities grew side by side, and it is difficult to imagine how any one man could have attended so assiduously, and so successfully, to a rapidly increasing business while abating nothing of his efforts on behalf of young men and adding daily to his interests in other religious institutions. That is the crowning wonder of the life of Sir George Williams.

Those who knew him only during his latter years, when his sons had relieved him of many of the most pressing anxieties of business and when he might be said to be giving the best part of his time, and certainly the greater part of his thought, to philanthropic work, can form no just estimate of the man as he was in the prime of life, when he ruled like a benevolent despot over a great company of workers in the establishment in St. Paul's Churchyard, keeping in constant touch with every detail, watching every turn and trend of one of the most complicated and exacting of trades.

He came to London without influence or capital, and amassed a fortune. His donations to all sorts and conditions of religious works were on the most lavish scale. And he died a rich man. Some few are born philanthropists; generosity is in their blood and they are dowered with the means of giving; some have philanthropy thrust upon them by a swift turn of fortune, by the exigencies of their position, by the necessity of living up to the world's interpretation of *noblesse oblige*. George Williams achieved philanthropy. He was never so wealthy that his generosity cost him little or nothing. He spared himself that he might spend on others, living always in the most quiet and simple fashion, utterly devoid of all ostentation or pride of success.

And even in those wonderfully prosperous years of Britain's most wonderful century, wealth was not attained by attending meetings or presiding at conventions. That he brought his religion into his daily life is perfectly true, but he would have been the first to admit that he considered his religion made him a better man of business. He believed, and stated more than once, that the lack of a well-grounded faith in

Photo by] [*Maull & Fox, Piccadilly*

SIR GEORGE WILLIAMS
From a photograph taken soon after the opening of Exeter Hall as the Headquarters of the Young Men's Christian Association

THE SUCCESSFUL MERCHANT

Christ, of definite Christian ideals, was one of the chief causes of commercial failure, believed with his father-in-law, the founder of the firm, that one of the greatest delusions of the day was that religion spoiled a man for business; that "the men of God, other things — natural ability and education and knowledge being equal — are the best men of business." He was not, however, inclined to make the mistake of trusting or employing a man merely on account of his religious training or convictions. He held fixedly to the idea that a Christian young man might be, and indeed ought to be, a good employee, and although he did all in his power to impress upon every one in his establishment the claims of Christ, he had, in these days of the making of his fortune, the keenest scent of the hypocrite and the highest appreciation of commercial capacity.

He built up his great business and he gained his high position in the world of commerce by unremitting work, and by his ability to gauge the capacity of the men who served him and the kind of treatment which would best develop their peculiar talents. When asked how he found time to control such an intricate business, he used to reply, "I manage the men who manage the business." George Williams was no petted favourite of fortune; he succeeded because he deserved success.

Towards the end of his life he was, more perhaps than most philanthropists, a prey to that noxious band, those camp followers and scavengers of the armies of Christ, men of the glib tongue and unctuous phrase, who have often been portrayed, and never, as some would have us believe, caricatured by the popular novelist. There came a day when Time blunted his keenness and when he found it almost impossible to refuse pecuniary aid to any who asked it, however unworthily, with the name of Christ upon their lips; when he gave, as it were, automatically, so strong had grown his habit of generosity, even to the most undeserving of rogues who could roll his tongue round a text. But until the last years he was most keen in his judgments, most careful in his charity. While like his friend Samuel Morley he gave in large measure, the mere giving of money was the least part of his philanthropy. Upon every cause in which he was interested he spent himself, his thought, his energy, taking delight in dispensing wisely and with discrimination.

At the time of the founding of the Young Men's Christian Association, he was, as we have seen, rapidly making his way in the house. Mr. Hitchcock, his employer, had taken a great personal liking to the bright, earnest young man who was adding so rapidly to the receipts and reputation of the business. It was natural that, when Mr. Hitchcock became Treasurer of the Association, he should invite the most energetic of its members to discuss matters with him at his private house. There George Williams met,

and fell in love with, his employer's daughter, Helen
Hitchcock. In due course, according to the fashion
of those days, he approached Mr. Hitchcock on the
subject, having obtained through his friend Mr. Tarlton, the Secretary of the Association, an assurance
that his suit would not be looked upon with disfavour.
There was a time, it is true, when he had noted in
his diary a determination not to marry, as he had
concluded that marriage might interfere with his
work among young men, but in Helen Hitchcock he
found one who sympathised with, and for over fifty
years did all in her power to help forward, the work
of his beloved Asscciation. He was married at the
age of thirty-two, having been made a partner in the
business some months previously. It is impossible to
write in any adequate terms of the love and devotion
of one who still lives, but I may be permitted to say
that throughout his long life Sir George Williams had
but one companion and but one confidante, and having
her, needed no other. His devotion to her was beautiful to witness, his old-world courtesy a thing to
dwell lovingly upon in memory. His wedding anniversary was the one holiday in the year with which
nothing was ever allowed to interfere. He always
spent it alone with his wife, generally visiting some
place of happy remembrance of their early married
days. Of Lady Williams all that may be said is that
she devoted herself day and night through more than
fifty years to her husband and to the work they both

loved, and that she was in every sense his second self — his helpmeet.

To them were born five sons who survive their father, three of them now active in the business, one a solicitor, and one a clergyman in the Church of England. The light of his life in later years was his youngest child, his daughter Nellie. And she died. It has been said that at the end of his days he could look back upon his long career with scarcely a sigh, that in all his life there was little of the tragedy of battle, little of darkness, scarcely a cloud. For a time, however, the deep sorrow of his daughter's death at the age of nineteen almost blotted out the sunshine of seventy years. She was one of those bright spirits whose memory is a gladness for ever. Those who knew her talk of her still; she is unforgotten, unforgettable. If she had lived — " The Lord gave and the Lord hath taken away; blessed be the Name of the Lord."

George Williams's time in the early years of married life was so crowded with engagements of every kind that his children saw little of him, except on Saturday night when he would read to them from one of the illustrated weeklies, impressing upon them the importance of keeping always in touch with the march of events, and upon Sunday morning when he always accompanied them to Portman Chapel, afterwards examining them upon what they had heard.

He held to the strict, old-fashioned ideas as to

their upbringing, and the Sabbath atmosphere was almost Scottish in its severity. He could always rejoice in the deep and devoted affection of his children. Those who were nearest him loved him best. That is the wreath they would place upon his grave.

And those who were associated with him in his business were almost as devoted as his immediate family. The head of a great concern is seldom a hero to his employees. But although George Williams stood in the fierce glare of his public profession of Christianity, his personality was most attractive and most beautiful to those who came in contact with him day by day, under all the testing, trying circumstances of the City's warfare. A few years ago, when he was in a very critical condition of health, one who was close in his business confidence said: " I have known him intimately these many years. I see him not merely every day, but almost every hour of the day and many times in the hour. I have seen him in touch with men of all classes and conditions, and it is my serious and sober thought that I shall never see his like again." There was almost a glamour about the man. By the magic of his personality he was able to retain the co-operation of many who served him loyally through the years and helped to build up the business and gloried in his success. Hard-headed men of business were willing to sacrifice themselves and their own immediate ends to help forward his schemes. He was surrounded by the most devoted set of business men which it has ever been the good fortune of an employer to have under his control, and this was due in large measure, no doubt, to his extraordinary success in measuring and weighing the abilities and possibilities of those with whom he came in contact.

He had the instincts of a great leader; he knew when to interfere and when to let alone, when to encourage and when to reprimand; he trusted men and believed in them, and the business he established is a monument to the excellence of his methods and a proof of the justice of his belief. He was, indeed, rarely mistaken in his judgment of men, never trusting to a sudden or hasty impulse. He was always watching men, and more than that, the men knew they were watched, and when a promotion was made, it was understood by all that the head of the firm had fully and carefully considered the capacity of the individual. He had a great idea of the value of responsibility. Once a man was placed by him at the head of a department, it was only in the rarest cases that he interfered with his methods of working. He accorded the utmost freedom to his buyers, and the yearly balance sheets of their departments usually justified his confidence. If they did not, he would immediately reorganise, again waiting a year or more before testing results.

No one will ever know one half of the story of his kindness to those in his employ. There must be living

THE SUCCESSFUL MERCHANT 247

to-day hundreds who owe to his help and guidance all that they have and are. Many are now engaged solely in Christian work; several whom he encouraged and whose expenses he paid are now in the ministry. A single case may be mentioned as typical of others. One day he happened to hear that a porter in the establishment had a real gift of preaching. He interviewed him, asked him of his ambitions and ended by sending him to college, where he soon took a high place. At this present time he occupies a distinguished position in the Church.

All who came to him, on whatever errand, were spoken to of their soul's salvation. And, as an American preacher once said, " he had within himself the right divine to speak to the most unfoolable lot of people the world knows — young men. No man had any doubt of his right to talk about the spiritual life."

Often he would spend much of his valuable time in the City office on his knees with some young fellow whom he would lead to his Master. He would look along the line of young men who waited outside his room seeking employment and always give the preference of a first interview to the one who appeared most discouraged and disheartened, and even if he could not offer him a situation the young man never left the office without a cheering word, without some practical help, some more than kindly expression of sympathy.

In his room hung a framed card illumined with the words "God First." Seldom has a man so fully lived up to the motto on his walls.

The Rev. A. R. Buckland, for many years the chaplain of the establishment and the personal friend of its chief, tells how, as a newly ordained curate, he first went to the great house of business in St. Paul's Churchyard to conduct an early morning service. "To me," he writes, "it was a new thing that an establishment of such a character and of such a size should recognise among the ordinary circumstances of its daily life a short religious service, should include among its organisations a strong aggressive missionary society, and should be known as giving men to the service of the Churches at home and in the mission field." That this element of religion was in no way a matter of formality was shown by the fact that the Rev. A. R. Buckland counted among his helpers a number of young men from Messrs. Hitchcock, Williams & Co.'s establishment, who, after a long day's toil in the City or at the end of their week's work, rejoiced to take part in the voluntary labours of his parish, which was at that time more largely inhabited by the criminal classes and by the pitifully poor than any other part of London. "It was obvious," he continues, "that the religious zeal of the head of the firm was not something which peered out only after business hours or upon Sundays. It penetrated his whole life. Some, no doubt, were embarrassed by, and some, perhaps, resented his inquiries, tender and fatherly as they were. Yet I do not doubt that many of these whom this concern for their souls filled first with a kind of alarm as well as astonishment, came in after years to thank God for the zeal thus shown."

These inquiries were by no means confined to his intercourse with the men in the house. His question, "What are *you* doing — what are you *doing* — for the Master?" became almost a form of greeting; his parting word was generally a text. It was his habit when paying the cabmen who drove him home, to ask whether they were married, for he was a great believer in marriage as a safeguard against temptation, and then whether they had found Christ. To all he met — to servants, to railway porters, to the casual acquaintance of his journeys, to omnibus conductors and cabdrivers — to all he put his searching questions. When he crossed the Atlantic he made a point of speaking to every soul on board from the captain to the stoker, from the poker-players in the smoking-room to the emigrants in the steerage. And the remarkable thing is that, although he must have spoken thus of their souls' salvation to tens of thousands, he could never recall a single instance when he received a rude or mocking retort, a splendid tribute to the way in which the world is quick to recognise and appreciate, and pay homage to, true Christian sincerity when accompanied, as it was in the case of George Williams, with the rarest tact and most modest courtesy.

Although he never was what is known as a society man, he had a keen appreciation of the social side of life, and would go a long way to be present at a wedding. He was very fond, too, of children, and when at the seaside might often be found addressing little gatherings on the sands. One of the last pictures we possess of him was taken at Filey, in his eighty-first year. It shows him standing on a sand castle surrounded by a crowd of children gathered together by the Children's Special Service Mission.

His constant aim was to make his business a model one in all respects. He was a strict disciplinarian in matters pertaining to dress, and had a weakness for tall, fine-looking men. He was himself almost sensitive with regard to his shortness of stature, and was, to the end, one of the best groomed men in the City. His one great abhorrence was tobacco, which he could not endure, and against which he waged incessant warfare. In the arrangements for feeding and sleeping the young men of his establishment he set an example of practical Christianity which was soon followed by other houses. He was invariably in the forefront of those who desired to improve the moral and material status of business young men, always contending that this made for their religious prosperity as well; and it is certain that not only he himself, but the Association he founded, did much to bring to the minds of employers their responsibilities towards their staff.

He was one of the mainstays of the Early Closing Association, and was among the very first to introduce the Saturday afternoon holiday into City warehouses. In the last report of the Early Closing Association it is stated that after his death the public press "failed to do justice to the liberal help rendered, not only by Sir George personally, but by the firm with which he was associated, in establishing on a national basis the early closing movement, and contributing in marked degree to the establishment of a weekly half-holiday." All the world knows that, revolutionary as the task of creating a half-holiday on what was still, in business phrase, "the heaviest day of the week" appeared to these early enthusiasts, it has in great measure been achieved, thanks to the devotion of the men responsible for the movement, among whom Earl Shaftesbury as President and George Williams as Treasurer were fellow-workers and conspicuous figures.

After the death of his co-worker, George Williams remained one of the chief forces of the Association during the stormy times that the movement was destined to encounter. The comparatively rapid success achieved by the pioneers of the Early Closing Movement in certain sections of the business community had created much impatience among less fortunate employees in other branches. A great outcry arose that the aid of Parliament should be invoked. The camp of early closers was almost fatally divided for purposes of continued effective warfare. Herein George Williams's deep personal interest in the work, and his counsel of moderation to the extremists of both sides, were of the utmost value to the cause of further progress. Although it may be that his preference lay in the direction of persistent voluntary effort, he, nevertheless, gave loyal support to Lord Avebury and others who sought legislation, and who were supported by the verdict of the National Early Closing Congress of 1888. A characteristic letter addressed by him, in 1867, to a firm inclined to withdraw from the agreement for Saturday early closing is worth quoting: —

"Having for a long period been identified with the early-closing movement," he writes, "we cannot refrain from expressing our regret that so eminent a firm as yours should have come to the determination to take the lead in what we fear will prove to be a retrograde course. We cannot close our eyes to the evils that have manifested themselves in connection with Saturday early closing — which evils are capable of correction — but we are convinced, and we think the public is becoming increasingly convinced, that the movement is a good one and deserving of support. We think it has been established beyond all question that the general results of early closing have been beneficial, both to the employer and the employed. It becomes, then, the prerogative and the privilege of the well-established and wealthy firms to lead the trade in this matter.

THE SUCCESSFUL MERCHANT 253

"They must always be in advance. Four o'clock amongst them leads to six, seven, and eight o'clock closing amongst the smaller tradesmen, but a relapse to the hours of seven and eight o'clock amongst the leading houses will, we fear, restore all the evils of ten, eleven, and even twelve o'clock Saturday shopping.

"We have allowed for a great number of years one third of our retail assistants to leave at two, but we find that so long as the establishment is kept open, others will keep open without allowing the boon.

"Hoping that you will be induced to reconsider your determination, and ultimately to close at two o'clock on Saturday,

"We are, yours most obediently,
"GEORGE HITCHCOCK, WILLIAMS & CO."

Always keenly interested in matters pertaining to the drapery trade, he was a Vice-President of the Linen and Woollen Drapers' Institution, presiding at its festival dinner in 1876. He was one of the pioneers of the Cottage Home movement, himself paying for two cottages at Mill Hill, his firm erecting another pair. He made a point of being present at the annual sports of the athletic association of his establishment and often took part in the meetings of its Literary and Debating Society. The St. Paul's Missionary Society, of which he had been one of the founders in his early days in the house, was much in his thoughts. On something like fifty occasions he presided at its annual meetings, taking peculiar interest and pride in its progress. Mr. Buckland states that his manner at these gatherings was that of a father assisting at a family function. " No one who ever saw his face on these occasions will readily forget the happiness which beamed from it; nor perhaps will the missionaries from many lands, who from time to time addressed these gatherings, soon find a parallel to the curious combination of missionary meeting and family party at which they assisted."

During his early and middle life his habits were most regular and punctual. For twenty years after the death of Mr. Hitchcock he bore alone the burden of the business. He was in his office every morning by nine o'clock, and was occupied till a late hour in the evening with correspondence and business interviews and the work and worry entailed in the management of an ever-increasing staff. His methods were always thoroughly up-to-date. He had, in unusual measure, that capacity of anticipating the market and the public taste, so valuable in every trade, so essential in the drapery business. The exhibits of his firm at the International Exhibition, held in London in 1862, at the Paris Exposition of 1867, and the Netherlands Exhibition of 1869, at all of which they gained high awards and prize medals, did much to enlarge the business, particularly in mantles, costumes, and all "made-up" goods, for which Hitchcock, Williams & Co. have held ever since a foremost position in the trade. Each of these exhibits cost the firm not less than £1,000.

The business is now one of the most important of

its class in the world. Gradually the wholesale side developed from an adjunct to the retail trade into a separate department, and then into dimensions which overshadowed the retail trade, although this has never been abandoned. The combination of wholesale and retail was one of the most striking examples of George Williams's commercial keenness. That it would be resented by many he regarded as inevitable, but it brought about a state of affairs which added immensely to the prosperity of the firm. It was in this wise. One of the most lucrative transactions in the drapery trade is often the purchase by tender of large bankrupt or other stocks, which are offered almost exclusively to wholesale houses. There came a time when such wholesale establishments began to feel the effects of competition from those who combined the wholesale and retail businesses. Pressure was brought to bear upon vendors of stocks sold in this manner, and a combination of the leading wholesale houses refused to tender unless they were guaranteed against the competition of such firms as Hitchcock, Williams & Co. No finer advertisement of the ability of these houses to pay good prices and purchase great quantities of goods could possibly have been offered, and the consequence was that, in many important cases, the stocks were in the first place offered privately to Hitchcock, Williams & Co., and, when they had had their pick of the best goods, the remainder was put up for tender. There can be no doubt that in keeping to his resolution not to sacrifice either the wholesale or retail side of his business, George Williams acted with uncommon foresight, for, as the *Draper* set forth in 1882, " it must occur to any person of experience in the trade that the wholesale and retail house combined possesses a great advantage, inasmuch as it is in daily, intimate contact with the public and hourly feels its pulse, as it were, with respect to its necessities, and so is able to provide the proper classes of goods for every freak and change of fashion. . . . The business of such houses immediately represents what the public stands in need of, as well as shows what the manufacturer can supply. Further, it is a capital medium for suggesting to the maker the precise needs of the consumer, which are not so readily found out by the exclusively wholesale dealer, who can only form conjectures of the public taste."

The foundations of George Williams's large fortune were, undoubtedly, laid in the time of the Franco-Prussian War, the effects of which upon British trade have never been justly appreciated. It was largely owing to the sudden cessation, at this juncture, of supplies from the two great Continental countries that Britain held her position for so long as the one great market-place of the world. For years Continental competition in the Colonies and in America was crushed, while the British retail draper, who in some cases had begun to buy direct from the Continent,

SIR GEORGE WILLIAMS. FROM THE PAINTING OF THE HON. JOHN COLLYER
Presented by the members of his house of business on
the Jubilee of the firm

THE SUCCESSFUL MERCHANT

finding his orders unfulfilled, was forced to fall back upon the home wholesale houses, holding as they did the only stocks available. The trade of the civilised globe passed, of necessity, through British hands, for the United States was then only feeling its way into outside markets. French and German ports were closed to commerce, and all British stocks of drapery goods, which are so largely of Continental manufacture, increased immensely in value, while orders poured into London from all parts of the world. These were the golden years of English commerce. George Williams seized the opportunity of adding immensely to the connections of his business, never speculating or undertaking hazardous ventures, but pushing forward in all directions, watching the returns grow as by magic under his hands, and in all glorifying God who had given the increase and giving back to Him nearer a half than a tenth of all he possessed.

These were arduous and stirring times for all commercial men, but, after a day full every moment of anxious work, he would leave his office, snatch a hurried meal, and spend his evenings at the Young Men's Christian Association or at meetings of other religious societies. It is no exaggeration to say that often several months would pass without a single evening spent at home. One who was much with him in these days remembers how one evening he was invited to have supper at Woburn Square. George Williams was very tired — " for once he seemed utterly dead-beat" — and was looking forward to a quiet evening. As soon as he reached the house, however, his wife, who examined his engagement book every day, reminded him that he had promised to be present at a meeting that night. The occasion was of no particular importance, and his absence would not have been of great consequence, but only serious illness was ever allowed as an excuse for breaking such a promise. He did not hesitate a moment. With only a mouthful to eat he started off again, taking his companion with him.

His interests were, as I have tried to show, by no means confined to the great and successful work with which his name will be for ever linked. They were, indeed, so many and varied that, if I were to attempt even a bare catalogue of the means adopted by this successful merchant to further the Gospel, there would be no bounds to the length of this book.

It was George Williams's pleasing habit to invite friends to lunch with him in his private room in the establishment, that room which has often been so graphically, though erroneously, pictured as the birthplace of the Young Men's Christian Association. It is true that it exists to-day much as it did in 1844, when, the membership having outgrown the Upper Room, it was used for one or two committee meetings before the Association obtained a room in St. Martin's Coffee House, but it is some way removed from the place of the actual bedroom in which the members first met, and in which the Association was definitely started. The Upper Room was demolished during one of the enlargements of the premises.

His most intimate friends had their regular lunch days, but the company was usually augmented by those who called to see him either on business or in connection with religious work. Here he would entertain old friends from the West Country, missionaries, evangelists, American visitors, secretaries of distant associations, representatives from the foreign mission field. He delighted in nothing so much as in listening to accounts of the progress of God's work. He loved to encourage and inspire God's workers. I have before me a number of letters from those whom he heartened in this way. "One of the rank and file," a missionary from Western China, writes of how the words of good cheer spoken in that little room had remained with him throughout the years of toil and persecution; another, a country clergyman, of the way in which his heart was made to glow as they talked together of the goodness of God and of the greatness of the work; a stranger from America of how he carried the blessing he had received at parting across the Atlantic. Many letters testify to his kindness in sending books to unknown correspondents; of the modesty and simplicity of his bearing when men spoke of the work he had accomplished; of how he would say, "The work is not mine, it is all the Lord's, and to Him we must give the glory"; of his unfailing courtesy to the youngest stranger who called upon him. After lunch it was his custom to spend fifteen minutes in prayer, to supplicate special mercies upon the varied work represented by those gathered round him. And then he would place his hand on the head of any who were journeying to distant lands and bless them with a truly apostolic benediction.

It is impossible to give more than one or two examples of the way in which Sir George Williams's influence permeated the religious activities of his time. He was connected, more or less intimately, with nearly every prominent evangelistic institution in the country and was the main support of many humbler endeavours. His contributions to the British and Foreign Bible Society were very large; he gave lavishly to missionary societies of all denominations. His generosity recognised no limitations of creed. He took part, for instance, in the reopening of Whitefield's Tabernacle and gave a large sum towards the erection of an Anglican church at Exeter, in which his son, the Rev. Charles Williams, was peculiarly interested. But perhaps more characteristic examples of his breadth of mind and wide generosity are to be found in the records of lesser known societies, such as the Commercial Travellers' Christian Association, the object of which is primarily the promotion of intercourse among Christian commercial men with a view to counteracting the special temptations of the "road"; of the Christian Community of those who work voluntarily among the poorest of London's poor, especially in the workhouses; the Seamen's Christian Friend Society, which ministers to the welfare of sick and destitute seamen and carries on missions in some forty British ports; of the Soldiers' Christian Association, with its four hundred branches scattered throughout the Empire; of the London Cabmen's Mission; of the London Tramcar and Omnibus Scripture Text Mission, whose object is to arrange for the exhibition of texts in trams, omnibuses, and railway carriages, and even of such a society as the Christian Cyclists' Union. These are but a few out of many similar institutions which had ever a warm place in his heart and which now mourn the loss of one who never wearied in forwarding the work by his counsel and never failed them in their hours of need. He was present, almost till the last, at all the important Committee meetings of the Aged Pilgrims' Society, and it was said that at the London City Mission he was, even as a very old man, one of the keenest and most acute examiners of candidates, one whose judgment of the suitability of an applicant for the post of missioner all held in honour. In earlier days he had conducted services in many of the London theatres and music halls, and he always took a prominent part in the supper given on Good Friday to theatre employees. Each year, immediately strawberries were obtainable, and before they became common and plentiful, he, with some ladies engaged in Rescue Work, gave a midnight " strawberry tea " to the women of the London streets. He spent the whole evening in the neighbourhood of the Strand inviting them personally, and afterwards served them himself with the choicest fruit that money could buy, treating all with noble courtesy, as if they had been the first ladies in the land.

And whatever the demands upon his time and purse, he did not forget or neglect the least ostentatious work with which he had ever been connected. One of his most intimate friends conducts a mission at Bromley, in Kent, and for twenty years without a break George Williams occupied the chair at its annual meeting, often postponing important engagements to be present, and, to the last, was as keenly interested in its welfare as if its work had been of world-wide dimensions.

He was appealed to from every side, and I doubt whether, in the years of his strength, a single genuine application from an individual or a society working on the old evangelical lines for the advance of Christ's Kingdom was ever refused.

He loved to brighten the life and strengthen the hand of some struggling minister of the Gospel. It mattered not by what name he was called, to what denomination he belonged. You could no more chain George Williams to a sect than you can tame the libertine breezes or control the wilful spring, as Morley Punshon used to say of Whitefield.

I have tried to show that he took no narrow or restricted view of Christian enterprise. He was, for instance, particularly fond of giving substantial, though unobtrusive, help to poor ministers and workers in need of a holiday, and one of the monuments of his generosity is " Hazelwood," the " Home of Rest and Recreation for Young Men " at Ryde, to which passing reference has already been made. This building was originally only rented by the Association, but George Williams became so convinced, during several visits to Ryde, of its value as a seaside home, that he determined to make a present of it to the young men of Britain. Accordingly he acquired the premises, at a cost of over £3,700, and handed them over to fifteen trustees, to be held by them for " the benefit of commercial young men, without any regard to religious distinction, under the management of a committee selected from members of the Young Men's Christian Association." In the entrance hall of Hazelwood a marble tablet bears this inscription: " Humbly and gratefully following the Divine example, and in hope of promoting the Glory of God and the welfare of young men, this home of rest and recreation for commercial young men has been purchased and placed in trust for their benefit by George Williams, Treasurer of the Young Men's Christian Association, London."

"Shaftesbury House," Margate — originally the Carlton Hotel — was another of his generous gifts to the Association. It was opened in 1882 by the Earl of Shaftesbury himself, and has since that time proved an invaluable boon to thousands of young men from the cities.

His office in St. Paul's Churchyard was like a crowded consulting-room. People from all parts of the country came to seek his advice. He was asked to settle family disputes, he was consulted by young men and women on most delicate and difficult questions, and, with the possible exception of the officers of the Salvation Army, to no one was so much of the hidden side of life revealed. To all who had fallen or who were on the brink he was unfailing in sympathy and consideration. He would sometimes ask the Secretaries of the Association what they knew of a certain young man who had been writing or calling for help. The report might be unsatisfactory, the present condition of want the result of flagrant misdoing, but his inevitable reply to the suggestion that the young man should be left alone would be, "No, no! As the Lord has been merciful to him, we must be merciful too. We don't know what the poor fellow may have had to struggle against. The Lord knows." He hated to hear evil of any man. He preferred to be imposed upon rather than to lose faith in humanity. "If you cannot say anything good of him," he would protest when his friends tried to enlighten him, "I don't want to hear anything else."

On one occasion it is remembered that, while a number of important customers and others were waiting to see him, his door remained closed for a long time and inquiries were made as to the cause of this unwonted delay. It appeared that a young man, a son of wealthy parents in the Midlands, had been compelled to leave home and had been subsequently discharged from his employment in London on account of dishonesty. In a state bordering on starvation, he begged an interview with George Williams. In spite of the pressure of business and other engagements the head of the house spent a considerable time talking and praying with this unknown young man, giving him sufficient money to obtain clothes and suitable lodgings, and telling him to come again in a week's time to report progress. Ultimately he was engaged in the house, but the kindness shown was not reciprocated, and trouble of one kind and another arose. George Williams would not despair, however, and for over a year everything that Christian sympathy could suggest was attempted to help this young fellow, who subsequently became reinstated in a respectable position.

George Williams made it a custom during later years to walk out in the neighbourhood of his home in Russell Square on Sunday afternoon giving away booklets and tracts to those whom he met, always keenly alive to any opportunity of getting into conversation with the young men he might encounter. One Sunday, while thus engaged, he came across a young fellow who appeared to be in a condition of abject need. He asked him if he could be of any service, and the young man at once replied, " They tell me there's a man called Williams living somewhere about here who will help a fellow when he's down. I wish I could find him." "Well," he answered, " my name is Williams. You had better come and see me in the City." And, as in thousands of cases, he devoted time and effort to help " the man who was down."

His correspondence was enormous. Every post brought some anxious inquiry from young men in search of guidance, often enough a letter from some mother who had lost trace of her son and was fearful of his fate in the City, from some head of a household who had failed in business and was near the abyss. All received an answer, and every reply spoke in eloquent sympathy of his keen realisation of the burdens of others and of his readiness to help to the utmost of his power.

These are but a few instances of the way in which he made himself beloved by all. The story of his benevolence, of his goodness to those in distress, is not for paper and print. Moreover, he was, throughout his life, careful to destroy every paper of private importance that came into his hands, and he had every justification for such a precaution, for he was the recipient of countless confidences which should be, and have been, buried in the grave. I cannot, and would not if I could, lift the veil that hides the multitudinous tragedies of life which came within his ken, and which, in manners known and unknown, he relieved and softened. There are living to-day many who came to him in the great and terrible crises of their lives and left him encouraged, strengthened, to start afresh on a new and nobler road. No finer monument to his memory can be raised than the simple statement that he who knew a thousand secrets never betrayed a single confidence.

In the last great gathering in St. Paul's Cathedral there were many who had thus visited him in their distress; there were none whom he had sent empty away. It is true that he never missed an occasion of speaking the word in season. There are not a few of whom the same may be said, and of some it is true that their religion ends with their speech. But he was above all things a doer of the Word, and the records of his deeds are graven on a thousand hearts, are living in a thousand lives.

THE YEARS OF TRIUMPH

CHAPTER XI

THE YEARS OF TRIUMPH

THE Jubilee of the foundation of the Young Men's Christian Association held in London in June, 1894, was more than a striking public recognition of the position attained by the society. The enormous gathering of delegates from all parts of the world, from every great nation on the Continent of Europe, from the United States and Canada, from India, Australia, New Zealand, China, Japan, Persia, and South and West Africa; the great meetings, honoured by the presence of the foremost men of many lands and marked by almost unparalleled enthusiasm — these were something more than a triumph for the Association. The celebration assumed almost unconsciously the form of an overwhelming testimony to the place George Williams held in the esteem of the people and in the personal affection of every member of the Association the world over. No wonder that his motto for the Jubilee year was, "They thanked God and took courage," for at the Conference the figures showed that the number of Associations had grown in the fifty years to over five thousand with a membership of half a million.

The Jubilee gathering was the largest delegated religious convention ever held in the British Isles. The interest it aroused was well reflected in the space given to reports of its meetings in the great London and provincial daily papers which, with one notable exception, wrote of its work in the most sympathetic manner. Shortly before the date fixed for the Jubilee the Queen offered to George Williams the honour of knighthood in acknowledgment of his "distinguished service to the cause of humanity." A few years previously he had been awarded the medal of honour of the "Society for the Encouragement of Good" for special services of merit. Mr. J. H. Putterill, one of the secretaries of the Association, to whose organising ability and admirable planning the Jubilee celebrations owed much of their success, was with him when he received the letter from the Earl of Rosebery communicating Her Majesty's pleasure. After reading it his face grew pale; his voice was choked with feeling as he spoke of its contents. The whole thing was so utterly unexpected by this humble Christian worker. Handing the letter to the Secretary, he said, "What do you think of that?" He replied, "Sir, it is a well deserved honour." "No, no," said George Williams, "it is not for me, it is for the Association. It belongs to our Master, let us put it at His feet." Then they knelt in prayer, and in humble tones he gave the recognition to Him to whom he felt it was rightly due. This was,

Photo by] [Ellis & Wallery

SIR GEORGE WILLIAMS IN COURT DRESS

Photographed on the day he received the honour of knighthood from Queen Victoria

THE YEARS OF TRIUMPH 273

indeed, his attitude in acknowledging all the honours bestowed upon him. He made no secret of his pleasure in these tributes, for he felt that each was a true compliment paid to the Association, that in praising him men were at last giving rightful recognition to the work he had founded and for which he had worked so well.

The knighthood conferred upon George Williams was one of the most popular honours of modern times. The two thousand delegates who reached London on the last day of May were delighted beyond measure; it placed the crown of rejoicing upon their celebration. And there was no one throughout Her Majesty's empire who did not feel that it was good thus to knight a good man. As the Archdeacon of London said at one of the early meetings of the Jubilee Conference, it had been suggested of late by certain members of the House of Commons that whenever such honours were granted by the Queen the reasons should be set forth in the patent conferring the title. In many cases this would be a very difficult task and sometimes, if the truth had necessarily to be told, the party leaders would have to admit reasons which would be ill-received by the general public. But in the case of Sir George Williams the statement would have been a plain one — the simple, incomparable record of good achieved and a life nobly lived.

It is doubtful whether there has ever visited London a more remarkable body of men than these representatives from Associations in many lands. Few of the foreign delegates spoke English with fluency, some were compelled to pin their faith to that most tantalising of guides, the phrase book. Some, no doubt, were a little uncertain of their reception in an unknown land, but wherever they were quartered — and for the most part they were divided among the homes of those interested in the Association — they were received with unbounded cordiality, and entertained in a manner which did full credit to British hospitality. There was not a delegate who returned to his home without a better understanding of the British nation and a higher regard for its people and its principles. It was inevitable that with such a concourse and amid such a confusion of languages, many amusing misunderstandings should occur, and there are houses in which you may still hear ludicrous accounts of the exciting episodes of these Jubilee days when the whole of the family's education was paraded in order to explain the simplest matters of daily routine and to entertain and enlighten their visitors.

The Jubilee was a triumph of organisation. Since its purchase by the Young Men's Christian Association, Exeter Hall has always been looked upon as a great organising centre, but never before or since have its resources been taxed to such an extent, and never have the efforts of its officials been crowned with such signal success. The labour involved in the preliminary work alone was enormous. A week's hospitality had to be obtained for two thousand guests, details arranged for their reception at the various stations, notices, tickets, and coupons printed in three languages, and provision made for meals, for information bureaux, for post-offices and writing-rooms in Exeter Hall. And from first to last there was not a single serious interruption in the programme arranged for the week.

The central figure of all the wonderful gatherings in that wonderful week was Sir George Williams. He seemed absolutely tireless. His whole being radiated joy and enthusiasm. He was in very deed the life and soul of the meetings, not missing a single one of any importance, and when relieved for a few hours from his really arduous position in the chair, still sitting near the central desk on the platform listening intently to the speeches as they were repeated in the three official languages of the Conference.

One of the most gratifying features of the celebration was the warm sympathy shown to the Association by all classes of the community. Early in 1894 Sir George Williams, as President of the Association, invited the clergymen and ministers of all denominations to preach special sermons commemorative of the work, and his letter received a cordial response from the Archbishop of Canterbury, who wrote wishing God-speed to such united efforts as the Association represented for Christianising and assisting young men. No fewer than fourteen hundred clergymen and ministers arranged to preach " Association" sermons on Sunday, the third of June, on which day a public thanksgiving service was held in St. Paul's Cathedral.

On the previous Friday the Bishop of London opened the celebration by a special sermon in Westminster Abbey, when over two thousand persons crowded the building, stretching away from the glimmer of transepts and choir stalls into the shadowy gloom of the Abbey's recesses. Immediately after the sermon the delegates were welcomed to London in Exeter Hall, where notices in many languages had been posted in the corridors, where secretaries, interpreters, porters, and commissionaires moved about in a perfect babel of tongues. Here was to be heard the clamour of Germans from North and South mingling with the more guttural tones of the Swiss, the elegant Parisian accent contrasting with the provincial speech of Vaudois and Meridional, and above all the ever-varying intonations of men from all parts of England, Scotland, Ireland, America, and the Colonies.

When Sir George Williams made his appearance, the whole audience rose and cheered vociferously. He was accompanied by Prince Oscar Bernadotte,

THE YEARS OF TRIUMPH

who had travelled from Sweden in a special steamer with more than two hundred delegates and newspaper correspondents sent to report the Conference for the Swedish Press, and by a representative gathering of friends of the Association, including Mr. William Creese and Mr. Norton Smith, two of its original members. His speech of welcome was probably one of the happiest and most characteristic he ever delivered. He was full of the pride of the work, of the welcome given to the delegates by the City of London, by "the nobles and great people," by the Prime Minister and by Her Majesty the Queen; full of thanksgiving to the delegates themselves, many of whom showed plainly that they had borne the burden of many days, working for years in obscurity, fighting an unnumbered host of difficulties, prejudices, and misunderstandings, but now rejoiced in this splendid consummation of their labours.

"I am," he said, "delighted to see you all. God bless you, and may God give us a wonderful Conference. They talk about religion being played out. Never a bit of it. Was it ever stronger or more to the front than it is to-day? Have the authorities and men in high places ever recognised the spiritual work which you are carrying on as they do to-day? And permit me to say as to the honour conferred upon me" — here a remarkable outburst interrupted him, the whole audience rising to a man, cheering themselves hoarse, and waving their handkerchiefs

— "permit me to say that there was no reason why I should have accepted that honour except for your sakes. It is given to me that I may share it with you, and we will all be partakers of it and feel that the Lord has brought honour upon His Name." Addresses of welcome were then delivered by the Archdeacon of London, who was particularly successful in addressing both the German and French delegates in their own language, and who spoke finely of the Association as a "living protest for unity of the spirit in the bonds of peace," and of its members as representatives of the grand truth of the spiritual priesthood of the laity and " of their right to preach and teach God's holy word in highways and byways without infringing on the settled duties of the ordained regular ministry."

The following day was given up to devotional and business Conferences, to a general report of the Central International Committee, and to reports from the various countries. The delegates were entertained each day to lunch and tea in the enormous marquee erected on the Thames Embankment on a site lent by the Corporation of London. The scene presented by this gigantic picnic and by the stream of delegates as they poured from the Strand along the Thames Embankment was a truly remarkable one. As showing the work entailed by these celebrations, it is worth recording that the statistics of the Jubilee catering showed that 12,500 lbs. of meat,

24,000 dinner rolls, and 2¾ tons of potatoes were consumed at these meals.

The speeches at the Jubilee Conference afforded an excellent survey of the work throughout the world and were thoroughly practical in character. It was a happy augury for the future success of the Association that little time was given to retrospect and none wasted in boasting. Throughout them all the note of thanksgiving blended into the trumpet-call of progress. The most eloquent plea for a forward policy came from the Continental delegates, and while there was no suggestion from any quarter of changing the Paris basis of the work, it was notable how broad had become the interpretation of the scope of the Association, how tolerant its views on many debatable points. From Scotland and from Ireland, from Austria and Hungary; from Belgium, where, in spite of much Roman Catholic opposition, an excellent evangelistic work was in progress; from the "arid and thankless ground" of Spain, with its seven societies; from Holland, with no less than 785 Associations and 16,000 members; from India, where the work was still in its initial stages, but full of vigour and promise; from Norway, Sweden, and Denmark, where the progress during the last years had been most startling, the work enjoying the practical support of the highest in the land; from Germany with its 65,000 members, and France which had nearly doubled its membership in four years; from

Australia and New Zealand, where the Association had been adapted to the special needs of new countries with remarkable success; from China, Ceylon, Syria, Persia, the Caucasus, Asia Minor and Kurdistan, from Turkey, Greece, Armenia, Argentina, Uruguay, Brazil, Hayti, Hawaii, and Madagascar; from Italy, the youngest Association, where, indeed, its continuance and, indeed, vigorous growth, was "almost a miracle"; from Japan, notable for its College Associations; from Russia and Finland, from the two large unions of French and German Switzerland, from Bulgaria and the shores of the Mediterranean, and from Africa, the encouraging records of increasing prosperity were received. Undoubtedly the most remarkable of all reports was that delivered from the United States and Canada. The speaker, in concluding a review of the work, said: "Speaking to you, Sir George, as the representative of the vast army of Christian young men in the United States and in Canada, who will probably never have the privilege, as we have, of looking upon your honoured face and of shaking you by the hand as I have, on their behalf and in their name I want to assure you of their heartiest love, and I want to say to you from them how your life shines in their hearts."

The Jubilee statement of the English Unions took the form of a survey of the history of the work from its earliest days and included an admirable statistical summary of its growth during the last ten

The Casket enclosing the Scroll conferring the Freedom of the City of London on Sir George Williams. Presented at the Guildhall, June 4, 1894.

THE YEARS OF TRIUMPH 281

years, from 316 to 893 Associations and from 46,000 to 87,500 members.

Many Conferences are remarkable chiefly for the sparsity of the attendance at the meetings, but this Jubilee celebration was crowded at every gathering in spite of the fact that every day there were three sessions, each of three hours' duration. The scene at Exeter Hall was, indeed, amazing. Every inch of the large hall was packed with representatives; the corridors and ante-rooms were full of a polyglot throng, speaking almost every known civilised language, and reminding a casual passer-by of a great Continental railway station at the height of the tourist season. The evening session of Saturday was devoted to a review of the missionary work of the Association, a work to which, perhaps, too small a share of attention has hitherto been devoted. It is not, indeed, generally recognised by the outside public, that what is probably the most remarkable missionary development of recent years is entirely due to the initiative of the Young Men's Christian Association, which in America has carried on its great missionary campaign under the general title of the Student Volunteer Movement. This movement, with its ringing watch-cry, "The evangelisation of the world in this generation," is pronounced by many of the sanest of critics to be the most wonderful since Pentecost. It was conceived and developed into its splendid proportions by the American College Young

Men's Christian Association. Unfortunately, as some think, its organisation has no official connection with the Association in Great Britain.

On Sunday more than three hundred special sermons were preached in the Metropolitan area, while in the Metropolitan Tabernacle the Rev. Thomas Spurgeon, and in the City Temple Dr. Joseph Parker addressed the delegates. Every moment was crowded with work. On that same afternoon the Rev. F. B. Meyer addressed a large meeting in Exeter Hall, a French meeting was conducted by Professor Barde, a Swedish gathering took place in the City Temple, and the German delegates held a large open-air meeting in Regent's Park. The evening of the following day witnessed a brilliant function at the Guildhall, some three thousand five hundred persons accepting the invitation of the Lord Mayor and Corporation to a reception and conversazione, for which entertainment the City Council had voted a thousand pounds. Seldom has the centre of the City's hospitality witnessed a more remarkable gathering. The amazement of the long line of foreign delegates as they watched the ancient civic ceremonies was delightful to behold. The reception was preceded by the presentation of the Freedom of the City of London to Sir George Williams. The Common Council "holden in the Chamber of the Guildhall of the City of London on Thursday, the 17th day of May, 1894," unanimously resolved that the Freedom of the City "in a suitable box" be presented to George Williams, Esquire, " in testimony of the appreciation by this Court of his life-long services in the cause of philanthropy and his special efforts for the welfare of the young men of this City." After making the usual declaration of allegiance to the Queen and the City and listening to the recital of the quaint old formula to the effect that he was " of good name and fame, and did not desire to defraud the Queen or the City," and that " he would pay his scot and bear his lot," Sir George was welcomed by the Chamberlain, who, in making the presentation, said: " The good you have been the means of effecting in the course of your long career, it is difficult to overestimate. I refer to the thirty-three societies such as the Band of Hope Unions, the Sunday School Union, and others with which you are connected and to which you have devoted your life. The Christian principles of fortitude, true temperance, chastity, and obedience inculcated by the Young Men's Christian Association have had a far-reaching influence upon society at large, and been productive of many blessings. The Corporation wish to do themselves the honour of adding your name to London's roll of fame, which, while it is crowded with kings, warriors, statesmen, and nobles, bears also such honoured names as your distinguished friend and fellow-worker, Anthony, seventh Earl of Shaftesbury, David Livingstone, George Peabody, and Angela Burdett-Coutts. Thus the Corporation delights to honour a citizen whose life work has been devoted to neither national nor political strife, but to the quiet spreading of those Christian and peaceful principles, that duty towards God and our neighbour which, after all, are the foundation of national and family prosperity, and which alone can bring a man peace at the last."

The casket which enclosed the scroll containing the Freedom of the City was of magnificent construction, and in after years occupied the place of honour in Sir George Williams's home surrounded by many trowels and golden keys, the memorials of his generosity. This public recognition from the City of which he was always so proud, touched Sir George as much as any of the tributes paid him, coming as it did from men who were for the most part not officially connected with any particular religious institution. In his reply to the Corporation Sir George Williams spoke of his work as a glorious service, wherein he had experienced the happiest moments of his life, spoke of the distinguished honour conferred upon him as signifying the sympathy of the City and its approval of the glorious cause in which God had enabled him and thousands of others to engage. There was a fine dignity in his closing words: "I accept your generous gifts so unanimously bestowed with feelings of gratification. It is an honour to which I never aspired, and which I never anticipated; nevertheless, as long as God may be pleased to spare my life, I trust I may ever uphold the rights and dignity of this City, and ever prove worthy of this high mark of your confidence and approbation."

In point of magnitude one of the most remarkable gatherings of the Conference was the public thanksgiving service in St. Paul's Cathedral, held on the evening of June 5th, when, to a congregation which filled every corner of the vast building, the Bishop of Ripon delivered one of his most brilliant orations. It was, however, on Jubilee Day, Wednesday, June 6th, that the most touching of the personal tributes to Sir George Williams were delivered, first of all in speeches by the Hon. John Wanamaker, of Philadelphia, by Canon McCormick, by Dr. Monro Gibson, and by Dr. Cuyler, the veteran American divine, and then by an endless stream of deputations and representatives from all kinds and conditions of religious organisations. The whole of the afternoon was given up to the reading of telegrams and messages from all parts of the world, from America, Canada, South Africa, and India, " salutations and good wishes " from the sons of the Alps, loving greetings from Stockholm and Hamburg, good wishes for a joyous Jubilee from Berlin, Milan, Neuchâtel, China, Antwerp, and from city after city in the United Kingdom. Then followed the deputations from the English, Scottish, and Irish Associations, Australian and American deputations, French, German, Danish, and Japanese deputations, most of them carrying illuminated albums and gifts for Sir George and in each case reading addresses of congratulation.

When all these had been received, it was stated that there were still nineteen societies wishing to express their gratitude and to address their greetings to Sir George Williams. These included the Young Women's Christian Association, the Society of Christian Endeavour, the Church Missionary Society, the British and Foreign Bible Society, the Religious Tract Society, the London City Mission, the China Inland Mission, the Commercial Travellers' Christian Association, the Church of England Young Men's Society, the Sunday School Union, the Ragged School Union, the United Kingdom Band of Hope and the National Temperance Union, the Zenana Bible and Medical Union, the Glasgow United Evangelical Association, and many others. Throughout the long afternoon Sir George Williams stood to receive these addresses. Other meetings during this wonderful week made more dramatic appeal to the emotion, but this was without doubt the most remarkable of all the tributes paid to the man himself, nearly every important and philanthropic religious organisation in his own country and all the Associations throughout the world joining in congratulation. Such homage had never before been paid to a humble worker for Christ, and it was obvious that, as deputation after deputation filed past him, he was much moved by such a display of affection and esteem. In a few simple words he thanked them all, finding no way fully to " express the gratitude of my heart for all this love."

In the evening of Jubilee Day a great demonstration was made at the Albert Hall. The vast building was packed from the floor to the topmost gallery. The culminating scene of the evening, when Lord Kinnaird presented a marble bust to Sir George Williams, in the name of those who had worked with him during the past fifty years and of all the five thousand Associations throughout the world, was preceded by what one of the speakers declared was a presentation in miniature of the work of the Association. Some, it is true, complained of the programme of the Albert Hall meeting as a strange mixture of prayer, gymnastics, song-singing, and music, but, as Dr. Monro Gibson said, it was time that " the ungodly divorce " of the sacred from the secular was abolished, time that every one should recognise that the Young Men's Christian Association had a threefold work to do — that those who guided and controlled its destinies realised that young men had bodies which ought to be in the most perfect state of training and efficiency for work for their God and their country; that they had minds which wanted improving and exercising; that, above all, they had souls which needed saving.

When Sir George Williams rose to reply, he was greeted with an enthusiastic burst of cheering which continued for many minutes. The scene was most impressive, the whole, densely crowded, mass standing and waving handkerchiefs, ending their demonstration with three ringing cheers for Sir George and three for Lady Williams.

His speech still lives in the recollection of thousands. It was the man himself, simple, modest, unaffected, and full of fire and the happiness of youth. There are many in distant lands who, when his name is spoken, picture him — " the little great man " — as he stood in the centre of that vast throng, gathered to do him honour, and spoke of his gratitude and of his abiding faith in the work.

" I do not know," said Sir George, " what I have done to deserve all this. When we commenced our Association, we never dreamt of anything like this. Just a few of us met in a small room, and then we took courage and we went as far as 2s. 6d. a week, and now it has grown into all this! Why, we could not have pictured such a thing, we could not have imagined such a thing. But the Lord has done it all from beginning to end. But why you should love me in this way I cannot understand. It is a total mystery to me. . . . With all these honours I seem to feel a young man yet, though I am a little advanced in years, and I hope I may be spared to do some good work still among young men.

"Now, beloved friends, we have had these large gatherings, we have had this Conference, which you have all so much enjoyed — for surely the Lord Himself has been with us. What is it all for? What does it mean? It must mean that there is a great future before this Young Men's Christian Association. It must mean that we are about to make a great advance forward. It must mean that we are about to occupy countries which as yet have not been occupied, or very little occupied. . . .

"This is our Jubilee Day, and we rejoice with exceeding gladness before God for it. God grant that we may go on prospering, and that He will give us friends who will help us to win young men all over the world for Christ. You know there is no doubt about it that if these young men are not won for Christ they will do harm. A young fellow must either do good or harm, and if he is won for Christ, what a blessing he will be to himself, and to all those round him. Now, I will give you only one instance. A young man at one of our meetings said this to me: 'I read all infidel books. I was well up in the infidel arguments and doctrines. I loved beyond anything to trouble and persecute the Christians. If a young fellow came into our office, it was my delight to tease and bother him all I could. Well, I found that my infidel opinions did n't help me to govern myself, and I fell over a precipice. But I seemed to catch hold of something, and hung on. Below was the awful abyss; below was the darkness and the gloom, but there I hung, and the arm of the Young Men's Christian Association reached down, caught hold of me, pulled me up, saved me, body and soul, and'—as he said it tears came in his eyes—'but for the Young Men's Christian Association I should have been in hell to-night. My sins would have carried me there, but the Association saved me, and here I am to praise the grace of God that saved me.' Who is that young man to-day? He is a magistrate. He is a large employer. He is exercising his beneficent influence in the country in which he lives. That is our work, beloved friends, saving young men whom the devil would destroy. Let us go on with this work and God will bless us."

The last day of the Jubilee Conference was spent at Windsor, where the Queen graciously accorded facilities for viewing the palace and grounds which had never before been so freely granted to any organisation, even the Mausoleum being thrown open. Lunch was provided in a monster pavilion specially erected in the Royal grounds, and after spending a glorious holiday in sight-seeing, the delegates gathered together for a vast photographic group and for the farewell service held at King George IV.'s gate, "under the walls of Britain's royal homestead where dwells," as one of the American speakers said, "that noble, pure, loving, gracious lady, the Queen, who is queen of hearts, even of American Republicans."

THE YEARS OF TRIUMPH

From first to last the Jubilee was a triumph. That grand old man of America, Dr. Cuyler, voiced the enthusiasm of all who had participated in the celebration when he said, "Its memory would warm the coldest night in Scandinavia, and the tale of its splendour be told far beyond the Rocky Mountains and in distant New Zealand."

But the memory which will last longest of all is of the frail figure of an old gentleman as he stood to receive from ten thousand of his fellowmen a demonstration of affection and pride without parallel in the history of religion — and who wondered why everybody was so kind to him.

FROM JUBILEE TO JUBILEE

CHAPTER XII

FROM JUBILEE TO JUBILEE

THE later years of the founder of the Young Men's Christian Association were crowded with honour. Their history is written in the annals of three great and notable public gatherings, and of one, no less remarkable, of a more intimate and private nature — four Jubilee celebrations, unique in human experience, which sum up triumphantly his life and his life's work.

In 1901 the American Young Men's Christian Association completed fifty years of work, carried on with the characteristic energy and fertility of resource of the Western continent. Sir George Williams's connection with the work of the American Association had always been of the most intimate and appreciative nature. He had been impressed, time and again, by its progressive features, and had introduced not a few of them to the notice of British and Colonial workers. He was not, as was the case with some of his friends, fearful of the results of the way in which these Associations were adapting the methods of the old world to the peculiar needs of the new. He held to his faith in the discretion of those responsible for their organisation, and he was never so foolish as to believe, as did some, that the work throughout the vast American continent could be controlled from Exeter Hall, while he was as firmly persuaded as any that Exeter Hall was not to be controlled, as some may have wished, by the organisation in New York. To the end he showed deep interest in all the details of the American work, and by correspondence and by closely questioning his many transatlantic visitors kept in constant touch with its rapid and, indeed, amazing progress.

His actual acquaintance with the United States dated from the year 1876, when, in company with his old friend, Mr. M. H. Hodder, he visited many of the Associations of the United States and of Canada and attended the Convention held in Toronto as the representative of "the London Association, the parent stock from whence has sprung the large and important organisations which now encircle the globe, and are everywhere banded in the name of the Lord Jesus Christ for the succour and well-being of young men." His journey through the States was in the nature of a triumphal progress. Everywhere, as he wrote to the Secretary of the London Association, he and his friends were received with the greatest consideration and kindness. They attended the annual meetings of the flourishing Boston Association, and he wrote home enthusiastically of his visits to the daily Prayer Meeting in New York, of the magnificent building erected in that city, of the Sunday afternoon Bible Readings, of the new building at Philadelphia, which "will, when opened, be by far the largest, and in many respects the most complete, Young Men's Christian Association house yet erected." From Philadelphia they went to Chicago, where they were met by the President of the Association, "who loaded them with kindnesses." They travelled West to the Rocky Mountains, and " found even there a Young Men's Christian Association," then to Kansas City and St. Louis and on to Toronto. The whole trip was always a memory of delight to Sir George Williams. He revelled in the newness of scenery and outlook. He filled every day with visiting and sight-seeing, went everywhere, talked to all sorts and conditions of men, examined everything, rejoicing in his new experiences with the ardour of a boy. While in the West he encountered some rough company, but never lost his happy knack of making himself at home in any surroundings and of getting into close touch with the most unlikely people, speaking to all of their soul's welfare. At Toronto he had a most inspiring reception. In the course of an address at one of the Convention meetings he remarked that if, as he supposed, one of the greatest pleasures that could come to a father was the realisation that his children agreed well and worked happily together, he surely enjoyed such a pleasure in no small degree, for "they all loved one another very much and were considerate for each other's happiness, and ever desirous of promoting the well-being of the brethren." Another pleasure he felt as a parent was that his children were getting wealthy, "not only with the wealth which they would be compelled some day to leave behind, but with that wealth of a better and purer kind which faded not away."

It is no wonder that he was impressed with the way in which the Association he had founded had entered deep into the heart and life of the American people. Although Sir George Williams was not able to be present at the Jubilee in 1901, he was represented by his son, Mr. Howard Williams, and took a personal and fatherly pride and interest in the great Congress of that year. No apology is needed for including in this biography some account of the work of the Association in America. That this work is due to the inspiration of Sir George Williams and originated as a direct outcome of the parent Association is acknowledged by every American. That it has succeeded even where others have failed and is now the most progressive and aggressive of all the Associations is acknowledged by every Englishman.

It is a pleasure to chronicle in connection with the American work that, in this instance at least, Christian young men have done something towards the elimination of geographical boundaries. For all practical purposes the Canadian and United States Associations may be regarded as one. Simultaneously they celebrated their fiftieth birthday, and it is within the covers of one book, entitled *The Jubilee of Work for Young Men in North America*, that the story of their rise and growth is told. On June 10, 1901, Mr. Howard Williams, in the name of his father, unveiled the tablet which forms an interesting record of the start of the Association in the North American continent, and was erected to commemorate the formation of the first Young Men's Christian Association in Montreal on November 25, 1851.

I have written elsewhere of the high hopes of 1851. It was in this year that the seed of the Association found its way across the Atlantic. On each of the tracts and pamphlets distributed by the members of the London Association to visitors at the great Exhibition of 1851, was an invitation to the receiver to examine the work and make use of the rooms of the Association. A gentleman from Montreal, who was spending a few weeks in the old country, received one of these leaflets, made inquiries as to the organisation of the work, and, as a result of his visit, started a similar Association in Montreal on his return.

In like manner the start of the Association in the United States is commemorated by a tablet in the Central Congregational Church at Boston, where the first Young Men's Christian Association in the

United States was inaugurated on December 29, 1851. As in England, so in America, there existed a number of societies for the spiritual and moral welfare of young men before the Young Men's Christian Association, as we know it to-day, was introduced into the country. In the land of its birth it cannot be said that the Association derived any particular benefit from these earlier societies, the founder and his friends being, probably, ignorant of their existence when they made their plans. But in the United States it was certainly upon a foundation of earlier efforts that the Association was built up. Those with a taste for historical records have traced the history of the religious work for young men in America back to the seventeenth century, when Dr. Cotton Mather wrote of the meetings for " ye services of religion " held at that time in Boston, where about the same time there existed a similar organisation for " ye prevention of ye mischief arising from vain company " and as " a nursery to the Church there." In later years the Nasmith Societies were organised under the title of " The Young Men's American Societies " by David Nasmith himself, when he visited America in 1831. They were, as a rule, short-lived, and were merged into the more aggressive Young Men's Christian Association, the Corresponding Secretary of the Montreal Nasmith Society, for example, organising the Young Men's Christian Association in that city in 1851 and in Toronto in 1853.

Montreal's example was quickly followed by Boston. Here the organisation resulted from an article describing the London Association and its work, written for a Boston paper by an American student in a Scotch University. As one of the speakers at the Jubilee celebration in Boston said: " The word was timely and was well directed; it fell upon the right ears. An Irishman, a sailor, heard the news and repeated it. It attracted the attention of an American business man, who shared his enthusiasm, and soon the first Young Men's Christian Association stood in its place and entered upon its enterprise. Mark the combination — an English merchant, an American student in a Scottish University, and a man of Irish descent with American associates — here is the parentage of this world-wide work."

As showing how, in the fifty years of its existence, the American Association had become one of the most important factors in the social as well as the religious life of the people, it is interesting to note that at the American Jubilee telegrams were read from President McKinley assuring those present of his deep interest and his hope that the Convention might devise means for even greater success; from King Edward VII., expressing his hearty sympathy with and encouragement to the Association; from the Emperor of Germany, who, in a characteristic message, expressed the desire that the American Association might in the future train for their great

Fatherland citizens " who are sound in body and soul, and of earnest convictions of life, standing on the only unmovable foundation of the Name of Christ, whose Name is above every name"; from King Emanuel of Italy; from Prince Hilkoff of Russia; and from Field-Marshal Lord Roberts.

At these meetings of 1901 the whole organisation of the Association, as it then existed in America, was reviewed in the ablest and most complete manner, and while, since those days, it has still further progressed and is still progressing, reports of that Convention may be taken as fairly representative of the work as it exists on the other side of the Atlantic.

The American Associations abide firmly by the first principles and the Evangelical test as drawn up in the Paris Declaration of 1855. That fundamental declaration remains, notwithstanding the extraordinary development of the Association, precisely in the position it held at the time of its adoption, and is still universally approved. It suggests, as one of the speakers at the Convention said, nothing about libraries or reading-rooms, gymnasiums, educational classes or lectures, and yet, as he was careful to point out, every one of these things in proper hands must tend to the promotion of the objects specified so clearly in the first Declaration of the Association, which came into being for the purpose of "uniting those young men who, regarding Jesus Christ as their God and Saviour according to the Holy Scriptures, desire to be His disciples in their doctrine and in their life."

In America, as in Britain, while the work has been chiefly the outcome of the efforts of laymen, it has had, from the beginning, the support and co-operation of the Church and clergy. It has been, from the first, a work of young men for young men; and while it was confined, in its early years, for the most part to commercial men, it soon proved itself adapted to meet the wants of other classes. The great outstanding fact about the American Young Men's Christian Association is its success in acting upon the conviction that wherever there are young men, of whatever grade or station, there it has a work to do which can be done, " emphasising always the essential quality of manhood, whether in overalls or a business suit." It has learnt the lesson of the new century, the supreme importance of specialisation, and has engaged the energies of men of the first rank, men of exceptional ability, education, and influence, who, under the leadership of such master minds as Mr. Robert McBurney and Mr. R. C. Morse, have made the Young Men's Christian Association, as a writer in the *Century Magazine* said, " an organisation in the forefront of the large powers of the century."

In a comparatively short time six or more distinct organisations have been established. First among these specialised agencies is one formed among students in the Universities, resulting in other important movements, including the Inter-Collegiate Young Men's Christian Association and the World's Student Christian Federation. Another organisation is composed exclusively of railroad men — railroad men working for Christ and for railroad men. This railroad work extends from Canada to the Gulf of Mexico and across the continent from ocean to ocean, and has at present a membership of 70,000. There is a separate department for soldiers and sailors operating throughout the United States and in Cuba, Porto Rico, and the Philippine Islands, in most cases occupying government property assigned for its use;[1] another for miners and lumbermen; while there are distinct organisations for work among men out of employment, young men in need of rescue from vicious surroundings, coloured people and Indians, young men in non-Christian lands,[2] and, most promising of all, a finely equipped special department and organisation for work among boys of between twelve and eighteen.

The work of the American Young Men's Christian Associations for the moral and physical uplifting of its members has been marked by extraordinary suc-

[1] Miss Helen Gould recently gave $413,000 towards a naval building for the Y. M. C. A. at Brooklyn.

[2] Over 60 American and Canadian secretaries are at present located in the foreign mission field, organising, administering, and supervising Association work. In Japan, India, China, and South America 300 Associations have already been formed through this agency.

cess; its athletic clubs, its gymnasiums, its reading rooms, are marvels of efficiency, second to none in all that land of progress; its central and departmental organisations are models of their kind, its buildings on a scale undreamed of in this country, its name honoured even by the most dishonourable, its standing respected even by the most disreputable. But if that were all, anything but a bare mention of its Jubilee celebrations would be out of place in a life of Sir George Williams.

It is not all. In spite of many misgivings, even the most conservative friends of the Association in Britain have come to understand that those who guide and control the affairs of the Young Men's Christian Associations of America have ever before them, in the words of Dr. Cuyler, " the one supreme aim of enthroning Jesus Christ in the hearts of young men." The purely religious work of the Association has been developed and strengthened on all sides with most encouraging results. Special success has attended the efforts put forth for the promotion of Bible study, first through Bible classes and then by means of an admirably equipped Bible Study department with systematic courses; while much excellent work is being accomplished in evangelistic work, by stimulating evangelistic effort in gospel meetings for young men, and by developing an ardent missionary spirit among the members.

The American Young Men's Christian Association

owes much to Sir George Williams, and in still insisting, with the power of its membership of four hundred thousand young men behind it, that the first principles of the work, as he laid them down in the upper room, are as essential to-day as they were then, it is nobly paying its debt to him and to his memory.

Two years after the American Jubilee, on June 9, 1903, Sir George and Lady Williams celebrated another Jubilee, the golden anniversary of their wedding day, when presentations were made by the Central Young Men's Christian Associations, and the National Council, who "united in thanking God for granting to Sir George and Lady Williams the joy of a long and blessed union, for the happiness and peace which had rested upon their home life, and for the many services they had rendered to every department of Christian work," and recorded their grateful appreciation of the self-sacrificing interest which for fifty years Lady Williams had shown in the work of the Young Men's Christian Association, "of the sympathy and encouragement constantly given to its beloved founder and President in all his efforts to further the interests of the organisation."

In the afternoon there was a large gathering of the members of the family and intimate friends at the house in Russell Square, where a service was conducted by the Rev. W. H. Griffith Thomas, B.D. Sir

George Williams was then in his eighty-third year, but his vigour, as he replied to the many addresses of congratulation, the cordiality with which he greeted his old friends, the delight which he manifested in the gifts they brought, surprised even those who knew him best. He looked like a patriarch, he spoke as a young man. For a few moments he was almost overcome as he surveyed the memories of the past years, as he asked forgiveness of any he might, unknowingly, have wronged, and spoke of the love which for half a century had brightened his life. Then his face lighted up, and, throwing back his shoulders, he faced the future, saying that he hoped he would be spared for some years to come. The old warrior would not lay by his armour while he had strength to bear it. He had long passed the allotted span of a man's life, but there was fight in him still. "So long as I have any strength left," he said, "I will fight. There is still much to be done. God helping me, I will fight the Evil One to the end."

He fought to the end. Speaking to the Secretary of the Seamen's Christian Friend Society, who congratulated him on the prospect of escaping from an English winter, he said, "What I do *not* like is that it interferes so with my work."

And he was eighty-three years old.

When, in April, 1905, the Jubilee of the World's Alliance of Young Men's Christian Associations was held in Paris, he determined to be present. His family and his friends endeavoured to dissuade him, fearing the strain upon his little store of strength, but to all he replied simply, "God willing, I mean to be there"; and although he was not allowed to take part in the general meetings of the Conference, he journeyed specially from the South of France to give a reception to all the delegates at the Hôtel Continental.

This, the close of his fourth Jubilee celebration, was the most moving scene in all his life. As, very slowly, supported on either side by his old friend Mr. Hodder and by his son Howard, he walked along the aisle, which had been left open for him by the thousand delegates of more than twenty-five different nationalities, to a daïs at the end of the reception hall, a great wave of emotion passed over the gathering. Men were beside themselves — they seemed unable adequately to voice their devotion and affection. They crowded towards him, stretching out hands of welcome, while cheer after cheer broke forth, until the voices were spent and there was a deep silence. It was a hero's reception.

"As a demonstration of personal feeling and affection," wrote an American delegate, "I have only once seen its equal, and that was the greeting accorded to Emerson as he passed out of the church at Harvard at the close of Longfellow's funeral."

He was very ill — he was on the border line of

Eternity — so feeble that those who accompanied him feared lest, at any moment, he might suddenly let slip his hold on life.

He had, with infinite pains, written out his last message to the Association. He knew his hour had come, but summoning up his remaining strength into a last mighty effort, he determined to bear a last testimony, to sound once more his splendid battle cry. With his last breath he would trumpet forth his challenge to the foe, his cheer to his comrades.

As he moved painfully through the swaying crowd of friends, his son asked him whether he remembered what he was going to say, reminded him that he had his speech written out, and that the paper was in his breast pocket.

"It is all gone from me," he replied sadly, "all gone. I cannot think of a word."

And then, as he stood on the platform and looked upon the representatives of the hundreds of thousands to whom he had been as a father in Christ, the old fire, the old radiance, came upon him. A touch of colour burned on each worn cheek, and, drawing himself erect, with his massive head thrown back and his arm upraised, his voice rang out clear and strong. For a few moments he had flung from him the heavy burdens of Time. Once more he was a young man. Speaking with an impressiveness which will never be forgotten, without glancing at his notes, or halting for a syllable, he uttered those words which will be passed down through generations:—

"Young men of France, I wish to say that, if you would have a happy, useful, and profitable life, give your hearts to God while you are young. My last legacy—and it is a precious one—is the Young Men's Christian Association. I leave it to you, beloved young men of many countries, to carry on and extend. I hope you will be as happy in the work as I have been, and more successful; for this will mean blessedness to your own souls and to the souls of multitudes of others."

Then, as quickly as it had come, the light died out from his face. His friends almost carried him to his room, where he lay as one dead.

REST

CHAPTER XIII

REST

THE touching and pathetic farewell meeting at the Paris Convention was a fitting close to the long public career of Sir George Williams. His speech to the delegates was, indeed, his last will and testament. A few months later he took the chair at the annual meeting of the Young Men's Christian Association in Exeter Hall, but he was distressingly feeble, and the cough from which he had suffered for years completely drowned his voice. As he stood on that platform which had witnessed so many wonderful scenes in his life, and endeavoured to address the meeting, the whole gathering rose to its feet, and cheer after cheer greeted him. But the effort was beyond his powers, and he was compelled to have the speech read for him — this last public utterance, so full of encouragement and undimmed enthusiasm, of overflowing thankfulness and praise.

"My word to you to-night," he had written, "would be 'Go Forward.' Expect great things from God. Next to the peace and joy which have come to me through my Lord and Saviour Jesus

Christ, my greatest happiness has been found in the work of the Association. I would, therefore, urge upon all young men to give themselves, body, soul, and spirit, to the Saviour who loved them and died for them, and to spend their lives in seeking to extend His kingdom. Thus shall come to them satisfaction and peace in this world and eternal glory in the life to come."

It was no surprise to his friends to learn that the doctors did not think it wise to allow him to attempt his usual winter trip to the South of France, and had suggested Torquay as a substitute.

His brain was not dulled, and at times there were sparkles of the old vivacity and alertness, but the little store of vitality soon flickered out. To his friend, Mr. Walter Hitchcock, who congratulated him on his eighty-fourth birthday with the words, "Oh, king, live for ever!" Sir George replied: "I fancy I have heard that before. That's what they say when they come to ask me for a subscription." An American friend, who spent some time with him in his London office after his return from the Paris Conference, records how Sir George Williams exclaimed, "Oh, you young men of America, you men of America, how greatly our Lord has used you in establishing the work there!" He then asked many questions about their buildings and membership, and was particularly interested in the recent developments in Bible study. Before parting he suggested that they might join in prayer together. "He led, and, as I recall it, I am still convinced that it was the greatest prayer that I ever heard. Feeble as he was, his voice low and trembling, he talked with God. He thanked Him for the great work accomplished throughout the world by the faithful men who were carrying the Gospel to every creature. He prayed most earnestly for the men of America; thanked God for their vision and consecration. He prayed for the young men of Russia and Japan; and earnestly pleaded that there might be peace on earth and good will to all men.

"After we rose from our knees, I asked him if he had a message for our young men in America, and, after a brief silence, he said, 'Yes; tell the men of America to seek first the Kingdom of God and His righteousness and not to think too much of the things that are temporal, for the true riches are only to be found in Christ Jesus.' He then said: 'My brother, we shall never meet on earth again. I am just waiting, waiting for His call.' Raising both his hands, as in benediction, he said, 'May God be with you, and make you and all your faithful workers very useful in His hands, to the salvation of precious souls.'

"As I looked back and saw him sitting before the open fire, with bowed head and hands clasped, I realised that when we should meet again it would be in the presence of our King."

Among the last Americans to visit him was Mr. James Stokes. "As I told him," he writes, "of the interest evinced by the King of Italy and the Emperor of Germany in the enlargement of the Association's service to the army, he said with deepest fervency, 'I thank God!' When the progress of the Association in St. Petersburg, with its enrolment of one thousand members, was made known to him, he exclaimed again, 'I thank God!' and again said, as I told him of the great progress of the Bible classes, 'I thank God for the young men of Russia!'"

When one of the earliest members and strongest supporters of the Association, Mr. Samuel Thompson, met him some little time before he left for Torquay, Sir George rallied him on his absence from recent meetings of the Association. Mr. Thompson explained that the doctors had told him to be careful, and that he was not to be out much at night. "Well, well," said Sir George, "that's what they say to me. But I'll tell you the best thing to do under the circumstances. I'll let you into my secret" — and he laid an affectionate hand on his friend's shoulder — "change your doctor, my dear friend, change your doctor!"

Mr. John R. Mott, who also saw him in London after the Paris Conference, tells how he was struck with his inability to attend closely to any subject of conversation, but how the master-thought and passion of his life still dominated his tired brain. "Are you," he exclaimed, suddenly breaking in upon the conversation, " are you ever thrown into contact with a man *without speaking to him about Jesus Christ?*"

The Hon. John Wanamaker took his last message to the young men of America — " Watch the adversary, love one another, keep true, fight on, win the battle. God bless my dear brethren."

As long as he remained in London he attended every important Committee meeting of the Association, but it was noticed that he found great difficulty in concentrating attention, and that he seemed weary almost to death. Every Sunday afternoon you might have met him in the neighbourhood of Russell Square, his hands full of tracts which he distributed with a kindly word to the passers-by, stopping now and again to speak to some cabmen on the rank or to address a word of Gospel invitation to a street loafer.

One likes to remember how — old and feeble as he was — he remained to the last one of the most progressive of all the members of the Association. On the outbreak of the war in South Africa the Committee met to consider a proposal to send out workers for evangelistic services among the troops, and it was suggested that large tents should be fitted up as reading, writing, and recreation centres for the use of the men when in camp. The suggestion met with considerable opposition, and it was only owing to the exercise of his remarkable influence that it was determined to make the experiment. So great was the success that attended this new venture that a large number of these tents were used throughout the campaign, and thus inaugurated a work which has since been introduced into all Volunteer encampments, where it has been the means of doing an incalculable amount of good.

He strongly disliked the special care exercised on his behalf by his friends, and he was known to accept invitations to preside at meetings on the definite understanding that his family should not be informed, lest they should endeavour to dissuade him. There is one now living who remembers well the flash of real annoyance which came over the old gentleman's face when he discovered that the policeman at the crowded crossing at Ludgate Circus had been instructed to watch for him every day and guide him safely through the traffic. It was only on the distinct understanding that his son needed it for his own personal use that he allowed a comfortable armchair to be introduced into his private sitting-room in St. Paul's Churchyard. In countless ways he was watched over and guarded by those who loved him. These attentions called for no little tact and innocent artifice, for he was not fond of being reminded that he had " climbed the white summit, the Mont Blanc of fourscore." To the end he loved life and living with an intensity which defied Death for many years.

A few days before he left for Torquay he walked

slowly through the warehouse, his eyes lighting up as he recognised, here and there, the old, familiar faces. His memory was wonderful, especially with regard to matters affecting his great circle of relations, and on that last day he inquired kindly after one of his great-nieces who had been ill, and after another who was shortly to be married.

On meeting an old customer from the country he took his hand, saying slowly and very impressively, "We must be faithful to the end." It was his last message to the City he had loved so long and worked for so faithfully.

The slight, bent figure walked down Paternoster Row. Men turned as they saw the fine, strong, white face, its deep, thoughtful lines more marked than ever, the eyes sunk under the heavy, white brows. And thus he passed out of sight of the business he had built and the scene of his labours for God and for man — and turned Amen Corner.

When he was asked about this time what was his chief thought in looking back on his long life, he answered, "Gratitude, thankfulness to God for His goodness in having used me, the least of His servants, in the promotion of His Kingdom amongst young men." Meeting Mr. J. H. Putterill, the General Secretary of the Association, on that same day, he asked eagerly and earnestly, "There is no abatement, is there?" "Abatement?" said the Secretary. "Yes, there is no abatement of zeal in the work, is there?" Mr. Putterill replied, "Oh no, we certainly have had the best year in the work we have ever experienced." Sir George exclaimed, "Thank God! thank God!" That was his farewell to the Association he had founded.

A few weeks later at Torquay his weakness became suddenly more apparent, and it was clear that the end could not be far off. As his mind wandered he imagined he was addressing assemblies of young men. Almost his last words were " Beloved young men!"

His sons were summoned, and in the evening he slept, and woke no more in this world. " He did but dream of heaven and he was there." What a joy it must have been to him to wake Beyond without weariness, to feel eternally young, to realise the glorious truth that " the oldest angels are ever the youngest "!

The articles on Sir George Williams in the press of many lands formed in themselves a remarkable tribute to the way in which this simple English gentleman had conquered the world. In years gone by it had been the fashion of certain newspapers to sneer at the narrow pietism which they were pleased to connect with the Association, but it is a pleasure to know that perhaps the most appreciative notices at the time of the death of its founder appeared in the so-called secular press.

The world has not sunk so low that it cannot

THE FUNERAL OF SIR GEORGE WILLIAMS AT ST. PAUL'S CATHEDRAL, NOVEMBER 14, 1905

appraise real goodness of heart, and the purity of
George Williams's long life, the splendour of his
aims, and the triumph of his attainments appealed
to all. It is good to hear the voice of the people
raised in honour of one whose chief claim to their
remembrance was that he went about doing good.
A still more remarkable tribute was presented on the
following day to the Dean and Chapter of St. Paul's
Cathedral. It was signed by the Lord Chancellor,
by the Lord Chief Justice, Count Bernstorffe, Prince
Bernadotte of Sweden, by Peers of the Realm,
Bishops, Deans, Archdeacons, and Prebendaries of
the Church of England, by the Lord Mayors of
London, Liverpool, Bristol, and Cardiff, by some
twenty Mayors of great cities throughout the land,
by Members of Parliament, and the most prominent
citizens and men of business of the three kingdoms,
and supported by resolutions from 400,000 members
of the Young Men's Christian Association in North
America, 20,000 members in Canada, 150 separate
Associations in India, and by representatives of the
Association in South Africa, Australia, New Zealand,
and every nation of importance on the continent of
Europe. It begged the consent of the Dean and
Chapter to the interment of " this well-known Christian philanthropist " in St. Paul's Cathedral.

This memorial contained a fitting summary of his
career, and of the work which was, as it states, " of
national, imperial, and world-wide importance."

After relating the beginnings of the work, it continued: " The last returns show that there are now in existence 7,676 Associations in forty-five nationalities, with a membership of 707,667, owning buildings valued at £6,800,000.[1] Any attempt to estimate the number of young men who during the past sixty-one years have benefited by the work of the Association would be impossible. It cannot be doubted that several millions have been helped spiritually, socially, and physically by the agencies employed. During recent weeks their Majesties King Edward VII. and Queen Alexandra have each made a special contribution to the funds, four successive Archbishops of Canterbury have spoken warmly in favour of the movement, President Roosevelt and President McKinley were active members of the Association, the Viceroys of India and Governors-General of Canada and Australia have testified to its usefulness, the French Government has conferred decorations upon the leader of the Association in Paris, the Emperor of Germany has on several occasions shown deep interest in the movement, and at a recent gathering in Berlin Prince Henry of Germany was one of the speakers. The Czar of Russia has given special permission for the work to be carried on in St. Petersburg, while his Highness Prince Bernadotte of Sweden is Chairman

[1] At the World's Committee of the Young Men's Christian Association held in Geneva in March, 1906, the latest official figures given were 7,773 Associations, with 722,000 members.

of the National Committee of the Association. It is a gratifying thought that the founder of the Association which has proved so beneficial to the young men, not only of our own beloved Empire, but of the nations of the world, should have been a citizen of London, pursuing a successful business career for upwards of sixty years in the near vicinity of London's Cathedral Church, leaving behind him a great example to young men of all time of a man 'diligent in business, fervent in spirit, serving the Lord.'"

The Dean and Chapter honoured themselves and their Church in granting the desired permission. That evening the last resting-place was chosen close to the place of Nelson's burial.

It was indeed fitting and right that the National Church in the name of the people should recognise that not only with sword and clash of arms is freedom bought and victory won. Much is spoken and written of the righteousness that alone exalteth a nation, but it is all too seldom that the nation nationally exalts righteousness.

The burial in St. Paul's Cathedral was the rightful honour paid to one of London's most noble citizens, a man who, in a thousand ways, some of wide renown, many untold or known only to the few, and, more than all else, by the personal example of his daily life, preached to men the possibility and the beauty of an upright life in the slippery places of modern commerce, and made straight the paths for many feet. It was but just that for such a man a resting-place should be found among the heroes.

On the following Sunday Archdeacon Sinclair preached a special memorial sermon to a great congregation in St. Paul's Cathedral. The sermon was the Church's answer to the people's memorial. "If," said the preacher, "any were to ask why the authorities of the Cathedral had granted to so humble and unassuming a Christian worker as Sir George Williams the rare and very exceptional honour of laying his remains among those of great heroes of sea and land, of illustrious churchmen, of eminent painters, musicians, and wise statesmen, the answer was that the Cathedral has a threefold duty in its sympathies and obligations: to the City, to the diocese, and to the Empire. In all three aspects the founder of that marvellous organisation, the Young Men's Christian Association, was pre-eminent. During his long business career he set an example to all City men of a simple, devoted Christian life, of wide and constant generosity, and of unswerving zeal for the welfare of those vast multitudes of young men whom the business of the City requires." Of the whole vast machinery and the great system of the Association Sir George Williams was not merely the founder, but to the end the inspiring genius, "constantly in touch with every part of the organisation, giving away great sums of money to help forward branch after branch, working daily for the whole, keenly interested in every centre of work, praying fervently every day for all.

"Throughout his life he was one of the humblest and most unobtrusive of men, living in the spirit of the New Testament, Gospels, Acts, and Epistles. Believing with all his heart and soul in the verbal inspiration of the Bible, he was never troubled with difficulties about criticism; to him the Bible was the Word of God; to him religion meant conversion, repentance, faith, hope, charity, prayer, the grace of God, communion with Christ, the gifts of the Holy Spirit."

"He was so direct, so straight, so unswerving in his faith, so serene in his courage, so strong in his trust, that he had a remarkable faculty for kindling enthusiasm. He had no care for his own ease or enjoyment. He was unsparing of time and money for the benefit of all those who needed a helping hand.

"His name stands for the abiding truth that a simple, heartfelt faith in the power and presence of Christ is possible at any age, under any circumstances, to any Christian man."

In spite of the throng and the press, the splendid tribute of the City and of many nations, in spite of the vast concourse of mourners, in spite of the grandeur of the place of his rest, it was the simple funeral of a simple English gentleman.

And that was fitting and right, for was not the keynote of his life, ever purposeful and strenuous, a rare Christian simplicity? It was because he was to the last a business man among business men, that he has written his name on the heart and life of the world. No sounding triumph, no sudden victory, no startling appeal to a people's passion or a country's gratitude gave him his place among the noblest of the nation's dead. It was his life, his life seen as a whole, his eighty-four years of battle for things that are pure and holy and of good report, that the world honoured in St. Paul's Cathedral on the 14th of November, 1905.

In the early morning of that day there gathered at Exeter Hall the vast company of members of the Young Men's Christian Associations.

Every branch of the mighty organisation was represented. From all parts of the United Kingdom, from the Colonies and from the Continent of Europe, from Asia and Africa came tokens of sympathy and sorrow. The great building was almost covered with wreaths and flowers. In addition to the members of the Young Men's Christian Associations there were representatives from ninety-nine different trade, religious, and philanthropic societies with which Sir George Williams had been connected in some official capacity, from such different societies as Dr. Barnardo's Homes, the Band of Hope, the Cabmen's Mission, the Omnibus and Tramcar Text Mission, the Children's Scripture Union, the Church Army, Missionary Societies of every denomination, the Commercial Travellers' Association, the Total Abstainers' Unions, from various societies in connection with the drapery trade, from the Early Closing Association, from the French Reformed Church, from the Irish Church Missions, one hundred missionaries from the London City Mission, delegates from Temperance Societies, Young Women's Associations, Rescue Works of all kinds, Theatrical Missions, Missions to Deep Sea Fishermen, Zenana Missions, and Missions for the Observance of the Lord's Day.

There is a fine impressiveness in the pomp and circumstance of a great military funeral, in the gorgeous trappings and equipments of Death, in the throbbing solemnity of Dead Marches played by massed bands. There were none of these things as Sir George Williams was borne through the streets of the City. Even more impressive, even more moving, was the unspoken tribute of a busy people who stopped for a few moments in the rush of life to wait in silent sympathy for the passing of a noble man. Never was funeral more sombre, never was Death less terrible. Covering the back of the hearse was a superb wreath sent by the staff of his house of business — a great heart of violets with the motto "Loved by all" shining out in flowers of white. As people turned to catch a last glimpse of the procession they must have felt that this indeed was the epitaph he himself would have coveted, and there were none to say that it was not a true and faithful summing up of his life.

The minute bells of the City were tolling, shops were shuttered in black, the roaring traffic of the City was stopped. In the gloom of the November day a great crowd lined the streets. As the hearse passed, many stood bareheaded in the rain.

Two thousand six hundred tickets had been issued for the service in the Cathedral. It was a service of men, men of all degrees and stations, men young and old. There was scarcely a glimpse of colour, save that provided by the Lord Mayor and Aldermen in their brilliant robes. Under the dome stood those who had served him in warehouse and factory. Close by were representative ministers of all churches and denominations. The grey light, streaming mistily through the windows, fell upon a vast assembly of men of note, heads of great business enterprises, merchant princes, men high in public esteem in the world of politics and commerce who came to render their farewell tribute. But it was the concourse of nameless men, men of the rank and file, men who thus expressed in the only way possible their heart's gratitude, which made the gathering so memorable.

The service was what those who knew and loved him best could best have wished. It was a service of rest.

THE LAST RESTING PLACE OF SIR GEORGE WILLIAMS IN
ST. PAUL'S CATHEDRAL

He was very weary, this warrior who had fought so hard, had toiled so long. And he had fallen on sleep. His friends could find no sorrow in the thought that night had come when he could no longer work.

The music was itself a service of rest. The exquisite singing of the choir, the majestic Equali for four trombones, that noble miserere written by Beethoven for All Souls' Day and played at his own funeral, rose to the dim heights of the dome, and echoed back like some sweet and tender melody from the golden city of rest. The lesson was read with wonderful impressiveness by Dean Gregory, himself two years older than Sir George Williams, while the actual burial service, conducted by Archdeacon Sinclair, whose voice seemed to take on an added note of power, spoke of the triumph of his rest, the rest which for one who had battled so long was victory indeed.

In the crypt, the members of the family and those young old men who had been his friends, had watched and worked and prayed with him for so long, said farewell. A single wreath was laid on the coffin, and as they passed out of the Cathedral their thoughts went out in affectionate sympathy to the lonely lady at Torquay, who had throughout the years wholeheartedly, unselfishly encouraged and helped him in his work, their work, always giving him freely, ungrudgingly, to the cause, their cause, Christ's cause — and now at the last had given him to the nation.

He had lived for the people, and in death the people claimed him.

> "Where shall we lay the man whom we deplore?
> Here in streaming London's central roar.
> Let the sound of those he wrought for,
> And the feet of those he fought for,
> Echo round his bones for evermore."

He rests from his labours and his works follow him.

THE MASTER BUILDER

CHAPTER XIV

THE MASTER BUILDER

"BLEST are the departed, who in the Lord are sleeping, from henceforth for evermore. They rest from their labours and their works follow them."

Those who heard the Cathedral choir sing the beautiful anthem of the Peace of Death and the Victory of Everlasting Life knew that in a special sense it was true of Sir George Williams that his works follow him.

For them there is no death, and in them he shall live for ever.

"What of Heroism, what of Eternal Light was in this man and his life is with very great exactness added to the Eternities."

He was the ideal Christian layman of his generation, one of those fine and forceful characters who bear their testimony for Christ "in the sphere of their daily calling," whose religious work is brought into the very heart of their business life and labour. It was this that made him to the last the acknowledged leader of thousands in foreign and distant lands to whom he was personally unknown, but to whom he was always, and will always remain, more than a name, always the expression, the type, of a splendid idea, an all-conquering truth.

While he was ever interested, generous, active in promoting the equipment and administration of the Young Men's Christian Association, he placed first emphasis upon the spiritual welfare of the individual young man.

He laboured for souls, not for systems.

He himself gave the example by personal intercourse with young men, in meeting and in Bible Class, and, in preference to all other means, in private conversation. He, as was once said of him, domesticated his religion in the building devoted to the business he so successfully carried on. His office was really the headquarters of the World Brotherhood of the Young Men's Christian Association. And in his office was the spirit of the Upper Room in St. Paul's Churchyard, where two young men came together to agonise in prayer for their companions.

Sir George Williams lives, and shall ever live, not only as the father and founder of the Young Men's Christian Association, but, in his personal life and faith, as its representative member. Methods will change, and are changing rapidly, organisations may differ, but unless the Young Men's Christian Associations in every clime succeed in showing young men how they shall serve and bear witness to Jesus

Christ in "the sphere of their daily calling," they dishonour the memory of their founder and their work is vain.

There is a splendid future for the Young Men's Christian Association. No one can doubt that. It is needed to-day even more than in 1844, and if carried forward on progressive lines it can meet to-day's needs more successfully than it met those of Sir George Williams's generation.

It belongs to the twentieth century as it did to the early Victorian era. It may renew its youth every year, for there is infinite adaptability in its programme. It has accomplished much during these sixty years. And much still remains to be done.

The past history of the Young Men's Christian Association is full of encouragement for the future. And, read aright, it is not without its warnings and cautions. From the beginning the movement has been characterised by growth. This development has not been uniform, not always rapid, but each year has seen advance in some direction, and each year the men who have preached progress in its counsels have prevailed. This will continue, this will increase. As the years pass, some of the old methods will lose their attraction in the eyes of young men, some of the old agencies will become time-worn and show signs of decay. Let those in authority face the unpleasant but undeniable fact that in such a society there is unceasing wastage, that from one cause or another men are always falling out of the ranks, that gaps in the files must be filled. New methods, new methods every year, are as necessary in the Young Men's Christian Association as in a house of business.

But these changes, changes of fashion it may be, do not entail any departure from the fundamental principles of the Association. These stand fast. They were never accepted, never acted upon, more loyally than they are to-day.

In this respect there will be no sign of wavering. The ideal before the members will always be the union of Christian young men for service in the extension of the kingdom of Jesus Christ among their fellow young men.

And that kingdom is to be extended by spiritual, social, intellectual, and physical agencies. In each of these there is fine promise of development, in numbers, in quality, and in equipment. It is safe to predict that during the next few years the most marked advance will be noticed in the social and physical sides of the work. There is no gainsaying the fact that these have not kept pace, especially in Great Britain, with the demands of the age. The crying and absolute necessity for amusement and recreation is the result of a state of affairs in the world we live in which no amount of argument or preaching will alter. The Young Men's Christian Association will never lessen by a hair's breadth the strain of our strenuous life. It may help men to

Photo by] [Elliott & Fry
THE LAST PHOTOGRAPH OF SIR GEORGE WILLIAMS

bear that strain. It will never abate one jot or one tittle of the fierceness of competition, of the cruelty of the conflict, but it can make men strong, mentally, physically, spiritually strong, so that they may the better fight. Among some there is a sinister idea that the Young Men's Christian Association does not welcome the fighting men, the men in whom the zest of life and the joy of the conflict is strong, that it is rather a hospital for the halt and the maimed than a place of rest and refreshing for the strong man who is weary but unconquered. The Young Men's Christian Association was the life-work of a successful young man, a man who struggled and toiled and battled towards success — and won. While it will always stretch out a kindly hand to the downtrodden and defeated, it is not merely or primarily a refuge for failures. In every possible manner the future leaders in Association work will preach and teach the great doctrines of competence and efficiency, will always insist that a young man should be better fitted for business because he is a member of the Association.

The men who are fighting to win are the young men who will be most welcome in the Young Men's Christian Association. And these men, these Christian young men, restless, active, strenuous, eager, and undaunted, whose days are crowded with toil, must have recreation, physical and mental. If the Young Men's Christian Association does not provide this on a satisfactory and attractive scale, they will go elsewhere, and, for its own sake as well as theirs, the Association must not lose hold on the workers, the young men who serve the Lord no less because they are diligent in business.

There is still much to be desired in the equipment of the Association buildings for such purposes, especially in Great Britain. This is largely a question, no doubt, of financial support. The Young Men's Christian Association has in the past appealed for the most part to those who give to definite religious agencies, give with amazing generosity. They are but few, and they are beset from all sides. The moral, physical, and social work of the Association will no doubt be brought more to the front, for herein it will commend itself to employers who are beginning to recognise, and who will shortly realise more strongly, the importance of providing in every community a counter-attraction to the many places of harmful amusement which are supported almost entirely by young men. It is a business man's Association. It was founded by a plain man of business; it is run on business lines for business men. Once an employer is persuaded from personal experience that it pays to employ one who spends his spare time at the Young Men's Christian Association there is every likelihood that he will help forward that institution in the most handsome manner.

For the purpose of commending itself to the outside public, as well as for the good of the people generally, it is to be hoped that the Young Men's Christian Association will take its rightful place as one of the recognised champions of moral right and religious liberty. There is a danger that determination to keep free from controversy may make it fearful. Young men delight in social work, in work for the community, for the uplifting of the race. Has not that part of the programme of a Christian young man been too little insisted upon? No one would advocate the entrance of such an Association upon the dusty arena of politics, or that it should take sides in the battle of sects, but the time has surely arrived when the Young Men's Christian Association may justly claim to make its voice heard on behalf of national purity and temperance, and give its weighty support to those who are fighting, under whatever banner, the tyrannies of evil. "Many evangelical Christians," said that prince of evangelical teachers, Dr. Dale of Birmingham, "have the poorest, meanest, narrowest conceptions of moral duty and are almost destitute of moral strength. If this defect is to be remedied, we Evangelicals must think more about Christian Ethics." The time has come when the old reproach that the Young Men's Christian Association prays and talks so much that it does nothing should be wiped away. It was never true. It is time the lie was killed.

In America one of the most striking advances of the next few years will, it is said, be in this direction of Social work. The Association refuses to be confined to its own building. It will provide men who will conduct physical work in churches, schools, public playgrounds, and settlements. By lectures and printed matter it will carry on its campaign of right living among all classes. It will give its members definite work to do in the physical and moral education of the people. It will interest itself as a society in measures for promoting good health and will co-operate in agencies engaged in such work. It will endeavour to minister to the recreative needs of the industrial and indeed of all classes. It will become an important factor in creating conditions where right ethics in sport will prevail.

By thus attracting into its membership many courageous, virile young men, and enlisting them in Christian service, it will introduce into the religious life of the Association the splendid elements of heroism and altruism, qualities of character which always make for the attractiveness of Christian service.

Something of the kind will surely manifest itself in Great Britain. Much interest has lately been aroused in what are termed Institutional Churches, and while there can be no doubt that occasionally, under strong leadership, Churches of this character may accomplish a successful work, it is equally true that the Church, as a whole, will never successfully maintain work of this character. The difficulties which will be encountered by clergymen, ministers, and Church officers will, in all probability, result in a wider recognition of the value of the Association and its adaptability for this class of work, and the Association will receive that moral and financial support from the Churches which has been in some measure lacking in the past.

The growth of the work in this direction will be accompanied by dangers against which Association workers will need to be constantly on their guard. Social and recreative work appeals strongly to young men, and having entered into the possession of large and well-equipped buildings, those responsible for ther management will be tempted to give undue prominence to the departments which most readily lend themselves to popularity. There is danger that the spiritual work of the Association may be placed in a secondary position.

The greatest care must be exercised by the leaders of the movement that the popular element, which, rightly, will occupy a more prominent position in the Association's programme, does not obscure the main plan, the essential object of the organisation.

And in this connection the experience of the Associations in America should prove useful to the workers in all parts of the world. There can be no doubt that during one period in the history of the American movement the purely religious work was overshadowed by the social, educational, and physical agencies. But it was recognised that the successful maintenance, even of the social work, was only possible by the development of the religious department, and strenuous efforts have been made during recent years to bring the spiritual work of the American Association into greater prominence. These efforts have been wonderfully successful. Not only have the Bible Classes in Association buildings grown in number and effectiveness, but more careful attention has been given to the systematic organisation of religious and missionary effort. More comprehensive and enterprising schemes for evangelisation will be set on foot in all directions. New types of Bible Classes and new courses of Bible study will be started to serve special groups of men who will be brought into the Association's sphere of influence. Classes will to a greater degree become objective and practical in character. The Association will be recognised as one of the chief training grounds for Christian work by laymen, each branch the centre of a great and widespread home missionary agency.

It may be predicted with confidence that future years will find the educational work of the Association organised and maintained with greater efficiency than at present. It is true that at the time of writing this department is lacking in signs of immediate growth. This is largely owing to the fact that members have been discouraged by seeing the educational work of the Association in Great Britain brought into competition with the Evening Classes established by the Educational authorities. There are, however, not wanting signs that the Association is beginning to realise that a wide field is open to-day for the provision of specialised forms of instruction designed to fit young men for the profession or business in which they are engaged. That there are great possibilities of successful work in this direction has been demonstrated in recent years by the Central Association, which by making provision for the training of young men for the Civil Service, and preparing candidates for the examinations of the Banker's Institute and of the London Chamber of Commerce, has secured for this department a degree of prosperity far exceeding that obtained when the curriculum was confined to ordinary commercial subjects.

But more than in any other direction the growth of the work will also be manifested in specialised effort by Associations, or by branches and departments of Associations, to reach definite and distinct classes of men. This specialisation has been introduced with almost unprecedented success in America, where experience has demonstrated beyond question that the Association can be adapted to meet the needs of young men of all degrees.

In the past there have been certain regretted episodes in Great Britain which will serve as a warning for the future. It is unfortunate that, owing no doubt to financial reasons, the work in the British Army and work among students has been allowed to pass out of the direct control of the Association. The Young Men's Christian Association has no business with affiliated Associations. It is capable of undertaking work among all classes of young men, and should be in a position to do so.

There are still, however, many distinct classes to which the Association can successfully appeal, and separate departments will doubtless shortly be started for men of special occupations who can only be reached by special methods, such as the police, the employees of the post-office, railway servants, and others.

The great artisan section is calling for the Young Men's Christian Association. The working-man will have his own Christian Association or none at all. Only those who have made a careful study of the subject have any adequate idea of the evil being wrought among the working-men of Great Britain by so-called social and political clubs.

Great encouragement for specialised forms of organisation in Great Britain is to be found in the success which has lately attended the work carried on in encampments of Volunteer Corps. Tens of thousands of men have thus been benefited, and the

Association movement has received a measure of popularity and publicity that has commended it to the whole of the Volunteer forces.

In the class Association and specialised department lies the most hopeful work of the coming years.

Probably no development of the work in the past brought greater joy to the founder of the Association than the establishment of boys' sections in connection with some of the larger branches, and no Association should be deemed well organised if it does not possess a well-equipped section for lads between thirteen and seventeen years of age.

In each new building in America between twenty and thirty per cent of the accommodation is now given to the boys' department, and the proportion of boy members is steadily increasing.

But the extension of the work is after all more a question of leadership than of anything else.

The increasing needs are obvious, and what is wanted is a steady addition to the number of men who will devote their energies to the work of leadership in the varied departments of the Association.

The Young Men's Christian Association offers a career to those who have decided to consecrate their lives to missionary work as arduous and certainly as full of opportunities for good as the foreign field. The work is ready and waiting for them.

Men cast in an heroic mould, whose religion is not of the hot-house variety but of the most manly and robust type, men of broad views of life, men capable of adapting themselves to new conditions as they arise, men of enthusiasm and generous sympathy, men young in thought and attractive in manner, with a happy appreciation of muscular Christianity and the good things of this life as well as of the next — these are the men whom the Association calls for.

And above all things these men must have faith in the young men themselves, faith in youth itself.

There are many who, like Solness, Ibsen's master builder, are fearful of the young men, " horribly afraid of the younger generation."

Sir George Williams would never have started the Association, could never have steered it through its dangerous and troublous years, unless he had had unbounded faith in the new generation, unshaken confidence in the future which is in their hands.

Solness heard the young men knocking at the door and — trembled. Sir George Williams, the master builder of the Young Men's Christian Association, welcomed them with extended hand.

According to the grace of God which was given unto him, as a wise master builder, he laid the foundation.

And another buildeth thereon.

But let every man take heed how he buildeth thereupon.

For other foundation can no man lay than that is laid, which is JESUS CHRIST.

INDEX

INDEX

ADELAIDE, First Association at, 167
Africa, Messages from, at the Jubilee, 285; represented at the funeral, 321, 326
"A. K. H. B.," 144
Aldersgate Street, new premises, 168, 169; noonday prayer meeting, 207, 208
Alexander, Dean, 144
Alexandra, Queen, 322
Alford, Dean, 144
Allcroft, J. D., 208, 224
America: Start of American Associations, 167; report from, at the Paris Conference, 1855, 171; at the Jubilee Celebrations, 280, 291; Sir George Williams's visit to, 296 *et seq.*; the American Associations, 299–305
American visitors (Sir George Williams's), 314, 315
Ashley, Lord, 62, 151–153; *see* Shaftesbury, Earl of
Ashway Farm, 6, 7, 11, 12
Associations, *see* Young Men's Christian Associations
Australia, 280, 321, 322
Avebury, Lord, and The Early Closing Movement, 252

BALE, Early association at, 169
Barclay, Rev. J., 116 *n.*

Barde, Professor, 282
Barker, Rev. J., 35
Barle, River, 4, 11
Bath, 145
Beaumont, Edward, 107, 110, 117
Berlin, 285, 322
Bernadotte, Prince, 276, 321, 322
Bernstorffe, Count, 321
Besant, Sir Walter, 53
Bevan, R. C. L., 136, 185, 208, 209, 221, 222, 224, 229
Bickersteth, Bishop, 144
Binney, Rev. Thomas, 28, 36, 37, 38, 39, 40, 41, 63, 71, 79, 136, 144
Blackfriars Bridge, 106, 107
Blackmore, R. D., 12
Blake, Admiral, 5, 10
Blundell's, The school of, 12
Boston, 167, 296, 299, 300, 301
Bradlaugh, Mr., 180, 217
Branch, Mr., 109
Brendon Hills, 5
Bridgwater, 3, 5, 6, 16, 17, 21, 23, 24, 25, 26, 27, 36, 45, 50, 52, 69, 233, 234
Bristol, 176, 321
Bromley (Kent), Sir George Williams's interest in a mission at, 262
Brown, Rev. Hugh Stowell, 144
Buckland, Rev. A. R., 248, 253
Burdett-Coutts, Angela, 283

INDEX

Cairns, Earl, 226
Canada, 280, 285, 304, 321; *see also* America
Canterbury, Archbishop of, 226, 276, 321
Carlyle, Thomas, 62
Century Magazine, The, 303
Ceylon, 280
Chalmers, Thomas, 62
Chicago, 297
China, 280, 285
Christian Cyclists' Union, 261
Christmas breakfast, 158
Cockett, F. J., 110
Commercial Travellers' Christian Association, 260
Companion for the Festivals and Fasts of the Church of England, A, 119
Copestake, Moore & Co., 205
Creese, William, 72, 79, 96, 101, 110, 115, 127, 135, 277
Cremorne Gardens, 59
Cutting, Mr., 104
Cutting, Mrs., 74
Cuyler, Rev. Dr., 285, 291, 305

Dale, Dr., 144, 155
Darlington, 214
Denmark, 279
Denny, E. M., 224
Denny, T. A., 223, 224
Diary, Extracts from Sir George Williams's, 71, 73, 76, 77, 78, 85, 86, 87, 88, 91, 92, 95, 96, 97, 111, 132, 134, 138, 139, 146
Dickens, Charles, 62
Dover, Association at, and the *Punch* incident, 194, 195, 196, 197
Draper, The, 256
Drapers' Evangelical Association, The, 115
Duff, Dr. Alexander, 144

Dulverton, 3, 4, 6, 9, 12, 13, 14, 16, 82, 233
Dykes, Dr. Oswald, 226

Early Closing Association, 53, 251, 252, 253
Ebury, Lord, 150
Edinburgh Conference, 188–199
Edward VII., King, 301, 322
Emerson, 308
Exeter, 46, 260
Exeter Hall, 143, 144, 165, 169, 203, 221, 222, 223, 224, 225, 226, 227, 228, 230, 231, 274, 275, 276, 281, 282, 296, 313, 326
Exhibition of 1851, 164, 165, 299
Exmoor, 7, 9, 13, 18

Filey, Sir George Williams speaking to children at, 250
Finney, Rev. Charles G., 30, 31, 32, 33, 34, 35, 36, 37, 38, 98
Fleming, Canon, 226
France, 139, 166, 167, 279, 308, 322
Franco-Prussian War, 256

Gale, Rev. Abner, 13, 14
Geneva, 220
Gerard, Miss, 25
Germany, 170, 279; Emperor of, 301, 316, 322; Prince Henry of, 322
Gibson, Dr. Munro, 285, 287
Glasgow, 118
Glasson, M., 110
Gloyn's Grammar School, 12
"Goose and Gridiron," 49, 99
Gough, J. B., 144, 222
Gregory, Dean, 329
Gresham Street headquarters of the Association, 153, 154
Gurney, Thomas, 133

INDEX

Hamburg, 285
Hamilton, Dr. James, 142, 144
Harman, William, 25
Harris, Miss, 25
Harrowby, Earl of, 150
Harvard, 308
Harvey, John, 110
Highbury Barn, 59
Hitchcock & Rogers, 45, 46, 47, 48, 49, 50, 54, 61, 68, 79, 95, 99, 108, 130, 133
Hitchcock, George, 46, 47, 48, 84, 85, 87, 102, 110, 133, 135, 136, 149, 182, 183, 184, 185, 242, 254
Hitchcock, Helen (Lady Williams), 179, 243
Hitchcock, Walter, 140, 314
Hitchcock, Williams & Co., 49, 104, 248, 253, 255, 256
Hodder, M. H., 296, 308
Holland, 166, 170
Holmes, Mr., 5, 22, 23, 45, 50
Hughes, Rev. Hugh Price, 195, 230

India, 285, 304, 321, 322
International Exhibition, 254
Italy, 302, 316

James, Rev. Evan, 26, 28, 29
James, Rev. John Angell, 144
Japan, 280, 304, 315
Jenny Lind, 222
Johnson, Dr., 59
Jubilee of the American Associations, 295-306
Jubilee of the World's Alliance, 307-310
Jubilee of the Young Men's Christian Association, 271-291

Kansas City, 297
Katerfelto, 13

Kingsley, Charles, 61
Kinnaird, Hon. Arthur F., 157, 158
Kinnaird, Lord, 287

Late hours of shop assistants, 54-61
Lectures on Revivals of Religion, 30
Lectures to Professing Christians, 30
Linen and Woollen Drapers' Institution, 253
Liverpool, 321
Livingstone, David, 283
London, 5, 28, 45, 46, 48, 49, 51, 52, 60, 68, 75, 80, 96, 121, 167, 168, 210, 214, 228, 254, 261, 262, 265, 271, 272, 273, 276, 277, 282, 316, 321, 323
London, Archdeacon of, 273, 278
London, Bishop of, 276
London Cabmen's Mission, 261
London City Mission, 118, 261
London, Lord Mayor of, 226, 230
London Missionary Society, 104
London Tramcar and Omnibus Scripture Text Mission, 261
Longfellow, 308
Lorna Doone, 4, 12

McCormick, Canon, 285
McKinley, President, 301, 322
Margate, Y. M. C. A. home at, 219, 264
Mather, Dr. Cotton, 300
May Meeting breakfast, 157, 158
Melville, Whyte, 13
Metropolitan Drapers' Association, The, 53, 126.
Metropolitan Early Closing Association, The, 53; *see also* Early Closing
Meyer, Rev. F. B., 282

INDEX

Milan, 285
Miller, Hugh, 144, 191
Modern Painters, 62
Monod, Pasteur, 166
Montreal, 167, 299
Moody, D. L., 210, 211, 212
Moore, George, 150, 205
Morley, I. & R., 205
Morley, John, 136
Morley, Samuel, 137, 150, 208, 224, 226, 229, 232, 242
Mott, John R., 316
Music, Sir George Williams and, 79
Mutual Improvement Societies, 103, 129, 137

NASMITH, David, 119, 300
Nasmith Societies, 119, 120, 121, 300
National Early Closing Congress, 252
National Scottish Church, 142
Nelson, Robert, 118, 119
Netherlands Exhibition, 254
Neuchâtel, 285
Newcome, Colonel, 59
Newman, Cardinal, 62
Newton, John, 156
New Zealand, 280, 291, 321
Nisbet & Co., 143
Noel, Rev. Baptist, 132, 137, 141
North Petherton, 45

OWEN, Prof. R., 144
Owen, W. D., 109, 110, 130, 133

PARIS, 139, 166, 167, 308, 322
Paris Conference, 139, 169–172
Paris Exposition, 254
Parker, Dr. Joseph, 282
Past and Present, 62
Peabody, George, 283
Pilkington, G., 69

Polytechnic Institute, 80
Poole, Mr., 82
Pressensé, Pasteur, 166
Prize Essay on the Evils which are Produced by Late Hours of Business, 55
Punch, 80, 194, 195, 196, 197
Punshon, Morley, 144, 263
Puseyism, 105
Putterill, J. H., 272, 319, 320

QUANTOCK Hills, 5
Quarterly Messenger, The, 194

RADLEY's Hotel, 117, 128, 132, 136, 160, 161, 162, 163
Record, The, 196
Reeve, Mr., 141
Revolution in Tanner's Lane, 37
Ridd, Jan, 4, 12
Ripon, Bishop of, 285
Roberts, Lord, 302
Rogers, Mr., partner of Mr. Hitchcock, 47
Rogers, E., 99–101, 110
Roosevelt, President, 322
Rosebery, Earl of, 272
Rotterdam, 169
Ruskin, 62
Russell, Earl, 144
Russia, 280, 302, 315
Russia, Czar of, 322
Rutherford, Mark, 37
Ryde, 219, 263

ST. LOUIS, 297
St. Martin's Coffee House, 112
St. Paul's Missionary Society, 253
St. Petersburg, 316, 322
Salvation Army, 26, 264
Seamen's Christian Friend Society, 261, 307
Sedgmoor, 10
Serious Call (Law's), 31

INDEX

Serjeant's Inn, Fleet Street, 135, 138, 140, 141
Shaftesbury, Earl of, 118, 151, 152, 204, 226, 230, 231, 251, 283; *see also* Ashley, Lord
Sherman, Rev. James, 73
Shipton, Edwyn, 139, 142, 159, 171, 176, 177, 220
Sinclair, Archdeacon, 324, 329
Smith, C. W., 110, 116
Smith, James, 109, 110, 112, 116
Smith, Norton, 110, 277
Smith, W. Hind, 186, 221, 224
Soldiers' Christian Association, 261
Spurgeon, C. H., 144, 179, 203
Spurgeon, Rev. T., 282
Stanley, Dean, 144
Stockholm, 235, 285
Stokes, James, 316
Stoughton, Rev. Dr., 143, 144
Sully, James, 28
Sweden, 279
Switzerland, 169, 280
Symons, J. C., 110, 112, 115

TARLTON, T. H., 133, 134, 135, 138, 140, 142, 145, 176, 177, 220, 243
Taunton, 10, 145
Teetotal Pledge, 69
Temple, Archbishop, 12
Tennyson, 4, 11, 62
Thomas, Miss, 22, 25
Thomas, Rev. W. H. Griffith, 306
Thompson, Samuel, 316
Timlett, Mrs., 12
Tiverton, 12
Toronto, 296, 297
Torquay, 314, 316, 318, 320, 329
Torrey-Alexander Mission, 21
Torr Steps, 11
Trench, Archbishop, 156

Tritton, J. Herbert, 221, 227, 229
Tussaud's, Madame, 80

UNITED STATES; *see* America

VALENTINE, Edward, 90, 100, 105, 110, 116

WANAMAKER, Hon. John, 285, 317
Watson, James, 144
Wesley, John, 95, 119
Whateley, Archbishop, 144
Whitefield, George, 31, 119, 263
Whitefield's Tabernacle, 260
Whittington, Dick, 23
Williams, Amos, father of Sir George Williams, 6, 12
Williams, Elisabeth, mother of Sir George Williams, 6, 9
Williams, Fred, 45
Williams, Howard, 298, 299, 308
Williams, Lady, 288, 306
Williams, Nellie, 244
Williams, Sir George: Home, 5; parentage, 6; boyhood, 8, 10; education, 12; religious training, 13; work on farm, 15; apprenticed to draper at Bridgwater, 16; life at Bridgwater, 22; conversion, 26, 27; joined Church, 28; spiritual homeland, 29; influence of Rev. C. Finney, 36; influence of Rev. T. Binney, 37, 39, 40, 41; with his brother Fred, 45; leaves Bridgwater, 45; first visit to London, 46; introduction to Mr. Hitchcock, 46; enters employ of Messrs. Hitchcock & Rogers, 46; business hours, 54; Sunday work, 72; secretary of Sunday School, 74; music and elocution, 79, 80;

356   INDEX

his letters to his relations, 81, 82, 83; business enthusiasm, 83; his popularity, 86; appointed drapery buyer, 87; first thought of Y. M. C. A., 96; method of praying for companions, 97; growth of prayer meetings, 98; influence over his fellows, 99; interest in missions, 104; Y. M. C. A. discussed, 106, 107, 108, 109; Y. M. C. A. founded, 110; his modesty, 110; tact and good humour, 126; critical time in business career, 132; takes charge of Bible Class, 140; ideas as to how a Bible Class should be conducted, 142; deputation work, 145; visits to his home, 81, 145; business prospects, 149; views for popularising Y. M. C. A., 151; tact in managing Committee work, 154; meetings he presided over, 161; visit to Paris, 166; starts branch of Y. M. C. A. there, 166; delegate to General Conference of Y. M. C. A. at Paris, 169; prominent work in connection with Y. M. C. A., 176; rules for daily life, 177; political views, 179; made partner in firm, 182; Treasurer of Y. M. C. A., 184; generosity to Y. M. C. A., 186; recreation, 213; speech at London Conference, 214; not an orator, 215; quotations from speeches, 217–219; idea of purchasing Exeter Hall for Y. M. C. A., 223; ovation at opening of Exeter Hall, 226; speech at opening of Exeter Hall, 227; Chairman of National Committee, 228; delegate at International Conference, Berlin, 230; elected President of Y. M. C. A., 231; speech at Annual Meeting, 231; Bridgwater Memorial Building opened, 233; work throughout country for Y. M. C. A., 235; business career, 240, 241; as a philanthropist, 241; married to Helen Hitchcock, 243; his family, 244; daughter's death, 244; devotion of employees, 245; his motto, 248; treasurer of Early Closing Association, 251; interest in drapery trade, 253; in Cottage Home Movement, 253; and in Literary and Debating Society, 253; methodical habits, 254; how he made his fortune, 256; his evenings, 257; help given to workers for Christ, 260; generosity to various societies, 260–264; presented "Hazelwood," Ryde, and "Shaftesbury House," Margate, to Y. M. C. A., 263, 264; his help and sympathy, 265–267; motto for Jubilee year, 271; knighted, 273; speeches at Jubilee celebrations, 277, 287, 288–290; presentation of the Freedom of the City of London, 282; golden anniversary of wedding, 306; present at Jubilee of World's Alliance of Y. M. C. A. at Paris, 308; last public speech, 310; last appearance on a public platform, 313; great feebleness, 313; last days in London, 319; last hours at Torquay,

INDEX

320; memorial sermon at St. Paul's, 324; funeral, 328; the works that follow him, 333
Windsor, 290
Wiseman, Luke, 144
Woodbridge Prayer Meeting, 71
Wren, Sir Christopher, 49

YEAST, 61
Young Ladies' Christian Association, 138
Young Men's Christian Association, 25, 26, 31, 41, 60, 69, 75, 80, 83, 96, 101, 104, 106; founded, 110; room engaged at St. Martin's Coffee House, Ludgate Hill, 112; first efforts to spread Association, 112; circular letter, 113; names suggested, 116; large room secured at Radley's Hotel, Blackfriars, 117; early work, 125; methodical prayer, 127; progress, 128; plans enlarged, 129; first tea meeting, 130; first report, 130; second social gathering, 132; Mr. Tarlton made secretary, 133; new offices secured in Serjeant's Inn, Fleet Street, 135; first Annual Report presented, 136; suggested extension of work, 137; Bible Classes started, 138; inception of Exeter Hall Lectures, 142; reputation, 144; definite forward movement, 145; interest of Earl Shaftesbury, 151; Annual Meeting first held in Exeter Hall, 152; headquarters removed to Gresham Street, 153; narrowness of some influential members, 155; public May meeting breakfast inaugurated, 157; Great Exhibition of 1851, 164; special lectures at Exeter Hall, 165; formation of branches abroad, 166; branch started at Paris, 166; work introduced to Holland, 166; branches in Adelaide, Calcutta, Montreal, and Boston, 167; formation of International Committee, 167; lease of new premises purchased, 168; Conference in Paris, 169; reports from Foreign Associations, 169–172; general correspondence started, 175; aim of Association, 181; financial trouble, 181; critical period, 187; attitude towards Church, 188; catholicity of Association, 191; objection to *Punch*, 194; Edinburgh Conference, 197–198; increasing usefulness and prosperity, 204; report for 1869, 206; educational work of Association, 208; Travelling Secretary, 209; work among Sunday excursionists, 209; visit of Mr. Moody, 210; Conference at London, 214; opening of Hazelwood House, Ryde, 219; International Committee established, 220; opening of East Central Branch, London, 221; history of Exeter Hall, 222; money raised for purchase of Exeter Hall, 224; Exeter Hall purchased as headquarters Y. M. C. A., 225; opening ceremony, 226; International Conference held at Exeter Hall, 228; International Conference held at Berlin, 230; election of Sir

George Williams as President, 231; appointment of Travelling Foreign Secretary, 235; Jubilee held in London, 271; organisation of Jubilee celebration, 274; Jubilee meetings, etc., 277-291; Jubilee of American Association, 295; growth of American Y.M.C.A., 298-306; Jubilee of World's Alliance of Y. M. C. A., 307; the future of the Association, 335

Young Men's Magazine and Monthly Record, 120

Young Men's Missionary Society, 103

ZION Congregational Chapel, Bridgwater, 23

www.ingramcontent.com/pod-product-compliance
Lightning Source LLC
Chambersburg PA
CBHW010741170426
43193CB00018BA/2909